EFFECTIVE
WRITING

EFFECTIVE
WRITING

CHOICES AND
CONVENTIONS

SECOND EDITION

Karen L. Greenberg

Hunter College

St. Martin's Press
New York

Senior editor: Mark Gallaher
Managing editor: Patricia Mansfield–Phelan
Project editor: Elise Bauman
Production supervisor: Katherine Battiste
Text design: Helen Granger, Susan Phillips
Graphics: Pica Graphics
Cover design and art: Nadia Furlan–Lorbek

Library of Congress Catalog Card Number: 90–71632
Copyright © 1992 by St. Martin's Press, Inc.
Manufactured in the United States of America.
65432
fedcba

For information, write:
St. Martin's Press, Inc.
175 Fifth Avenue
New York, NY 10010

ISBN: 0–312–04838–6

Acknowledgments

Excerpt from "Why I Can't Write" by Patricia Cummings. Reprinted by permission of the author.

Excerpt from *Writing with Power: Techniques for Mastering the Writing Process* by Peter Elbow. Copyright © 1981 by Oxford University Press, Inc. Reprinted by permission. Excerpt from *Writing without Teachers* by Peter Elbow. Copyright © 1973 by Oxford University Press, Inc. Reprinted with permission.

"Interview with Maya Angelou" from *Like It Is* by Emily Rovetch. Copyright © 1981 by Central State University. Used by permission of the publisher, Dutton, an imprint of New American Library, a division of Penguin Books USA Inc.

Excerpt from *Write to Learn* by Donald Murray. Reprinted by permission of the author.

Drawing by Booth; © 1976 The New Yorker Magazine, Inc.

Excerpt from "Little David" in *And the Walls Came Tumbling Down* by Ralph David Abernathy. Copyright © 1989 by Ralph David Abernathy. Reprinted by permission of Harper-Collins Publishers Inc.

"How I Write" by Lynn Z. Bloom. From *Writers on Writing*, ed. by Tom Waldrep. Copyright © 1985. Reprinted by permission of McGraw-Hill, Inc.

"Dancing Grandma" by Karen Buchanan. In *Student Writers at Work*. Copyright © 1984. Reprinted with permission of St. Martin's Press.

Excerpt from *Lives on the Boundary* by Mike Rose. Copyright © 1989 by Mike Rose. Reprinted with permission of The Free Press, a Division of Macmillan, Inc.

Acknowledgments and copyrights are continued at the back of the book on page 390, which constitutes an extension of the copyright page.

 The text of this book has been printed on recycled paper.

PREFACE

As I noted in the Preface to the first edition, the title of this text, *Effective Writing: Choices and Conventions*, echoes Mina Shaughnessy's belief that effective writing grows out of the choices and decisions writers make in their selection of words, sentence structures, and rhetorical strategies. In addition to making choices that are consistent with their purposes and with the expectations of their readers, writers must also edit their writing so that it conforms to the conventions of Standard Written English. The second edition, like the first, encourages writers to try out a variety of forms and strategies, to examine the relationships between their choices and their intentions, and to cast their choices in the conventions of academic English.

This second edition of *Effective Writing* presents a variety of strategies and activities that are designed to meet the diverse linguistic and intellectual needs of today's students. Throughout the book, instruction and assignments represent current theory and practice in composition. The writing tasks enable students to examine their writing processes and to expand and improve these processes in specific writing contexts. In addition, the content of every writing assignment and exercise comes from the "real" world—from the workplace and from the academic areas of the physical and social sciences and the humanities. Thus, the text provides intellectual challenges while encouraging students to learn about writing from their own efforts to compose and revise.

One unique feature of this text is its format: every exercise is composed of a paragraph or an essay, allowing students to practice skills within the connected discourse of paragraphs rather than in the isolated, arhetorical sentences found in most other composition texts. Writing teachers know how common it is for their students to complete textbook exercises correctly, only to produce paragraphs full of the very errors that they had just seemingly mastered. Part of the reason for this failure to "transfer" knowledge is that the learning context of arhetorical, disconnected sentences eliminates the relationship between content and form. In the exercises in this text, the practice of skills is merged with genuine rhetorical goals. Finally, all of the writing assignments in this book are student-centered—even the research assignments ask students to draw upon personal experiences as they plan and compose—and the many models of student writing provide realistic examples of the skills that student writers can attain.

Overview of the Text

The organization of this text reflects the findings of recent composition researchers that developing writers need to begin from the "top down" with "large" elements (elaboration of ideas, details, and rhetorical objectives) and move to "smaller" elements (features of syntax, grammar, and mechanics). This progression also represents the most logical pedagogical approach. It is pointless to ask writers to begin the semester examining subjects and verbs, especially if they have not yet done much writing that requires them to use subjects and verbs. If the purpose of writing is to communicate one's ideas and feelings effectively to specific readers, then writing instruction and texts should begin by acknowledging this purpose and by presenting students with purposeful, meaningful writing activities. Working on grammar or syntax has little purpose or meaning if it is divorced from writers' efforts to make their writing more appropriate for their readers.

This text is organized into four parts: "Drafting," "Revising," "Editing," and "Applying Your Writing Skills." Each part presents writing as a recursive process of thinking, writing, rethinking, revising, editing, and rewriting. Each chapter within these parts begins with a shared writing task for groups of students to work on collaboratively (or for a whole class to try together), and each chapter includes a variety of different tasks to assign to individuals. In addition, every chapter ends with a stimulus relating to the topic of the chapter—a picture, a cartoon, a piece of writing—for students to think and write about; each also includes guidelines to help students develop and organize a response to the stimulus.

Every chapter also presents students with a revising checklist to help them examine and improve their writing, and every chapter (except the first) ends with suggested issues for students to explore in their journals. These issues come from two sources: some of them are based on ideas that have been presented in the preceding chapter, and some of them present issues that will be discussed in the chapters that follow. This variety in suggested journal topics encourages students to think and write about the material that they have recently finished reading in the text. It also enables them to record and explore their immediate responses to controversial issues that will be presented in writing tasks throughout the book.

The second edition of *Effective Writing* incorporates many new features and changes that reflect the responses and suggestions of teachers and students who used the first edition.

- More than a third of the reading selections in this edition are new, including longer professional and student drafts and revisions.
- Each chapter ends with a new reading and a new writing assignment relevant to the chapter's theme. These essays illustrate the various stages of the writing process and serve as models for paragraph and essay development.
- The organization and structure of the chapters on paragraph and essay development have been expanded and reorganized. The new, detailed treatment of paragraph development, accompanied by new examples and exercises, will help students master a variety of patterns of exposition and argumentation.
- The concept of revision is discussed more comprehensively than in the earlier edition. Both paragraph-level and sentence-level revision are described in greater detail.
- The treatment of research writing has been expanded and integrated with instruction on writing across the curriculum.
- A new chapter on writing essay tests and writing competency tests presents illustrations from various local and statewide tests and describes the process of writing a timed test.
- Specific instruction on writing with a word processor at the end of every chapter will guide students in composing, revising, and editing on a computer screen.

As in the first edition, every chapter in this book stresses the recursive processes involved in writing and helps students see the relationships between improvements in their processes and improvements in their products. To help reinforce these goals, the book ends with a series of individualized progress logs that students can use to keep track of their writing problems and progress; separate logs are provided for considering the composition of paragraphs and essays, for noting particular spelling problems, and for thinking about conference discussions.

ACKNOWLEDGMENTS

Many friends and colleagues helped me with the second edition of *Effective Writing*. As in the past, I am indebted to Harvey Wiener—

master writer, gifted teacher, and loyal friend—for his inspiration and his advice. I am also grateful to my editor, Mark Gallaher, whose many valuable suggestions for improvement guided this revision, and to project editor Elise Bauman for her skillful management of the project. I also want to acknowledge the contribution of Virginia Rubens, my talented copy editor. I thank my colleagues in the Developmental English Program at Hunter College, who contributed many excellent recommendations for this edition, and I am especially indebted to the students in my composition courses who offered sound and useful advice.

I also want to thank the following reviewers whose thoughtful comments and suggestions helped me improve the first edition: Laura Anderson, Trinidad State Junior College; Douglas Garrison, College of the Desert; Joseph La Briola, Sinclair Community College; Larry Silverman, Seattle Central Community College; and Kathy Anne Simpson, Northern Virginia Community College.

Finally, I thank my husband Kenneth and our son Evan for their endless patience, support, and love.

K. L. G.

CONTENTS

PART ONE

DRAFTING

CHAPTER ONE

EXPLORING YOUR THOUGHTS AND FEELINGS ABOUT WRITING

Writers kid themselves—about themselves and other people. Take the talk about writing methods. Writing is just work—there's no secret. If you dictate or use a pen or type or write with your toes—it is still just work.

SINCLAIR LEWIS

Writing is the hardest work in the world not involving heavy lifting.

PETE HAMILL

WRITING ATTITUDES

Everyone is a "born writer." Young children love to tell stories, and young storytellers are thrilled when someone else can read their squiggles and understand their stories. Some of us manage to preserve this sense of the magic of the written word and, as we grow older, continue to find pleasure in expressing our experiences in writing. Others lose touch with the magic because no one delights in our stories or because the criticisms we receive start to overwhelm us. Gradually, we lose our natural spontaneity, and writing becomes more and more difficult.

How do you feel about writing? Attitudes toward writing usually influence writing habits and processes, so it is important for you to understand your beliefs and feelings about writing. For example, are you one of the many people who believe that "good" writers always enjoy writing and have the ability to create perfect prose every time they write? This is simply not true! In fact, many professional writers (like students) sometimes have trouble developing and organizing their thoughts and getting them down on paper. Here is a discussion of this problem by a professional writer who also teaches writing:

> I can't write. I'm trying to begin, I can't think of anything to say. No—there's too much to say, but first I have to find a good title, a good first word, an arresting, unforgettable first sentence. And then everything has to be beautifully organized—how? I can't do this, it's too hard, too confusing, too frightening; I put up a good front most of the time, my friends believe me, I've hoodwinked my teachers (some of them; or they were kind); but if I write badly I will, finally, be exposed; people will laugh, or they will feel sorry for me—and I will vanish.
>
> I can't simply say what I want to say (whatever that is), I have to say it cogently, intelligently, brilliantly. I can't.
>
> Somehow, growing up, I lost both my fluency and my spontaneity when it came to writing—it was all those red penciled comments in the margins. Eventually those can be useful, when it comes to editing; but the real problem is to get something to edit—words—on paper.
>
> Patricia Cummings
Free Writing!

Another misunderstanding that some people have is that writing is a neat, orderly process. It usually isn't; in fact, writing is often a messy business. Even fluent writers who enjoy writing usually write notes all over their first drafts and draw circles and arrows connecting new ideas to old ones. Most successful writers have to write several **drafts** (preliminary versions) of a story, an essay, or a report. In each draft, they get closer and closer to what they want to say and how they want to say it. Also, most experienced writers show their drafts to concerned readers who help them revise, edit, and proofread their writing.

Students who have misunderstandings about the process of writing often become overwhelmed by the prospect of trying to produce a "perfect" piece of writing in one draft. They become convinced that they cannot write well and may develop negative attitudes toward writing—fear, anxiety, contempt. These negative attitudes make it even more difficult for them to produce and to shape ideas.

Regardless of whether you think that you write well or poorly, you may have some attitudes about writing that are interfering with your ability to express or to revise your ideas. In order to change these attitudes, first you need to understand them. This chapter is designed to help you examine your feelings and beliefs about writing and explore your writing habits.

PAIRED WRITING TASK   **INTERVIEWING A PEER ABOUT WRITING ATTITUDES**

In order to discover how other people feel about writing, interview a classmate and take notes as you interview the person. Before you begin, examine the questions below and decide which ones you want to ask. If you think of any other questions about writing attitudes or habits that are not on the list, write them down in the space provided at number 12. When it is your turn to be interviewed, tell the truth. There aren't any "correct" responses to these questions. If you feel uncomfortable about answering a particular question, tell your classmate to skip that question. As you interview your classmate, write your notes about his or her responses on a separate piece of paper.

Feelings
1. How would you describe your feelings about writing?
2. How do you feel when you sit down to write something?
3. How do you feel when you finish writing?

Habits
4. How would you describe your writing habits?
5. What kinds of writing "rituals" do you follow? For example, do you do certain things to prepare for writing? Do you need quiet or some kind of noise? Do you write in pen or pencil, or do you use a typewriter or a word processor?

6. What do you do when you begin writing? How do you know when you are finished writing?
7. To whom do you show your writing? Who helps you with it?

Beliefs

8. Do you think that you write well? Why or why not?
9. Do you think that anyone can learn to write well? Why or why not?
10. Do you believe that a person has to like to write in order to be able to write well? Why or why not?
11. Do you usually revise or edit your writing? Why or why not?
12. _____
    _____

   When you are finished with the interview, use your notes to write a description of the person's writing attitudes and habits. The classmate you interviewed will use your paragraph to help get a better understanding of his or her writing attitudes.

SOME STUDENT RESPONSES

How do your feelings about writing compare with those of the students who wrote the brief uncorrected essays that follow?

I have mixed feelings about writing. Sometimes I like to write, especially when I am writing to friends and have something very important to tell them. But sometimes I hate to write and those times are usually when I am writing an essay for school or for work and I know that the person who will read my writing will judge me by it.

Even when I am writing something that I enjoy, I find it hard to write. It's so much easier to talk to people. I never seem to have any trouble thinking up ideas or organizing them when I am speaking, but I always have trouble when I am writing. I think I get so nervous about having to write that my mind clams up.

I hope that my writing courses will make it easier for me to write and will help me improve my writing. I envy writers who can sit down and pour out their ideas on paper and polish them up so that when you read them you understand exactly how the writer's mind works. I also believe that writing well is a skill that will be very valuable to me in college and my future. I am studying to be a nurse and nurses must know how to write clearly and effectively. So I am putting a lot of effort into improving my writing.

                                                     Aida Vasquez

I usually do not enjoy writing. I have great difficulty getting my thoughts together and putting them down on paper. When I know I have to write something for school, I get very nervous about it and put it off till the last possible minute. Then I sit down and write very fast and try to get all of my ideas out of my head before I lose them. If I think that the teacher is going to look at my writing, I'll go over my paper before rewriting it. After I hand it in, I try not to think about it.

My approach to writing is very different from my approach to things that I like doing. For instance, I love to run. I'm on the track team and the way I prepare for a race is almost the opposite of the way I prepare for writing a paper. I start thinking about the race and planning for it about a week in advance. I stay calm and do lots of practice runs. I give the race everything I've got and if I lose, I try to

```
figure out what went wrong and how to win the next time.

I wish I could write as good as I run.
```

Allen Parkinson

WRITING ACTIVITY   **EXPLORING YOUR FEELINGS ABOUT WRITING**

Write two or three paragraphs about the ways in which your feelings about writing are similar to or different from the ones expressed by Aida Vasquez and Allen Parkinson in the preceding paragraphs.

WRITING HABITS

Everybody has writing habits—unconscious behaviors and conscious rituals that they follow every time they write. For example, I begin *every* piece of writing by biting my nails and scribbling notes in green ink on a yellow legal pad. Some writing habits are productive, in that they enable writers to begin and to continue their writing processes. However, some writing habits interfere with people's ability to get their ideas down on paper. The next time you begin writing, try to become more conscious of your writing habits and to consider how each helps or hinders your writing process.

EXERCISE   **ANALYZING YOUR WRITING HABITS**

Below is a list of writing habits that may be interfering with your ability to get your ideas down on paper and develop these ideas clearly. In the space before each description, check "Yes" if you have this habit or "No" if you do not.

Yes   **No**

___   ___   I get nervous and worry a lot about what I am writing.

___   ___   My lips keep moving but my pen or pencil doesn't.

___   ___   I frequently erase and correct what I have written.

___   ___   I keep wondering whether my writing is good or bad.

___   ___   I pause a long time after each word or sentence.

___   ___   I often cross out what I have written and start over again from the beginning with a new idea.

___ ___   I often recopy what I have written and hope that I can catch all the errors.

Some of the writing habits in the list above may be causing you problems with writing. Try to concentrate *more* on figuring out your ideas and details and *less* on worrying about errors or whether your writing is good or bad. If you want to improve your writing, you have to change some of your negative attitudes and behaviors. Chapter 2 of this text will help you master some useful writing habits.

PERCEPTIONS OF THE WRITING PROCESS

People's attitudes toward writing are influenced by their perceptions of how writing "happens." Most students and some teachers have misconceptions about the writing process. They think that clear, correct writing flows magically from the pens of successful writers. Indeed, successful writers may foster this belief because they usually do not talk or write about the thinking, planning, and organizing that they do before they sit down to write. In fact, skilled writers *may not even be aware of* the **prewriting** that they work through—all of the thinking, deciding, focusing, organizing, and developing that they do—before they begin to write. However, prewriting activities such as thinking, planning, and focusing are absolutely necessary for the production of effective writing. These activities enable writers to come up with enough ideas and information so that when they start writing, they have the luxury of selecting and arranging only the most promising ideas. Writers who don't do any prewriting have no clear idea of what they want to say and have very little sense of why they are writing or of the audience who will read their writing.

In addition, many people also do not understand the importance of **revising**. They think that revising consists of correcting errors in spelling and grammar or "polishing" their writing. In reality, error correction (**editing**) is usually the *last* stage in the writing process of most skilled writers. Before they edit their errors, skilled writers usually read and revise their work over and over again.

As they revise, experienced writers often move from the draft as a whole to its specific components:

- First, they reshape their ideas and organization, making sure that they have communicated their meaning.
- Then, they may cross out whole sentences and paragraphs and add new ideas and details.

- Next, they may revise their sentences and words, checking for accuracy and appropriateness.
- Finally, they may decide to throw out what they have written and start all over again.

If a piece genuinely matters to them, skilled writers may revise it nine or ten times before they are satisfied that it has expressed their ideas and concerns. For example, here is the fourth draft of the paragraph that I turned into the list above:

```
           FOURTH DRAFT OF MY PARAGRAPH

     Also, many writers do not understand the importance

of postwriting activities.  These people think that revising

means correcting errors in spelling or grammar.  They are

wrong.  Skilled writers usually read and revise their work

over and over.  Then, they reshape their ideas and

organization.  Then, they look at sentence structure or

vocabulary.  Some throw out everything that they have written

or add new sentences or paragraphs or new details.
```

How does my fourth draft of this paragraph differ from the final version that precedes it?

Another misconception that causes problems for some writers is their perception of writing as a series of four separate stages or processes: prewriting, writing, revising, and editing. They believe that writers start with the first activity and move on to the next without any backsliding or returning to a previous activity. This description of the writing process is also inaccurate. Most experienced writers move back and forth among these activities whenever they write. In other words, they may do some planning and writing, stop, and then do some more planning. Next they may do some revising and then more planning and organizing and writing. Although this book discusses "writing" and "revising" separately—Part One (Chapters 1–5) takes up writing, and Part Two (Chapters 6–9) covers revising—in reality, the two processes often occur simultaneously.

A PROFESSIONAL RESPONSE

Read the following essay from *Writing Without Teachers* by Peter Elbow, a well-known writing teacher. How are his writing processes similar to or different from your own?

In high school I wrote relatively easily and—according to those standards—satisfactorily. In college I began to have difficulty writing. Sometimes, I wrote badly, sometimes I wrote easily and sometimes with excruciating difficulty. Starting early and planning carefully didn't seem to be the answer: sometimes it seemed to help, sometimes it seemed to make things worse.

Whether or not I succeeded in getting something written seemed related only to whether I screwed myself up into some state of frantic emotional intensity: sometimes about the subject I was writing about; occasionally about some extraneous matter in my life; usually about how overdue the paper was and how frightened I was of turning in nothing at all. . . .

My difficulties in writing, my years as an illiterate English teacher, and a recent habit of trying to keep a stream of consciousness diary whenever life in general got to be too much for me—all combined to make me notice what was happening as I tried to write. I kept a kind of almost diary. There were two main themes—what I called "stuckpoints" and "breakthroughs." Stuckpoints were when I couldn't get anything written at all no matter how hard I tried: out of pure desperation and rage I would finally stop trying to write the thing and take a fresh sheet of paper and simply try to collect evidence: babble everything I felt, when it started, and what kind of writing and mood and weather had been going on. Breakthroughs were when the log-jam broke and something good happened: I would often stop and try to say afterwards what I thought happened. . . .

Trying to begin [to write] is like being a little child who cannot write on unlined paper. I cannot write anything decent or interesting until after I have written something at least as long as the thing I want to end up with. I go back over it and cross it all out or throw it all away, but it operates as a set of lines that hold me up when I write, something to warm up the paper so my ink will "take," a security blanket. Producing writing, then, is not so much like filling a basin or a pool once, but rather getting water to keep flowing *through* till finally it runs clear.

THE PROBLEMS CAUSED BY PREMATURE EDITING

A common misconception that many inexperienced writers share is that skilled writers revise and edit while they are writing. Certainly some professional writers do stop after every paragraph, or even after every sentence, to make sure that it expresses their meaning accurately. However, most experienced writers write and revise a first draft in its entirety before they look for any errors in it. This is because they know that they are discovering their ideas *while* they are writing. Furthermore, most experienced writers develop their own methods or systems for noting problems that they will return to in order to clarify or correct them when they are finished writing. For example, when I am writing or revising, I use the following system. I put

- a ✓ in the margin next to any sentence that I haven't thought out clearly;

- an ✗ in the margin next to any word that sounds wrong or funny to me;

- a ⌒ around any word that I am not sure how to spell; and

- a — in place of a word when I can't think of exactly the right word to use in the sentence.

This system allows me to keep writing without stopping to edit (which would break my train of thought).

Here is an example of how I use this system:

```
       THIRD DRAFT OF THE PARAGRAPH ON PAGE 10

   Also, many writers whom I have had the opportunity to  ✗

talk with don't understand the importance of _____ activities.

They are (inaccurate.) Skilled writers usually revise their  ✓

work by reshaping their ideas, organization, and coherence.
```

```
Then they may look at their sentence structure and vocabulary.

Or they might throw everything out and start again.          X
```

Unfortunately, many inexperienced writers keep interrupting their writing in order to edit or to correct their work prematurely. Their main concern is avoiding errors that teachers often circle in red. Given some teachers' preoccupation with "rules" and with correctness, it's no wonder that many writers—professional and inexperienced—worry more about correcting errors than about communicating clearly. Some people worry so much about their errors that they find it agonizingly difficult to commit words to paper. If you are one of these people, try to relax. Allow yourself to make mistakes. In fact, assume that you *will* make mistakes and that you will learn from these mistakes. Don't let your fear of making mistakes or your concern with editing your errors cripple your writing abilities.

SOME DIFFERENCES BETWEEN SPEAKING AND WRITING

A common misconception about writing is that it is merely "speaking with the pen instead of the tongue." While both speaking and writing involve the creative use of language to express ideas, they are different processes. Speech develops naturally: All children go through the same stages in speech development. No matter what language children hear, if they are physically normal, they will begin to speak that language at about eighteen months of age, and they will have mastered its basic grammatical structure by about the age of five. In contrast, five-year-old children have little formal writing ability, because writing must be learned and practiced. Furthermore, regardless of one's age, writing is a skill that requires patience, training, and feedback.

Writing and speaking differ in other ways that can make the process of writing much more difficult than the process of speaking. When people speak, they can see their audience and know the extent to which they share experiences, attitudes, and beliefs about the world. Writers have to consider how much their audience of readers is likely to know about a topic, or, if they know their audience, they have to figure out exactly what their readers need to know. Moreover, speakers can look at their listeners' expressions and know immediately when they are being unclear, incomplete, or confusing. Writers rarely get this immediate feedback, so they must make their ideas as clear and as explicit as possible.

Writing skills are far more complicated and difficult to acquire than speaking skills. The exercise below will give you a better understanding of some of these differences.

EXERCISE: **IDENTIFYING DIFFERENCES BETWEEN SPEAKING AND WRITING**

Work on this exercise with a classmate. First, read aloud the conversation transcribed below and the course handout that follows. (Note that stressed words have been italicized.) Then, circle every word or phrase (group of words) that makes this teacher's speech sound very different from her written handout.

CONVERSATION OVERHEARD
ON THE FIRST DAY OF ENGLISH 100

"What's *this* course about? What are we gonna be . . . I mean, what will we *do* in here?"

"This is a *writing* workshop. So we'll be doing a lot of writing and . . . and a lot of revising."

"But what's the *syllabus*? I mean, aren't you gonna hand out a *schedule* of readings and assignments?"

"No, but . . . well, the *schedule* depends on *your* interests and progress. *You'll* be responsible for *thinking up* the topics and for *writing regularly*. Let's just say that you'll be *writing* in every class session and every night."

"But what if I *can't think* of anything to *write about*? You know, if I don't have anything to *say*."

"Well, then you'll write about *that*. About *not* having anything to say. And then, you know . . . you can write about *whatever* it is that you were thinking about *before* you started writing."

"That, uh, doesn't *sound* like it's gonna help me *write* better."

"Well, it depends on what you mean by *better*—doesn't it? Let me try to explain. . . . *Continuous* writing or *freewriting* might not help you *correct* your writing . . . but it will help you get in *touch* with your *ideas* and *feelings*. What I mean is that it will help you figure out what matters to *you*."

"Is that *important*?"

"Writing something that *matters* to *you* is *very* important. If your writing *doesn't* matter to you, why should it matter to *anyone else* who reads it?"

"Oh . . . I guess *this* course is gonna be *real* different from my *other* English courses."

HANDOUT FOR ENGLISH 100

This course is a Writing Workshop: We will be doing a great deal of writing and revising. Students will be responsible for writing every day, in class and at home, on topics of their choosing. Techniques for getting started will be taught and students will do extensive freewriting to get in touch with their ideas and feelings and to learn how to write about things that matter to them.

EXERCISE   EXPLORING SPEAKING AND WRITING DIFFERENCES

Ask a friend, a family member, or a classmate to let you make a tape recording while he or she is speaking. Ask the person to speak for one minute on *one* of the following topics:

- What do you like best about yourself?
- What would you like to change about yourself?
- What angers you more than anything else?
- What is your favorite activity?

If you do not have a tape recorder, ask the person to speak slowly while you try to write down the words. After you have recorded the speech, ask the person to write for one minute about the same topic. When he or she is finished writing, compare the speaking with the writing. Make a list of the similarities between the two and a list of the differences.

"STANDARD WRITTEN ENGLISH" (SWE) DIALECTS

Some people feel that they don't write well because the form of English that they use is different from the kind used in books, newspapers, and magazines. In reality, however, the English language consists of many forms or *dialects*—the social, regional, and racial variations of the language. These dialects can differ in pronunciation, in vocabulary, and in grammar. Here are examples of four current American English dialects:

1. I be the one who leave class first, but today I gonna hang out and talk to the teacher.
2. I no want to stay late most of the time, but today I stay and talk to the teacher.

3. Usually, I'm the first one outta class, but today I'm going to hang around and talk to the teacher.
4. Usually, I am the first person to leave the class, but today I am going to stay late to talk to the teacher.

Some of these examples may sound strange, but each is an example of an English dialect that is found in America today. These dialects, as well as all the other dialects of our language, are governed by rules, and all are equally logical. No dialect is superior to any other, but they are not all equally appropriate for academic or business writing. The fourth example is **Standard Written English (SWE)**. This is the dialect of our language that is appropriate for professional, business, and academic writing. Nobody *speaks* Standard Written English. For example, no one always speaks in complete sentences or pronounces the final letter of every word. However, many people learn to "translate" their spoken dialect into SWE when they write.

Everyone's spoken and written dialects are governed by contextual factors that include the age, sex, race, and social background of the speaker or writer and of the audience. Depending upon whom we are addressing and what we are discussing, we can switch from the most informal slang to the most formal language. The correct use of SWE is a survival skill necessary in most academic, professional, and business situations. Chapters 10–12 in the "Editing" section of this book will help you improve your ability to translate your spoken dialect into SWE.

WRITING ACTIVITY **TRANSLATING SPEECH INTO WRITING**

Below is the opening paragraph of a novel entitled *Sitting Pretty*, by Al Young. Although this paragraph is fiction, it is characterized by many of the conversational features of genuine speech and it also includes features that identify it as a dialect that differs from Standard Written English. On a separate piece of paper, rewrite this paragraph in Standard Written English. You will have to make changes in spelling, punctuation, grammar, vocabulary, and sentence structure.

Maybe it was on accounta it was a full moon. I don't know. Its a whole lotta things I use to be dead certain about—like, day follow night and night follow day—things I wouldnt even bet on no more. Its been that way since me and Squirrel broke up and that's been yeahbout fifteen-some-odd years ago, *odd* years—July the Fourth.

When you finish your translation, write a brief answer to this question: How does your paragraph differ from Young's?

SOME GOALS TO CONSIDER

For most people, the goal in taking a writing course is to improve their academic writing ability. The best way to achieve this goal is to work at mastering smaller, more manageable tasks like the ones listed below.

TEN IMPORTANT WRITING GOALS

1. Try to care more about writing. Every time you sit down to write something, try to find something to say that matters to *you*.
2. Try to understand and to change the negative writing attitudes and behaviors that are causing your problems.
3. Take more time to think about what you want to say in your writing.
4. Focus more on getting your ideas down and less on worrying about whether your writing is good or bad.
5. Try to develop many specific details to support your ideas so that your readers will understand your generalizations.
6. Work on organizing your details in a logical order so that your readers can follow the development of the ideas.
7. Get into the habit of writing several drafts of any piece of writing that matters to you.
8. Revise a piece over and over again until it says what you want it to say in a way that is appropriate for you and for your readers.
9. Edit your *final revision* for correct Standard Written English grammar, usage, spelling, and punctuation so that your readers will be able to comprehend your ideas.
10. Keep an open mind about the strategies offered by your teacher and by this text, and try them out even if they seem silly or irrelevant.

As you succeed in achieving these ten goals, you will probably feel better about writing and you will improve your writing performance in *all* of your courses and in your job.

READ BEFORE YOU WRITE

Maya Angelou is a writer, actress, teacher, and songwriter, whose autobiography, *I Know Why the Caged Bird Sings*, was an immediate critical and commercial success. Here is an excerpt from an interview with Angelou conducted by Arthur E. Thomas. As you read it, underline the sentences with which you most agree.

Thomas: Beautiful, brilliant, fantastic black woman—why does it make you almost want to cry, and sometimes cry, when reviewers tell you that you're a natural writer?

Angelou: Well, because it costs so much to write well. It is said that easy reading is damned hard writing, and of course that's the other way around, too. Easy writing is awfully hard going to read. But to make a poem or an article, a piece of journalism, sing—so that the reader is not even aware that he or she is reading—means that one goes to the work constantly: polishing it, cleaning it up, editing, cutting out, and then finally developing it into a piece that hopefully sings. And then one shows it to an audience and a critic says, "She's a natural writer." There's nothing natural about it. It costs a lot.

Thomas: There's a tremendous amount of work in writing.

Angelou: Hard work. It's hard work. I think everything is hard work. Everything that I've seen that one wants to excel in. I push toward excellence. Always. I think that we've become a country which accepts mediocrity, rudeness, crudeness, coarseness as the norm. We have stopped asking not only for excellence from others, we've stopped demanding excellence from ourselves individually. Too many of us, that is.

Thomas: I know you have worked all day and sometimes more than one day on just two lines.

Angelou: All day! I've worked on one poem six months. One poem. Because, first, I never wanted to write dust-catching masterpieces. And I'm happy that my work is required reading at almost every university in this country, either the autobiographies or the poetry. When I write a poem, I try to find a rhythm. First, if I wanted to write a poem about today and my experience in southern Ohio, just today, I would write everything I know about today: every picture I've seen, every person I've met, what I know about the new friends I've made, how my mother's responding to this trip, you, the car—I would write everything. That would take about fifteen pages. Now I might end up with four lines.

But then I would find rhythm. . . . *Then* I start to work on the poem, and I will *pull* it and *push* it and *kick* it and *kiss* it, *hug* it, everything. Until finally it reflects what this day has been.

It costs me. It might take me three months to write that poem. And it might end up being six lines.

WRITING ASSIGNMENT   DESCRIBING YOURSELF AS A WRITER

In this chapter, you have explored your writing attitudes and those of your classmates. You have also learned about the differences between speaking and writing and about the qualities of effective writing. You have examined your writing habits and processes, and you have read about the writing processes of two well-known authors. Using the information that you have read and written for this chapter, write a draft describing your writing attitudes, abilities, and processes. Use the Prewriting Guidelines below to help you plan, focus, and develop your ideas for this draft.

Prewriting Guidelines

1. The audience for this description is your instructor. Think about the information you will have to provide so that he or she understands who you are and why you feel the way that you do.
2. Try writing *nonstop* for ten minutes about the topic to get your ideas flowing.
3. Reread everything that you wrote for this chapter and take notes as you are reading. Then, write a list of all the ideas that pop into your mind when you think about the assignment.
4. Keep reminding yourself of your purpose: to describe your attitudes and feelings about writing and your writing abilities and processes for a reader who does not know you very well.
5. Examine the description written about you by the classmate who interviewed you. How accurately did your classmate describe your writing attitudes and habits? What details did he or she omit? What details would you emphasize differently?
6. When you write the first draft of this description, make a conscious effort *not* to revise or edit as you are writing. Don't worry about problems or errors. Just concentrate on getting your ideas down on the page.

When you finish the draft, **reread it aloud**. Then, revise it until it is as clear and as detailed as you can make it.

GETTING STARTED

*I sometimes begin a drawing with no
preconceived problem to solve, with only the
desire to use pencil on paper and make lines,
tones, and shapes with no conscious aim; but
as my mind takes in what is so produced, a
point arrives where some idea becomes
conscious and crystallizes, and then a control
and ordering begin to take place.*

HENRY MOORE

*I know very dimly when I start what's going
to happen. I just have a very general idea, and
then the thing develops as I write.*

ALDOUS HUXLEY

FINDING TOPICS

The most common student complaint in English courses is "I can't think of anything to write about." When teachers ask students to write about a topic of their own choosing, many students freeze. If this happens to you, one way to overcome the problem is to think about the people in your life and to write about them, or to think about experiences that you have had that made you intensely happy or sad or angry. You are unique, and your daily experiences can provide you with a multitude of writing topics. Here is some advice about "collecting" writing topics from Donald Murray, a teacher who has written newspaper and magazine articles, short stories, poems, and academic essays and books.

We are all writers whether we know it or not. We collect information so that we can survive. What is that noise? What is that smell? Did that shadow move? We learn what brings punishment and what brings rewards, what streets are dangerous, what behavior makes you popular. We learn how to dress and walk and talk and laugh. We learn how to make a dress, pass a basketball, make money, get through school. Our brain stores everything we see, smell, hear, taste, touch; and it also stores how we feel and think. Your brain has already collected enough information for thousands of books.

The cartoon on p. 22 by the famous cartoonist George Booth, offers additional advice for finding topics in your daily experiences.

GROUP WRITING TASK   **FINDING TOPICS TO WRITE ABOUT**

Form a group with two or three classmates so that you can share ideas and learn from one another. Below are four categories of possible topics. For each category, jot down a list of ten topics that come to your mind when you think about the category. Choose one person to record the group's responses to each category on a separate piece of paper.

- Things that puzzle or confuse me
- Things that I want to change
- Things that I want to know more about
- Things that make me furious

"Write about dogs!"

TECHNIQUES FOR GETTING STARTED
AND FOR DEVELOPING IDEAS

Writers can get ideas from private or public sources. The most private sources are feelings, perceptions, and insights: writers can think about these and record them in diaries or journals. The most public source is the library, where writers get ideas and information by taking notes from books, magazines, newspapers, files, and other public documents. In between the journal and the library are many types of sources: people whom writers can interview, and places and things that writers can observe and describe. You can get ideas for writing simply by opening your eyes and your ears to what is going on inside of you and all around you. However, if you don't keep a record of your observations, experiences, and reactions, then your best ideas may be lost to you forever. Here are some strategies for recording and developing ideas.

Journal Writing

Writing in a journal constitutes the best way of "talking to" and "listening to" yourself, of examining your ideas and emotions. A journal is simply a notebook in which writers record their observations, thoughts, and feelings. It differs from a diary in that a diary is a record of each day's events. A journal, on the other hand, is used to record particularly interesting or meaningful events or observations *and* the writer's reactions to these events. For example, here is an entry from my diary:

6/11 I finished the first section of Chap. 2. It's a tough chapter. I picked up Evan from nursery school. He had a fight with his teacher—remember to call her. Ate out at Burger King—again!

And here is an entry from my journal for the same day. How does it differ from the diary entry above?

6/11 A lovely golden day, a day for dreaming outside. But I had a rough day today—spent most of it writing (when Evan wasn't demanding attention). Chapter 2 of the new book is going very slowly. Why is it so difficult? Is this chapter touching a raw nerve—reflecting on my own anxiety about "getting started"? After fifteen years of writing professionally, I still get so nervous and cramped when I sit down to write. Can I work out some of this problem by following my own advice in this chapter?

You can also use your journal to record pieces of writing that you like: poems, quotations, paragraphs from books and magazines, road signs, and graffiti. Everything you read and record becomes material for you to sort and develop when you need ideas for essays. For example, here is an old journal entry of mine that I recently expanded into an essay on sexist language:

> 9/15/83   A sign I passed on the parkway today said "Slow—men working." Evan was in the back and wanted to know what the sign said, so I read it to him. As I slowed down by the construction, I saw two men and a woman in bulldozers, tearing up the shoulder of the road. My first reaction was "That sign's inaccurate—it's not true" (always the English teacher, looking for accuracy!). Then, I started to think about the effects of the sign. My young son—and all the kids who see the sign or get their parents to read it to them—are going to learn that only *men* work on roads and build and construct. Why can't the signs in our country read "People Working"?

The most important thing about journal writing is to do it regularly, at least once or twice a day. The point of recording your thoughts and responses in a journal is to "behave" like a writer: to get into the habit of recording feelings and impressions in writing. A journal is the place to let your ideas percolate, the place to write reactions to a topic, a class, a reading, or a piece of writing on which you are working. The more regularly you write in a journal, the more comfortable you will be with exploring your ideas in writing. A journal also provides a permanent record of your ideas and observations—a record that is always available to you when you need a topic or some ideas for an essay or term paper.

Although a journal should never be graded or evaluated by others, some teachers do check students' journals to make sure that they are writing regularly or to learn about their concerns and reactions. If you write anything in your journal that you do not want others to read, fold over the page on which the entry is written and staple it or tape it.

A STUDENT RESPONSE

Here is an uncorrected entry from the journal of a student who wishes to remain anonymous:

2/10 I am still so nervous about writing in this little book. I know that it's a private place and I can try out new ideas and stuff in it. But whenever I write, I always feel like someone's going to grade it or criticize me. I don't even want anyone to look at this book. I'd just die. I'd be so embarrass. I want to use this journal to figure out who I am and what I am becoming. I want to put down all the scary feelings that I have that aren't okay or ready for anyone else to read. Greenberg says that doing this will help me get over my awful fears about writing. Well, we'll see.

JOURNAL-WRITING REMINDERS

1. Write in your journal every day.
2. Write about things that matter to you and always tell the truth.
3. Include details about what you see, hear, feel, taste, smell, and think.
4. Write about your reactions to your observations and experiences.

WRITING ACTIVITY   WRITING JOURNAL ENTRIES

If you do not keep a journal, start one today. Get a notebook that you will use only as a journal. Put today's date at the top of the first page, and write at least two entries for today. For your first entry, you might want to record your reaction to this writing assignment: how do you feel about keeping a journal? Why do you think you feel this way? If you are having difficulty getting started on your journal entries, think about something that really bothers you or upsets you. Explain what that thing is and why it annoys you so much. Other possible journal topics include a wonderful or terrible experience or a person whom you like or dislike very much.

EXERCISE **COLLECTING SENSORY OBSERVATIONS IN A JOURNAL**

A journal is an excellent place to record images—sensory descriptions of people, things, places, and events. Images are a writer's most important tools because they enable readers to experience the writer's perceptions and feelings. Sensory details make writing interesting. How sharp are your senses? Before you can create images with words, you have to sense them fully. Here is an exercise that will help you do this.

Carefully examine the picture of the scene on page 27. In your journal, answer the following questions about this scene:

1. What details are most striking about this scene? Which objects and shapes seem particularly interesting? Why?
2. Imagine yourself in the scene. What sounds do you hear and what do these sounds remind you of? What odors do you smell and what do these odors remind you of?
3. Still imagining yourself in the scene, describe the way the things around you feel. What do the surfaces feel like?
4. What does this scene (or a particular part of the scene) remind you of?
5. What is your overall impression of this scene?

If you start a journal and then find that you are having trouble writing in it regularly, set aside a specific time every day (or every other day) to write in it. For example, I write in my journal for at least ten minutes at 8:30 p.m. every evening during the week. (I usually skip weekends.) Thus, keeping a journal has enabled me to create a special time and place for me to reflect on my thoughts and feelings. I review my day, consider how satisfied or dissatisfied I am with my behavior and accomplishments, and think about the next day.

Freewriting

Often, writers feel that they know what they want to say, but they're not sure about how to express it. Freewriting can help writers with this problem. Freewriting means writing continuously about whatever is in one's mind. Here is what the professor who created the term freewriting—Peter Elbow—has to say about it:

Freewriting is the easiest way to get words on paper and the best all-around practice in writing that I know. To do a freewriting exercise, simply force yourself to write without stopping for

ten minutes. Sometimes you will produce good writing, but that's not the goal. Sometimes you will produce garbage, but that's not the goal either. You may stay on one topic; you may flip repeatedly from one to another: it doesn't matter. Sometimes you will produce a good record of your stream of consciousness, but often you can't keep up. Speed is not the goal, though sometimes the process revs you up. If you can't think of anything to write, write about how that feels or repeat over and over "I have nothing to write" or "Nonsense" or "No." If you get stuck in the middle of a sentence or thought, just repeat the last word or phrase till something comes along. The only point is to keep writing.

Teachers may collect students' freewriting and may write comments on it or ask questions about it. However, freewriting is never graded. Here is an example of some freewriting that I did before I wrote the first draft of this section:

> Let's see me practice what I preach—or is it practice what I teach. How shall I begin this section? With a reading? an example. a student piece. myself—no I'm too boring. Uh oh, I'm running out of ideas and I just started writing. Get back to it. To what? What do I think will help my readers. I guess <u>whatever it is that helps me and other writers</u> that I know. <u>journals, charts, clusters.</u> And of course <u>freewriting.</u> OK. so now I know my topic, but what am I going to say about it? I guess I better do some more freewriting about it. How can freewriting help me and my students? Well, it gets a person connected to her ideas and feelings and to thoughts she might not have realized were on her mind. Oh, Karen, get your act together!

Freewriting is a warm-up activity: it loosens up your hand and your mind, and it gets you into the habit of thinking on paper. In addition, it solves the two most serious writing problems: getting started and getting ideas. If you get used to freewriting regularly, you won't panic when you are faced with a writing assignment. Instead of staring anxiously at the topic, you can record your immediate responses to the topic, your questions about it, and all of the associated ideas that occur to you. Also, by freewriting, you can find your own "voice"—your own way of seeing and saying things. Just remember that the only "rule" for freewriting is to keep writing for as long as possible or for as long as your teacher specifies. If your mind goes blank, that's what you write about ("I can't think of anything to say. My mind is blank. Help. What can I write about?"). Your goal is to get all of your ideas down on paper as quickly as possible. When you are finished freewriting, read over what you have written and underline any word or sentence that strikes you as particularly important or interesting. These underlined ideas can serve as starting points for further thinking and writing.

FREEWRITING REMINDERS

1. Write *nonstop* for as long as you can.
2. Use words and phrases; don't worry about writing complete sentences.
3. Write as quickly as you can about everything that comes into your mind.
4. Don't evaluate your ideas or your writing; just write.

EXERCISE **FREEWRITING**

Take out a piece of blank paper and write continuously for five minutes. During this time, do *not* put your pen or pencil down, and do *not* go back to read over what you have written. Write about whatever occurs to you. When you are finished writing, consider the number of times you started to worry about using the wrong word or making errors. Set yourself a goal of reducing this number.

WRITING ACTIVITY **FREEWRITING**

Choose *two* of the following topics and do five minutes of freewriting about each.

1. a childhood experience that you remember clearly
2. a recent or old dream that disturbs you
3. a favorite activity or hobby
4. a job you really liked or disliked
5. a favorite place
6. a problem that you have overcome
7. a belief or principle that guides your life
8. a characteristic or quality that is unique to you
9. a characteristic of yours that you want to change
10. a reason why you are going to school

A STUDENT RESPONSE

Here is a student's uncorrected five-minute freewriting about her favorite place:

> Candy T. — My Favorite Place
> My real favorite place is the dance floor at the Gaslight Club – great music, terrific dance floor. I was there last night, I go three or four nights a week. I better not write that cause then Prof. Greenberg's gonna ask me when I have

time to do all of my homework! Well I
make time. Because I love to dance.
I learn all the new dances from my friends
and from watching people at the club.
And then I get on the dance floor and
fly. I feel the music in my heart
and my head and my feet fly. I feel
like a bird. Dancing is so easy for me,
it makes me feel light and free. I could
dance all night every night. Maybe I should
think about becoming a professional dancer.
Only I don't like it when I have a clumsy partner.

GROUP EXERCISE **RESPONDING TO FREEWRITING**

Get into a group of three, and talk about your responses to doing
freewriting. You do *not* have to share your freewriting (unless you want
to). Simply share your responses to the questions that follow:

1. What did you think about Candy T.'s freewriting?
2. How did you feel while you were freewriting?
3. What do you think about this form of writing?
4. How might freewriting help you to become a better writer?

Brainstorming

Brainstorming is freewriting with a focus. It works best in a
group of three or four. Either you or your teacher specifies a topic, and
then each person in the group calls out every idea that he or she can
think of about the topic. Often one person's ideas stimulate the others
to think up different ideas about the topic. The trick to brainstorming
is to write down the group's ideas and your one-or-two-word responses
to them. You can be as messy as you need to be; no one but you will ever
read your notes. Your goal is to list as many ideas as possible, as fast as
everyone in the group says them aloud.

Brainstorming has one rule: no criticism is allowed. All ideas get
written down, regardless of your reaction to them. When the brain-

storming session is over, you will have pages of ideas about the topic. At that point, you can reread the list and circle the ideas that you find most interesting or that you think you might want to write about.

GROUP EXERCISE BRAINSTORMING IN A GROUP

Get into a group of four. Brainstorm together for five minutes about the benefits of exercising. Write down every idea that your classmates mention. When your group finishes brainstorming, circle the best ideas on your list.

EXERCISE BRAINSTORMING

Do five minutes of brainstorming about your favorite place and what it means to you. Here are some questions to help you get started:

- Exactly what do you see when you're in this place? What sights stand out? Describe these sights in detail (colors, shapes, sizes, textures, etc.). Why do these sights have special meaning for you?
- What sounds do you usually hear in this place? How nearby or far away are these sounds? What do the sounds remind you of? How do they make you feel?
- What can you smell in this place? What does the air smell like?
- What textures can you feel? What do the surfaces and the edges of things in this place feel like?
- What does being in this place make you think of?
- What does being in this place make you feel?
- Why do you like this place so much?

When you are done, think about the main impression that you have of the place—how do you feel about it and what makes you feel that way about it? Write down this main impression, and then do five more minutes of brainstorming about it.

A STUDENT RESPONSE

Here is an example of a student's individual brainstorming list that was done in response to the assignment "Describe your favorite place." Note that after he was finished brainstorming, the writer grouped similar ideas together and gave each group a label.

MY FAVORITE PLACE: MY CAR

*see
smell*

89 Corvette--my first car!!   My own money!

great condition--they took good care of it

big blue machine   new paint   sparkles

V-6 fuel-injected engine that's takes off

inside--clean blue leather

my favorite smell--leather and oil

great stereo--Akai cassette deck

new speakers!

*what
I do in
my car*

sit in the car and blast the radio

think and dream   my OWN space

or cruise the streets with Lynne

or go places cars and buses just can't go

or race friends at the drag strip

always wanted to be a race-car driver

*how I
feel
about
it*

CHALLENGE, speed, power

No one bothers me in my car   it's PRIVATE!

good place to hide, get away and think

lots of space and privacy--I love that feeling

I even like just being alone in my car and not

doing anything--just sitting in there and

thinking

My real home   MINE!

Allen Brower

Purpose

Try to make people understand how I feel about

my car and why I feel so strong.

BRAINSTORMING REMINDERS_____
1. Concentrate on the topic.
2. Say anything that comes to mind about the topic or problem, no matter how silly or irrelevant it seems.
3. Write words and short phrases, not sentences.
4. Don't judge, evaluate, or ridicule anybody's ideas (including your own).

A STUDENT RESPONSE

Here is a brainstorm that was written in response to the assignment "describe an experience that changed your life" by a college freshman named Joan Brown:

Tommy's birth - problems - different
   Found out he's retarded

Mongeloid - never be normal - slow to develop
   Family upset   physically &
                        mentally

Special kid - sweet, happy, good, loving

Mom and Dad had to work - I had to take care of him

My Favorite brother - I fed him, washed him
                        dressed him, played with him

Now - he's walking and talking
   learning (slowly)

Future - who knows his potential?
   (Doctors sure don't - they've been
   wrong about him all along)

I'll always take care of him

He made me grow up   Gave me courage

   faith

Special love.

Clustering

Clustering is a form of brainstorming that enables you to see different kinds of relationships among your ideas about a topic. You begin a cluster by writing your topic in the middle of a page and by putting a circle around the topic. Then you record all of your ideas about the topic in other circles around the topic and connect them. If you get stuck in one branch of a cluster, go back to your central topic and begin a new branch.

When you run out of ideas, stop and evaluate what you have written. First, decide if the central circle is still the most important focus of the cluster. Maybe one of the other circles would make a better topic to write about. Next, try to note the theme of each of the main clusters and decide which ones are most interesting. Make separate clusters for each of these main clusters. Creating these clusters will help you to generate new ideas and to see the relationships among these ideas.

A STUDENT RESPONSE

Here is a cluster that a student wrote about his decision to go to college.

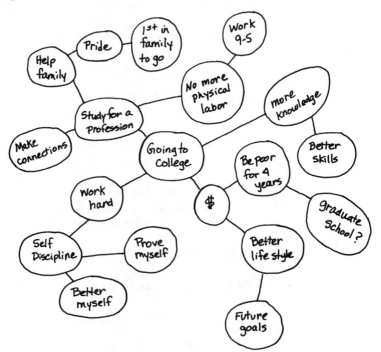

As you can see, clustering may be messy. Just make sure that you can follow the connections among your ideas.

CLUSTERING REMINDERS _____

1. Write as many words and phrases as you can think of, no matter how irrelevant they may seem at first.
2. Try to develop a cluster around each circle.
3. Keep the connecting lines in each cluster clear.

EXERCISE CLUSTERING

Choose a topic, or ask your teacher to suggest one, and make a cluster for it on a separate piece of paper. If you get stuck, ask yourself some of the questions that were discussed in the section on brainstorming. Try to continue clustering for ten minutes. Fill up the entire page with connected clusters. When you are finished, look for the group of circles that seems most interesting or that seems to connect several logically related ideas. Give that group a label, and write a sentence explaining the main point of the group.

Write a sentence or two describing the different types of paragraphs that you could use to develop the different groups of circles in your cluster.

TECHNIQUES FOR DEVELOPING A DISCOVERY DRAFT

A discovery draft consists of a writer's first attempt at developing an idea in paragraph or essay form. After you have explored your thoughts and feelings through freewriting, brainstorming, and clustering, you are ready to put some of your ideas together in sentences and paragraphs. However, as the name of this draft implies, you are still discovering what you want to say about a topic. In fact, as you write a draft, you should continue to ask yourself questions about the topic, questions such as these:

- What points do I want to make about this topic?
- Who are my potential readers and what do they want or need to know?

- What do I want to make my reader think or feel or do about this topic?
- What else do I need to know about this topic in order to write intelligently about it?
- Why is this topic important?

Remember that your goal in writing a discovery draft is to write details that develop the ideas in your drafting activities. Therefore, it is extremely important that you do not edit prematurely at this stage: do *not* worry about spelling, punctuation, or grammar. Just concentrate on selecting, developing, and connecting the ideas that you wrote about in your freewriting, brainstorming, and clustering. Your discovery draft can be as messy as you like, since it will be revised several times before other people read it. However, remember to leave wide margins on all four sides of your paper for the comments and symbols that you will be writing on it. Also, skip lines (or type with triple spaces) so that you will have room for revisions.

STUDENT RESPONSES

Below is an uncorrected draft that Joan Brown wrote, based on her brainstorming on page 33 of this chapter. Note that she did not edit any errors.

A Special Birth — Joan B.

When my little brother Tommy was born my life change. He is a Mongeloid, he's retarded ~~and different~~ and he will never be normal and he's developing very slowly—both physically and mentally. At first my family (and I) were very upset. He has so many problems that the family has to take ~~good~~ special care of him. I have helped him the most. Since my Mom and Dad have to work, I have been responsible for feeding him.

washing him dressing him and playing with him. He's such a wonderful kid - he's gentle and happy and loving and I adore him. He made me grow up. Taking care of him taught me about life and made me strong. I love him. I'm glad he's my brother. His life definitely change mine for the better!

Here is the uncorrected discovery draft that Allen Brower developed from the brainstorming list on page 32 of this chapter.

```
          FIRST REVISION: MY FAVORITE PLACE

     My favorite place in the world is my car.  Its the first

car that I have ever owned and I really enjoy being in it.  I

like to sit inside and breathe the smell of the leather and

oil.  The car is a 1989 Corvette and its previous owner took

care of it.  The blue paint gleams and the chrome sparkles.

Its really smooth.  The blue leather is worn but clean.  And

the stripes on the sides of the car really look fine.  Also

there's an stereo radio and cassette deck with four speakers

that can blast me to heaven.  I feel like this car is my real

home.  It's private.  No one bothers me when I'm driving

around or even sitting in the car.  I can use it to go places

that buses and trains just can't go.  Its a terrific place to

think and dream.  Also, I like to race friends in the local
```

drag strip. Even when I'm doing this, I feel alone and I love

the feeling of space and privacy. I zoom along feeling

powerful and free. I also use my car simply as a place to

hang out, cruising the streets with my girlfriend. And I

enjoy being alone in the car. Its my own space and my own

machine and I love it.

Allen Brower

GETTING STARTED WITH A WORD PROCESSOR

If you have access to a computerized word processing program, you already know that it can make planning, drafting, and revising easier and more fun to do. Although the word processor does not automatically make people better writers, it does enable them to experiment more—to play with words, phrases, and paragraphs until they are genuinely pleased with what they have written. And a word processor makes writing less stressful, because it removes the need to rewrite and retype a composition every time the writer revises. Here are some guidelines for getting ideas for discovery drafts using a word processor:

1. Make sure that you know your word processing program well. If it has *tutorials*, practice them slowly and carefully (and take written notes if you need to). Make lists of all the specialized writing features that your program includes, and try to memorize the combination of keys that activates each feature.
2. Try out a special form of freewriting called "invisible writing." Turn the screen's *brightness control* until the screen is blank. Then type in your freewriting. You will not be able to see what you are writing, and this may encourage your creativity by helping you to concentrate solely on generating new ideas.
3. *Save* every freewriting list, every brainstorming list, and every discovery draft *as soon as you complete it*. Give each file a separate name or coded title, and include the date of creation. Every five minutes, *save* everything you write.
4. If your program has *windows* or *split screens*, put your freewriting and brainstorming notes into a window or split screen so that they remain on the screen when you begin to draft.

> 5. When you finish a prewriting or drafting session, make *back-up* copies of your files. Then, print out *hard* copies of them.
> 6. Read your *printouts* carefully, and make notes on them to guide your next session at the word processor.

READ BEFORE YOU WRITE

On the preceding pages you read a student's description of a person and an experience that changed her life. Here is another writer's response to this topic. The excerpt that follows is from *And The Walls Came Tumbling Down*, the autobiography of Ralph Abernathy, the famous clergyman and civil rights leader. As you read this description, underline the sensory language that enables you to share Abernathy's perceptions of his subject.

I learned about strength, independence, and moral earnestness from my father, while my mother taught me kindness, love, and gentility. She was the sweetest and most caring person I have ever known; and from the beginning her presence at my side flooded my life with warmth and sunlight. For as long as she lived, I belonged to her, and when she died my youth and innocence died with her.

Her maiden name was Louivery Valentine Bell (she was born on St. Valentine's Day), and she married my father on New Year's Eve in 1905. She bore him twelve children who survived infancy, and I can never recall that they quarreled or raised their voices in anger against one another. As a result of this domestic peace our family was close-knit and loving. The familial harmony that exists today among my brothers and sisters is in large measure a legacy of my mother's.

Not that she submitted without protest to my father's strong hand when she believed he was wrong. But she would never challenge him in front of the children, I suppose because she knew it might undermine his authority in our eyes. But in her quiet, endearing way, she was as strong as he was, something I found out when I was around six years old and entering school for the first time.

Like every younger child in a large family, I lived with hand-me-downs; I wore them and played with them. But when I went to school I wanted my own books—brand new ones with perfectly white inside covers where I could write my own name without first scratching out the name of my brother. Books were special to me, and my mother understood how I felt.

My father, on the other hand, was more pragmatic. He had housed, fed, and clothed ten of us, with two more coming up; and he saw no reason why he should have to buy more books when there were perfectly legible copies of what I needed stacked up in one of the closets. "You use William's books," he told me. "It's foolishness to waste money on new ones."

I tried to protest, but he simply didn't want to listen. There were other needs, other priorities. He was immovable and my eyes filled with tears.

Then I noticed my mother watching me with anguish on her face; and I was amazed to see her dabbing her eyes with her apron. She was crying because of me! I believe it was the first time in my life that I understood what love really meant, that capacity to feel the suffering of others as if it were your own. I was stunned with the sheer beauty of it, and a little frightened as well. My father wheeled and walked quickly out of the room, on his way to saddle his mule for a ride around the farm. He left behind a room filled with cold air.

Then my mother, without a word to me, charged after him. Through the window I could see her rushing to catch up to him as he walked toward the open field where the mule was grazing. Because I knew that my father's word, like the Good Lord's, was absolutely and eternally true, I turned from the scene and went somewhere to brood.

The next day, when I didn't have the right books, I was scolded by the teacher. I assured her that I would have the books by the next day, though my heart was in despair, because I knew my father all too well. However, when I came in the front door after school I saw them piled in a neat stack on the dining room table: all the books I needed, their jackets untorn and unwrinkled, their pages still white and unsoiled.

I knew immediately who was responsible, and I went into the kitchen to hug my mother. Later, when my father came in from the fields, I thanked him as well, but he merely nodded his head and brushed the matter aside. That afternoon I understood a little more about the world in which I lived than I had that morning.

WRITING ASSIGNMENT **WRITING A DISCOVERY DRAFT**

The topic for this discovery draft is the same one that Joan Brown and Ralph Abernathy wrote about: a person or an experience that affected your life or that taught you something important. Your purpose is to let readers see what you saw, hear what you heard, and experience what you felt. Your audience for this draft is your teacher.

Prewriting Guidelines
1. Do some freewriting on the topic. Write for fifteen minutes about everything that comes into your mind when you think about a person or an experience that changed your life.
2. Select several ideas from your freewriting that seem to explain why the person or experience had such an impact on your life. Do five minutes of brainstorming or clustering about these ideas.
3. Reread your freewriting *and* your brainstorming or clustering. Select the most interesting ideas and connect them into a paragraph. Do *not* worry about spelling, punctuation, grammar, or sentence structure.
4. Get feedback on your discovery draft by following the guidelines below.

How to Get Feedback about Your Discovery Draft
   Read the directions below carefully *before* you begin.
1. Get into a group of two or three students, and take turns reading your discovery drafts aloud to one another. When it is your turn to read, speak slowly and clearly, and don't interrupt your reading with comments about the draft. Just read it through in its entirety.
2. When it is your turn to listen to a classmate, put your draft away where you cannot see it. Try not to think about your draft; instead, concentrate on your classmate's draft. Listen closely to each classmate, and try to understand the ideas that each is trying to communicate. Do *not* write while your classmate is reading. Do not evaluate or judge his or her writing. Do not make any criticisms.
3. *After* each person reads his or her draft, you have three minutes to take notes on what you have heard. Write down what you think were the author's main points and important details. Write down any words or phrases that you remember clearly. Also write down any point or sentence that seemed particularly interesting or that you want to know more about.
4. After everyone in the group has finished reading and writing, take turns reading what you have written about each person's draft.
5. When it is your turn to listen to your classmates' responses, take out your draft and write notes on it. Note the ideas, sentences, or words that your classmates point out and note the places where they may have misunderstood you or where they want more information.

   The goal of giving and getting this feedback is to help members of the group become more aware of the strengths in their writing and more aware of the impact of their writing on readers. After you go through this "group feedback" experience, you will have a clearer sense of your discovery draft as a "whole" piece of writing. Your classmates' comments should help you see where it is strong and where it is confusing or misleading. You can use your classmates' comments to help you revise your discovery draft.

ISSUES FOR YOUR JOURNAL

Use your journal to record things that stimulate your thinking: ideas, observations, notes, questions, outlines, quotations, lists, signs, titles, and anything else that you might want to think or write more about at a later date. At the end of every chapter in this book, I have included several ideas for you to explore in your journal. These issues and questions are based on material discussed in the preceding chapters and on paragraph and essay topics in the chapters that follow. In other words, you can use your journal to think and write about most of the writing assignments in this book.

1. What is your impression of your writing course or of this writing textbook so far? What do you like about the course or the book? What do you dislike about either one (or about both)?
2. How did you feel about working with your classmates? How did you react to giving or getting feedback on each other's writing?
3. What interesting or strange things have been happening in your life recently? How have you reacted to these events?
4. Look at the list of topics on page 29 of this chapter. Choose one of them to write about in your journal.
5. Who is the person you care about most in your life now? In your journal, describe this person in detail. What is it about this person that makes you care so much about him or her? Why is he or she so special? What have you learned about yourself from caring about this person?

ADDITIONAL READING

In the reading that follows, Lynn Z. Bloom describes the sources of her ideas. Bloom is an English professor who has written numerous books and articles on writing, biography, and autobiography.

A writer is always writing. I write when I swim, I write when I cook (favorite daily activities); I write when I dream, asleep or awake, especially during an hour of semiwakefulness I've come to cherish early every morning after five or six hours of sound sleep. James Thurber has described well the process of incessant writing:

> I never quite know when I'm not writing. Sometimes my wife comes up to me at a party and says, "Dammit, Thurber, stop writing." She usually catches me in the middle of a paragraph. Or my daughter will look up from the dinner table and ask, "Is he sick?" "No," my wife says. "He's writing something."

Sometimes my mental writing consists of random speculations, searching for a golden needle in a haystack that is mostly straw. At other times it means looking at a more familiar subject from a deliberately unusual perspective, or series of perspectives, to see anew—because I don't want to see—or say—the same old thing. Often, one idea will lead to another.

When I get a good idea, one that seems right, or so obvious that I wonder why no one ever thought of it before, I recognize it immediately. Aha! It took me five years and one minute—the latter six hundred pages into the final rewrite—and a catalytic suggestion from a friend to discover the right title for my most recent book. I take casual, fragmentary notes on this thinking, usually jotting down key words and phrases, and names of books and authors to consult. If ideas don't come, I read. When the material is relevant I continue to take sketchy notes, or to dog-ear pages. When the material is irrelevant—the daily papers or a novel when I'm wrestling with a critical issue in autobiography—the reading is merely a diversionary activity, a facade for the thinking about the *real* issue that I'm working on beneath the surface. If good ideas still don't come, or if I find it hard to concentrate creatively, I stop and turn to something entirely different, maybe even a less demanding kind of writing. I know the hard part will continue to simmer on a mental back burner until it's pliable enough to work with.

From time to time I stop and simply sit and think; it looks as if I'm not doing anything. Or I take a brief nap, or drink tea and read the newspaper, or exercise, or cook, or do (horrors!) housework. And let the ideas cook awhile. Sometimes I discuss my ideas with my husband, a social psychologist who's been not only my best friend but my best—and most unsparing—critic for nearly thirty years. During this casual-seeming time of intense gestation

I try to keep out distractions, especially those that involve concentrated thought and effort in other areas of life. Indeed, to the extent that I can, I try to compartmentalize categories of major effort; teaching and paper grading get done on teaching days; writing gets done on writing days; social activities and errands get pushed into gaps between these larger blocks of time.

OPTIONAL WRITING ASSIGNMENT

Write a page or two about the prewriting strategies that you learned in this chapter: How can you fit these strategies into your daily life or into your writing habits? How might using them change your writing attitudes and behaviors?

CHAPTER THREE

SHAPING IDEAS

How do I know what I think until I see what I say?

E.M. FORSTER

We do not write in order to be understood, we write in order to understand.

C. DAY LEWIS

Faith. Hardest of all for me. Faith that I can write, that I have something to say, that I can find out what it is, that I can make it clear to me, to a reader, so that I can write so that the reader is not aware of the writer but the meaning.

DONALD MURRAY

FOCUS, PURPOSE, AUDIENCE, AND SUPPORTING DETAILS

Once you have gotten your ideas flowing in a discovery draft, you can begin to shape your material so that it has a focus and a development that a reader can follow. Your discovery draft may seem clear and logical to you, but chances are that it may not make much sense to anyone else. As you prepare your writing for readers, you have to clarify the connections between your ideas. You also need to consider your readers' concerns and attitudes and to develop examples and reasons that will convince readers of your points.

Most experienced writers begin shaping a draft for readers by thinking carefully about their focus, purpose, and audience. Sometimes referred to as the "thesis," the **focus** is the main point that the writer wants to make about a topic. When you were writing your discovery draft for the assignment in the previous chapter, you may have had a vague notion of the central point that your draft would develop. Now, reread your draft to find out if it does have a focus—a clear main point—or if it does not (that is, if it jumps from point to point without making any clear assertion about the topic). Ask yourself which sentence in the draft interests you most. Does it serve as the focus for all of the other details that you have written? If not, then you need to write more details to expand upon your focus. Or maybe you need to choose a different sentence in your discovery draft to serve as the focus of your revision.

Writers must also think about their **purpose** or reason for writing. Why are you writing the draft? To explain something? To tell a story? To describe something or someone? To analyze something? To convince someone of something? Sometimes, writers do not know their purpose until they begin writing—as they sort out their ideas and figure out what they want to say, they discover their purpose for writing a particular piece. Whenever you write something, ask yourself how you want readers to feel or what you want them to think or do after they finish reading your writing. Even if you are writing to yourself—to explore an idea, to clarify your feelings, or to learn something—you should keep your purpose in mind.

Finally, writers must consider their **audience** (their readers). Are you writing to yourself, your family, your friends, classmates, teacher, or employer? When you write for these people, you have a sense of how familiar they are with you and with your topic. If you don't know your audience, then you have to invent one. Keeping an audience in mind while writing helps writers figure out how much information their readers already know about the topic. It also helps them analyze what their readers want to know or need to know about the topic. In addition, keeping the audience in mind enables writers to select details and words that their readers will understand and that will not offend their readers in any way.

One's focus, purpose, and audience influence everything that one writes, from the first discovery draft to the final revision. The activities in this chapter will help you clarify your focus, purpose, and audience and will give you many options for developing appropriate details.

GROUP WRITING TASK   **EXAMINING FOCUS, PURPOSE, AND AUDIENCE**

Work on this activity with two other students. Think about the essay that you might write for each of the topics below. Brainstorm a list of all of the details that you would include in each essay.

- Topic 1: Write a description of your town or city. The purpose of this description is to share your feelings, impressions, and observations about your town. The audience consists of people your age who live in your town and whom you know.
- Topic 2: Write a description of your town or city. The purpose of this description is to inform your readers about your town and to explain why it is an appealing or an unappealing place to live. The audience consists of couples who have young children and who are considering moving to your town.

When your group has finished writing the two lists, discuss the ways in which the lists differ. Consider the following questions:

- How does the information included in the lists differ?
- How does the vocabulary in the lists differ?
- How formal or informal is each list?
- Which list was easier to write? Why?
- How did the purpose influence the details in each list?
- How did the audience influence the details in each list?

TECHNIQUES FOR INVENTING AUDIENCES

If you do not know your audience (because you do not know the intended reader or because the audience has not been specified in your writing assignment), then you have to invent some readers. You will have to make up a person or a group of people who might be interested in or concerned about your focus, and you will have to consider their knowledge, attitudes, and feelings about the topic. Jot down some notes about the members of your imaginary audience:

- How old are they?
- What are their cultural and religious backgrounds?
- How much education have they had?
- What do they do for a living?
- What books, magazines, and newspapers do they read?
- What are their political and moral beliefs?

EXERCISE   **INVENTING AUDIENCES FOR DIFFERENT PURPOSES**

This exercise will help you gain experience inventing and visualizing unknown audiences. Think about each audience and purpose, and then write an answer to each of the questions.

1. Focus: The pleasure or the harm of cigarette smoking
   Purpose: Explain why you do or don't smoke cigarettes
   Audience: A nurse in your school's medical office
   a. What does this reader already know about you and about cigarette smoking?

   b. What is this reader's attitude toward smoking?

   c. What might this reader want to know or need to know?

2. Focus: The joy of a concert
   Purpose: Describe a concert starring your favorite musical group
   Audience:
   (Invent an appropriate group of readers or an appropriate magazine for this description)
   a. What do these readers already know about this topic?

   b. How do these readers feel about this topic?

   c. What might these readers want or need to know?

WRITING ACTIVITY **WRITING FOR DIFFERENT AUDIENCES**

This activity will help you improve your ability to invent and visualize unknown audiences and to shape details to fit their needs. Choose a topic that you know a lot about, and decide on a purpose for writing about it. Then write one sentence about the topic that will serve as your tentative focus. Next, write two paragraphs for two different audiences. First, write a paragraph about your focus for readers who know almost nothing about your topic. Then write a paragraph—about the same focus—for readers who are experts on your topic.

When you finish the paragraphs, answer the following questions:

1. How did the examples and reasons in your two paragraphs differ?
2. How did the organization of the two paragraphs differ?
3. How did the vocabulary in the two paragraphs differ?

OPTIONS FOR DEVELOPING DETAILS

Your audience and purpose determine the kinds of details that are appropriate for the focus of any writing that you have to do. For example, suppose you were asked to write a brief essay on "my best friend." As you do some freewriting, brainstorming, and clustering about this topic, you might realize that you have many ideas about it and points that you want to make. You would also begin to see that you have a variety of options for narrowing your focus and for developing your points:

- You could describe the way your best friend looks, sounds, and behaves.
- You could describe an incident or a scene involving your best friend.
- You could compare and contrast your best friend with other types of friends.
- You could describe different ways in which best friends act toward one another.
- You could explain some of the reasons why you (or people in general) chose a best friend.
- You could explain the effects or consequences of having a best friend.
- You could use a combination of all the strategies above to support your ideas about people's need for best friends.

How do writers select the best option (or combination of strategies)? Successful writers think about their purpose and their audience and ask themselves questions as they write.

DEVELOPING DETAILS: FOUR QUESTIONS TO ASK YOURSELF

1. What do I want to convince my readers of?
2. Which details will be most convincing to these particular readers?
3. Which strategies fit my purpose, ideas, and details?
4. What ideas and words are appropriate for this audience?

WRITING ACTIVITY   **CREATING DIFFERENT DETAILS**
FOR DIFFERENT PURPOSES AND AUDIENCES

The focus for these two writing tasks is your best friend. For this activity, you will be writing two different descriptions of this person.

Task 1

Your best friend has asked you to write a letter of recommendation for a part-time job that he or she really wants and needs. Write this letter to an imaginary employer (whose name, business, and address you will have to invent), and try to convince the employer to hire your friend immediately. (You will also have to invent the job title.)

Task 2

This same friend is depressed because he or she has recently moved to a new city and doesn't have any friends yet. You decide to help your friend by writing and sending a letter to the "People in Our Town" column of the local newsletter. Write a letter to the editor of this newsletter describing your friend in a way that will convince people to call him or her and make plans to get together.

When you finish both tasks, identify the similarities and the differences in your two descriptions of your best friend.

A STUDENT RESPONSE

The description below was written in response to the following assignment: "Describe your best friend and relate an experience that supports your impression of him or her." (The audience was "class-mates.") After reading it, answer the questions that follow.

My best friend and I look so much alike that we're often mistaken for sisters. We are both 5'6" tall and weigh 120 pounds. And we both have shoulder-length curly red hair. But our resemblance is only skin deep. Emotionally we're very different. Unlike me, my friend Lizette is cool and calm. She doesn't have many highs and lows whereas I'm always either really excited and happy or down in the dumps. But even though Lizette is so easy-going and self-controlled she still has very passionate feelings. She loves her family and friends deeply and she would sacrifice her own happiness for theirs. For example last week she won tickets to see a jazz group that we both really like and she told me to take the tickets and go with my boyfriend. She said "You like them better so you go. You'll enjoy it more." And she wasn't just saying that. She wouldn't stop pestering me about the tickets until I finally agreed to take them. She is always doing things like that. I guess that's why she's such a wonderful friend and why her friendship is so important to me. She helps me stay sane and stable and I know that she'll always care for me, no matter what happens or what I do.

Luisa Lord

1. What was the writer's focus?
2. What was the writer's purpose in this description?
3. What was her audience?
4. What types of details were most effective? Why?

TYPES OF SUPPORTING DETAILS

As Luisa Lord's paragraph illustrates, effective writers support their ideas with a variety of different types of details including facts, experiences, and observations.

Facts are details that express "truths"—statements that can be verified (checked for their truth or their accuracy). Facts often refer to specific names, dates, amounts, and statistics, or to actual things, places, and events. Writers often use facts to convince readers of their points or their arguments. Lord included several facts—statements that could be proved true—to support her point: "We are both 5'6" tall and weigh 120 pounds."

Experiences are details that tell the story of an incident or an event that the writer has experienced or witnessed. Writers use these kinds of details to let the reader "see" the actions and "hear" the words of the people involved in the incident. There are three kinds of experiences that can be used as supporting details:

- *direct*—experiences that the writer actually had
- *imaginary*—experiences that the writer dreamed, thought, or wondered about
- *vicarious*—experiences that the writer heard about from others, read about or saw in a movie or on television

In her narration of a direct experience that she had with her best friend, Lord provides specific details about the way her friend acted and spoke, and these details allow readers to understand how and why she feels as she does.

Observations are sensory details that reveal writers' impressions about their topic. These kinds of details let the reader know how the writer perceives the topic and how the writer feels about it. Lord's paragraph is filled with observations about her friend's physical and emotional characteristics. These images and illustrations enable readers to share the writer's perspective and believe her conclusions.

In Chapter 2, you practiced sharpening your senses and improving your ability to create sensory images for your readers. Observations are often composed of these images, and the more specific they are, the easier it is for your reader to sense them and almost experience them. For example, which of the following details gives you a clearer impression of the writer's observation?

1. The sun shone brightly through the light blue afternoon sky.
2. The sun seemed like a dazzling orange ball shining brightly over the pearl blue sky and the iridescent clouds.

What picture do you "see" from the details in the second sentence? How is this different from the picture that the first sentence communicates to you? In the second sentence, the writer used "pearl blue" to describe the color of the sky. She could have used a different shade of blue. In fact, the *Dictionary of Color Names* lists over 500 different shades of blue. Below is a sample listing of some different blues. Examine this list and decide which of these shades best describes the color of the sky today.

blue ashes	bright bluish violet
blue black	chrome blue
bluebird blue	dark bluish gray green
blue chill	dull blue green black
blue drab	dusky blue green

When you describe an observation or an experience that you had, try *showing* readers what you saw, heard, and felt instead of *telling* them. Let your readers share your experience; don't simply summarize it for them. Details that "show" are far more interesting to read than are details that "tell." Concrete, sensory language enables readers to share the writer's perceptions and experiences. For example, here are two sentences that "tell" about a scene:

The yard between the tenements was very narrow and it was filthy and dusty. Lots of sunlight shone brightly into it.

Below is the actual paragraph that these sentences summarize. Note how the author, Alfred Kazin, uses details to "show" the reader the scene as he perceived it:

The yard smelled of brick and was thickmatted with clotheslines. On every side the white backs of the two tenements rose up around you, enclosing you in a narrow circle littered with splintered crates, loose sheets of old newspaper, garbage cans, and the thin green ooze left behind by the cats. Great shafts of light poured through the space between the roofs, rewhitening the sheets hung across the yard. Every particle of light falling into the yard seemed to dissolve into the color of that dusty white brick at the back, revolving in the air as if shot out of a great open bag of flour. When you were in the yard, you could look only straight up, the clotheslines seemed about to strangle you—the place was so narrow, so narrow; held you in a cylinder of white dust and the noise from the back windows.

EXERCISE **ANALYZING DETAILS THAT "SHOW"**

Below is an excerpt from a book by the Pulitzer Prize–winning writer, Norman Mailer. This paragraph describes his first impression of Senator Robert Kennedy. Notice that Mailer's observations are composed of very specific sensory details and that these details reveal his subject's personality.

So it had begun well enough, and the reporter had been taken with Kennedy's appearance. He was slimmer even than one would have thought, not strong, not weak, somewhere between a blade of grass and a blade of steel, fine, finely drawn, finely honed, a fine flush of color in his cheeks, two very white front teeth, prominent as the two upper teeth of a rabbit, so his mouth had no hint of the cruelty or calculation of a politician who weighs counties, cities, and states, but was rather a mouth ready to nip at anything which attracted its contempt or endangered its ideas. Then there were his eyes. They were the most unusual. His brother Teddy Kennedy spoke of those who "followed him, honored him, lived in his mild and magnificent eye," and that was fair description for he had very large blue eyes, the iris wide in diameter, near to twice the width of the average eye, and the blue was a milky blue like a marble so that his eyes, while prominent, did not show the separate steps and slopes of light some bright eyes show, but rather were gentle, indeed beautiful—one was tempted to speak of velvety eyes—their surface seemed made of velvet as if one could touch them, and the surface would not be repelled.

Get into a group with two or three classmates and choose someone to write down the group's responses to the questions that follow:

1. To which senses does Mailer appeal?
2. Which sensory words are most effective in conveying Mailer's perception of Robert Kennedy?
3. Based on this description, describe Robert Kennedy's personality.

WRITING ACTIVITY **DEVELOPING DIFFERENT TYPES OF SUPPORTING DETAILS**

Think of one person whom you know very well. Write the person's name on top of a piece of paper, and next to this name, write your dominant impression of the person—the quality that you think of most immediately when you think of this person or when you see him or her. A dominant impression is the characteristic that best describes a person (for example, "gentle," "fierce," "sexy," "aggressive," "bubbly," "depressed").

Next, write the heading "Facts" on your paper, and list as many facts as you can think of that contribute to your dominant impression of this person. These facts can be statements about the person's physical characteristics, gestures, behavior, or actions. Make sure that the details you are listing are not merely your opinions—each detail must be one that other people would agree is true.

When you finish listing facts, write the heading "Experiences," and write down the details of one or two experiences in which the person said things or displayed behavior that revealed your dominant impression of him or her. Make the experience "come alive" by including sensory details about the setting, the people involved, their actions, and their exact words.

Then, write the heading "Observations," and list all the other details that contribute to your dominant impression of the person. What physical characteristics contribute to this impression? List sensory details that show how this person looks, behaves, and sounds.

A PROFESSIONAL RESPONSE

Read this excerpt from *The Joy Luck Club* by the novelist Amy Tan. Then answer the questions that follow.

I didn't tell anyone about the things I saw, not even my mother. Most people didn't know I was half Chinese, maybe because my last name is St. Clair. When people first saw me, they thought I looked like my father, English-Irish, big boned and delicate at the same time. But if they looked really close, if they knew that they were there, they could see the Chinese parts. Instead of having cheeks like my father's sharp-edged points, mine were smooth as beach pebbles. I didn't have his straw-yellow hair or his white skin, yet my coloring looked too pale, like something that was once darker and had faded in the sun.

And my eyes, my mother gave me my eyes, no eyelids, as if they were carved on a jack-o'-lantern with two swift cuts of a short knife. I used to push my eyes in on the sides to make them rounder. Or I'd open them very wide until I could see the white parts. But when I walked around the house like that, my father asked me why I looked so scared.

I have a photo of my mother with this same scared look. My father said the picture was taken when Ma was first released from Angel Island Immigration Station. She stayed there for three weeks, until they could process her papers and determine whether she was a War Bride, a Displaced Person, a Student, or the wife of a Chinese-American citizen. My father said they didn't have rules for dealing with the Chinese wife of a Caucasian citizen. Somehow, in the end, they declared her a Displaced Person, lost in a sea of immigration categories.

My mother never talked about her life in China, but my father said he saved her from a terrible life there, some tragedy she could not speak about. My father proudly named her in her immigration papers: Betty St. Clair, crossing out her given name of Gu Ying-ying. And then he put down the wrong birthyear, 1916 instead of 1914. So, with the sweep of a pen, my mother lost her name and became a Dragon instead of a Tiger.

In this picture you can see why my mother looks displaced. She is clutching a large clam-shaped bag, as though someone might steal this from her as well if she is less watchful. She has on an ankle-length Chinese dress with modest vents at the side. And on top she is wearing a Westernized suit jacket, awkwardly stylish on my mother's small body, with its padded shoulders, wide lapels, and oversize cloth buttons. This was my mother's wedding dress, a gift from my father. In this outfit she looks as if she were neither coming from nor going to someplace. Her chin is bent down and you can see the precise part in her hair, a neat white line drawn from above her left brow then over the black horizon of her head.

And even though her head is bowed, humble in defeat, her eyes are staring up past the camera, wide open.

"Why does she look scared?" I asked my father.

And my father explained: It was only because he said "Cheese," and my mother was struggling to keep her eyes open until the flash went off, ten seconds later.

My mother often looked this way, waiting for something to happen, wearing this scared look. Only later she lost the struggle to keep her eyes open.

1. What is the narrator's dominant impression of her mother? (What is the main point that she wants to make about her mother, Betty St. Clair?)
2. Which words in the description enable you to *see* Betty St. Clair?
3. What kinds of supporting details—facts, observations, or experiences—did the narrator use most often in this excerpt?
4. Try to describe Betty St. Clair in your own words (in a sentence or two).

SUBJECTIVE VERSUS TECHNICAL DESCRIPTION

Description is always influenced by the speaker's or the writer's audience and purpose. For example, think about how you would respond if you walked into your home and discovered that it had been burglarized while you were away. Your room is wrecked: everything has been ripped or broken, and the place is a mess. Imagine that you call the police and then you call your best friend to describe the burglary. How would you describe the scene to the police officers who come to your home? How would you describe the scene to your best friend? Probably, the details that you would give to the police officers would be **technical** ones: the extent of the damage, the location of every item, the ways in which things had been moved or broken. The police officers would need to know specific details about how your room looked before and after the burglary. They would not be too interested in how you feel about what happened. Your best friend, on the other hand, would probably want to know your personal response to the burglary—what it means to you and to your life. The description that you would give your friend would be **subjective;** it would convey your feelings and impressions. Whenever you write descriptions of people, places, or things, you have to decide whether your purpose and your audience require technical or subjective details or a mixture of both kinds.

WRITING ACTIVITY **EXAMINING SUBJECTIVE AND TECHNICAL DETAILS**

Here are two descriptions of a place. The first is a technical description, the second a subjective description. How do they differ?

Pennsylvania is roughly rectangular in shape and its area of 45,333 square miles ranks it 33rd in size among the States. Situated astride the Appalachian Mountains, it has access to the Atlantic Ocean, the Great Lakes, and the Ohio River Valley.

Altitudes range from sea level in the Philadelphia area to 3,213 at the summit of Mt. Davis in Somerset County. Although there are lowlands near the Atlantic Ocean and the Great Lakes, most of the State's terrain is mountainous. Its mean altitude is about 1,100 feet.

Except for a narrow lowland in the northwest corner of Pennsylvania, the western and northern parts of the State are occupied by a plateau. The Appalachian Mountain Range, averaging about 70 miles in width, trends north and northeast across the central and east-central parts of the State. East and southeast of these mountains, low rolling hills and shallow valleys extend to the Philadelphia area. A narrow lowland in the southeasternmost part of the State is part of the Atlantic Coastal Plain, which fringes the Delaware River and Delaware Bay.

U.S. Department of the Interior

Pennsylvania means many things to different people. To one it means the glow of steel mills along the Monongahela at night or strip

mines in Venango County or the milky water of the Clarion at Johnson-
burg. To another it means the trout streams of Centre County, duck
hunting at Pymatuning, a cabin on the upper Allegheny, maple trees at
Myersdale in autumn, the long beach bordered by cottonwoods at Pres-
que Isle, or the ski slopes at Ligionier when the snow lies deep upon the
mountains. Or it means an eagle seen from Mt. Davis fighting its way
through a thunderstorm, a deer starved and winter-killed in Elk
County, acres of trillium along Thorn Creek, or the pink mountains of
Bedford County when the wild azaleas bloom. For each of us there is a
favorite picture or recollection. Mine takes me back a good many years.

Edwin L. Peterson

1. How did the first description make you feel? Which details made
   you feel this way?
2. How did the second description make you feel? Which details
   made you feel this way?

EXERCISE   **DEVELOPING TECHNICAL AND SUBJECTIVE DETAILS**

Below is a picture of a family that lost its home in a flood. On a
separate piece of paper, make two lists. For the first list, note details
that describe exactly what you see in the picture. For the second list,
write details about how the picture makes you feel. When you are finished writing both lists, write a paragraph describing the picture
based on *one* of your lists.

WRITING ACTIVITY SHAPING SUBJECTIVE AND TECHNICAL DESCRIPTIONS

Do five minutes of freewriting about your home town (your neighborhood or your city). Then do some brainstorming and clustering about your town. Focus on the town's advantages. You will be using your freewriting, brainstorming, and clustering to write the two different descriptions below. For each one, consider your purpose and your audience, and decide how subjective or how technical your description should be.

Description 1

Write a description of your home town for the real estate newsletter *People and Places.* This newsletter will be distributed to real estate agents across the country. They will be handing it out to their clients—mostly people aged 25–35 who are interested in buying a new home or renting an apartment. The editor of this newsletter has asked you to write a description that will convince these readers to buy or rent a home in your town.

Description 2

Write a description of your home town for the magazine *Money-Making Opportunities.* The people who subscribe to this magazine are mostly middle-aged business people who have some money to invest and who are looking for investments that will make a lot of money. Several builders are considering building a new shopping center in your town and they want to convince readers of this magazine to invest in their center. They have asked you to write a brief description of your town, convincing readers that it is an excellent place for new buildings and growth.

When you are finished writing both descriptions, reread them and list all of the differences between them.

SHAPING IDEAS WITH A WORD PROCESSOR

A word processor can help you shape your discovery draft. When you retrieve the draft, INSERT the focus, purpose, and audience for the draft at the top or in a WINDOW or a SPLIT SCREEN. As you add details, keep checking to make sure that the new information is relevant to your focus, fulfills your purpose, and is appropriate for your readers. Here is an example of a split screen (below the text) showing focus, purpose, and audience.

```
FILE NAME:     My Street, Draft # 1

FILE DATE:    · 3/4/90


At night, Lawrence Avenue wakes up.  Music blares from

apartment windows, rolling out in frenzied waves.  Cars race

up and down, their screeching noise punctuated by the

machine gun shots of backfiring engines. Laughter pours.

\-----+-----+-----+-----+-----+-----+-----+-----+-----+----/
Page: 1      Line: 3      Col: 2      Layout: 7


FOCUS:        The sights and sounds of my street at night

PURPOSE:      To convince readers that my street is exciting

AUDIENCE:     Classmates who have never been on my street

\-----+-----+-----+-----+-----+-----+-----+-----+-----+----/
Page: 1      Line: 1      Col: 4      Layout: 2
```

READ BEFORE YOU WRITE

Below is an essay by Karen R. Buchanan about her grandmother. Buchanan was a student at Highline Community College in Washington when she wrote this essay in her composition course. The essay, entitled "Dancing Grandmother," won a Bedford Prize in Student Writing and was published in an anthology of essays written by students. As you read the essay, underline the words which enable you to see and hear the writer's grandmother.

Grandma celebrated her fifty-third birthday just weeks before Grandpa died of cancer in 1965. Although his passing was tremendously difficult for her, I think their shared struggle to prolong his life taught Grandma that good health was not to be taken for granted, and she vowed to live the remainder of her own life as fully and as long as she could. Although we always suspected Grandma had dutifully subdued a zest for living during the long years of Grandpa's illness, we were hardly prepared for the personality that emerged from within her after he died. When she announced her decision to invest part of Grandpa's life insurance benefits in lessons at the Fred Astaire Dance Studio in Portland, Oregon, where she lived, we rolled our eyes in embarrassment and helplessly wished she would just stay home and bake cookies as normal grandmothers did. Many years filled with countless dance lessons passed before we learned to appreciate the wonder of having a dancing Grandma.

I suppose Grandma's primary motivation for wanting to learn to dance was social. She had been a shy girl, always very tall and heavy, and had married into Grandpa's quiet lifestyle before developing any grace or confidence in her personal appearance. Dancing, on the other hand, filled her life with glittering lights, wonderful parties, beautiful gowns, dashing young dance instructors, and the challenge of learning. Although the weekly dance lessons did not diminish her ample, two-hundred-pound figure, Grandma surprised everyone with energetic performances on the dance floor that soon gave her as much poise, grace, and confidence as any Miss America contestant.

Never one to lack confidence in her own decisions, Grandma signed up from the beginning for enough weekly dance lessons to last for years. She learned the rumba, the cha-cha, and various waltzes easily and was soon participating in dancing contests all over the Northwest. When I was fourteen, Grandma proudly invited me to watch her compete in one of these contests to be held in the grand ballroom of Seattle's Red Lion Inn. My attitude was still unenthusiastic at that point ("Grandmas aren't supposed to dance," I often grumbled), but to make her happy, my mother and I attended the competition. As if to prove me wrong, Grandma made a spectacular showing in every event she entered. The one dance that I particularly remember was a Spanish dance involving a dizzying amount of spinning, dipping, and fast-paced twirling. Her timing was perfect, her sparkling smile never wavered, and her lovely handmade black and red dress shimmered under the spotlights, swirling in rhythmic complement to every movement. I thought she was truly the belle of the ball during that dance, and my thoughts were echoed by the judges a short time later when she was awarded a glistening gold trophy for her outstanding performance.

Grandma's dance costumes were dazzling, and most were her personal creations. Because she was never conservative in her choice of colors or styles, designing glittering, eye-catching ballroom dance dresses came as naturally for Grandma as baking apple pies comes for ordinary grandmothers. Since a costume was rarely repeated from one dancing event to another, she had huge cardboard boxes of tissue-wrapped dresses in her basement, most of which had been worn only once. I discovered those boxes while helping her move from Portland to Seattle in 1975 and was promptly given my own private showing of the vast collection. As she tenderly unfolded each dress and held it up for me to admire, her eyes glowingly expressed the well-earned pride she felt toward each costume and the vividly remembered moment on the dance floor that it represented. Consequently, I felt warmly honored several months later when Grandma wore one of her favorites to my wedding, although she nearly stole the show when she stepped majestically down the church aisle in the stunning dress of glossy white satin, boldly printed with bright red roses and billowing about her to the floor. Topped with her crown of snow-white hair and wearing her proudest smile, Grandma was an unforgettable picture of dignity and grandeur.

Occasionally, I still long for a grandmother who rocks cozily in a rocking chair next to a warm fireplace, knitting afghans and feeding everyone chocolate chip cookies that she has baked herself. Then I think of my own version of a grandmother and burst with pride for her in spite of myself. Although it took many years for me to appreciate the wonder of having that very unique and talented lady for my grandmother, I will never again begrudge her chosen path in life. In fact, someday I may follow in her dancing footsteps.

WRITING ASSIGNMENT **SHAPING A DISCOVERY DRAFT FOR A SPECIFIC PURPOSE AND AUDIENCE**

Your purpose in this writing assignment is to describe your dominant impression of someone you know well. This description can be about the same person whom you described for the activity on pages 54–55, or it can be about someone else. Your goal is to focus on the one characteristic that best describes this person.

Prewriting Guidelines

Your first job is to specify your focus:

- Whom are you describing?
- What is this person's relationship to you?
- What is your dominant impression of him or her?

Next, determine your audience:

- Who might be interested in knowing about the person you are describing?

- What does this reader (or group of readers) already know about the person?
- What do they need to or want to know?

Then, refine your purpose for writing this description and decide exactly what effect you want to have on your reader:

- How do you want your readers to see this person?
- What do you want your readers to think or feel about this person?

Begin by using the prewriting techniques that you learned about in Chapter 2: Write down the person's name and your dominant impression of him or her. Underneath that, write your audience for this description and your purpose (what you want your readers to think and feel). Then develop some supporting details by doing some freewriting, brainstorming, and clustering. Take the most interesting details and include them in a discovery draft. Next, get your classmates' responses to this draft by following the guidelines for "How to Get Feedback about Your Discovery Draft" previously discussed on pages 41–42. Use classmates' feedback to help you revise your draft.

ADDITIONAL TOPICS TO WRITE ABOUT

Here are some more topics for descriptive paragraphs:

1. Describe the best course that you ever took in school.
2. Describe the person (living or fictional) whom you admire most or whom you would most like to be.
3. Describe a teacher or an employer whom you really respect.
4. Describe a place that has special meaning for you.
5. Describe a place where you would like to live (now or in the future).

Reminders

Specify your focus:
1. Whom or what are you describing?
2. What is your dominant impression of this person, place, or thing?

Determine your audience:
1. Who might be interested in knowing this person, place, or thing you are describing?

2. What does this reader (or group of readers) already know about him, her, or it?
3. What do they need or want to know?

Refine your purpose:
1. What do you want your reader to think or to feel about this person, place, or thing?
2. What do you want your reader to see, hear, smell, touch, or taste?

After you finish your discovery draft, get your classmates' responses to this draft by following the guidelines for "How to Get Feedback about Your Discovery Draft."

ISSUES FOR YOUR JOURNAL

1. For most of the writing activities in Chapter 2 and in this chapter, you were asked to describe things, experiences, and people. Which descriptions did you most enjoy writing? Why? Which ones did you dislike writing? Why?
2. Who is the best teacher you ever knew (in *or* out of school)? Who taught you the most about something or about life? What did you learn from this person?
3. What is the most interesting thing you learned in one of your classes this week? Why do you find it interesting?
4. What would be the ideal career or job for you? If you could have any job in the world, what would you choose? Why?
5. Why are you going to college? How do you think it will help you? What do you expect to gain from the experience?

ADDITIONAL READING

The description below is excerpted from the book *Lives on the Boundary* by Mike Rose, a writer, teacher, and good friend.

Jack MacFarland couldn't have come into my life at a better time. My father was dead, and I had logged up too many years of scholastic indifference. Mr. MacFarland had a master's degree from Columbia and decided, at twenty-six, to find a little school and teach his heart out. He never took any credentialing courses, couldn't bear to, he said, so he had to find employment in a private system. He ended up at Our Lady of Mercy teaching five sections of senior English. He was a beatnik who was born too late. His teeth were stained, he tucked his sorry tie in between the third and fourth buttons of his shirt, and his pants were chronically wrinkled. At first, we couldn't believe this guy, thought he slept in his car. But within no time, he had us so startled with work that we didn't much worry about where he slept or if he slept at all. We wrote three or four essays a month. We read a book every two to three weeks, starting with the *Iliad* and ending up with Hemingway. He gave us a quiz on the reading every other day. He brought a prep school curriculum to Mercy High.

MacFarland's lectures were crafted, and as he delivered them he would pace the room jiggling a piece of chalk in his cupped hand, using it to scribble on the board the names of all the writers and philosophers and plays and novels he was weaving into his discussion. He asked questions often, raised everything from Zeno's paradox to the repeated last line of Frost's "Stopping by Woods on a Snowy Evening." He slowly and carefully built up our knowledge of Western intellectual history—with facts, with connections, with speculations. We learned about Greek philosophy, about Dante, the Elizabethan world view, the Age of Reason, existentialism. He analyzed poems with us, had us reading sections from John Ciardi's *How Does a Poem Mean?*, making a potentially difficult book accessible with his own explanations. We gave oral reports on poems Ciardi didn't cover. We imitated the styles of Conrad, Hemingway, and *Time* magazine. We wrote and talked, wrote and talked. The man immersed us in language.

Even MacFarland's barbs were literary. If Jim Fitzsimmons, hung over and irritable, tried to smart-ass him, he'd rejoin with a flourish that would spark the indomitable Skip Madison—who'd lost his front teeth in a hapless tackle—to flick his tongue through the gap and opine, "good chop," drawing out the single "o" in stinging indictment. Jack MacFarland, this tobacco-stained intellectual, brandished linguistic weapons of a kind I hadn't encountered before. Here was this *egghead*, for God's sake, keeping some pretty difficult people in line. And from what I heard, Mike Dweetz and Steve Fusco and all the notorious Voc. Ed. crowd settled down as well when MacFarland took the podium. Though a lot of guys groused in the schoolyard, it just seemed that giving trouble to this particular teacher was a silly thing to do. Tomfoolery, not to mention assault, had no place in the world he was trying to create for us, and instinctively everyone knew that. If nothing else, we all recognized MacFarland's considerable intelligence and respected the hours he put into his work.

OPTIONAL WRITING ASSIGNMENT

Write a description of the most unforgettable person you have ever met. Make sure that all of your details relate to your focus, purpose, and audience.

CHAPTER FOUR

WRITING PARAGRAPHS

Content and form, form and content—which comes first? The answer has to be content. Form is not an empty jug into which the writer pours meaning; form grows out of meaning, so much so that many writers come to believe that form, in a very real sense, is meaning.

DONALD MURRAY

The writer writes more like a sculptor who finds form while sculpting than like a bricklayer who piles bricks to construct a wall.

WILLIAM IRMSCHER

STRATEGIES FOR DEVELOPING EFFECTIVE PARAGRAPHS

What is a paragraph? The simplest answer to this question is that a paragraph is a group of sentences that develop a single topic or idea. Academic paragraphs usually range from about one hundred to three hundred words, although a one-sentence paragraph can be used effectively to emphasize a point or to state a conclusion. Since a paragraph illustrates or supports a single specific point, the number of sentences in a paragraph depends on the complexity of the point and on the reader's knowledge about it. (This paragraph has only eighty-six words in it, not including this sentence.)

As a reader, you know the reason why paragraphing is important; you know how annoying it is to read a very long piece of writing that has no paragraph indentations. Readers need paragraphs to help them know when a writer has completed discussing a topic and is moving on to the next topic. Paragraphs also serve an important function for writers: they help writers focus on a topic and consider the relationships among their ideas about the topic.

Nobody speaks in paragraphs. Paragraphing is a visual cue—five spaces indented at the beginning of the first sentence—that is possible only in writing. This fact gives inexperienced writers some difficulty in deciding where to begin and end paragraphs in their discovery drafts. This chapter will help you improve your ability to shape your ideas into effective paragraphs that help readers understand your key points and your reasoning.

GROUP WRITING TASK   DECIDING WHEN TO PARAGRAPH

Get into a group with two or three other students and read the following piece of student writing. Together, decide which sentences should be grouped into paragraphs. Write in the symbol ¶ (which means "Begin a new paragraph here") at the beginning of each sentence that should begin a new paragraph.

DISCOVERY DRAFT

If you want to succeed at a new job, there are several

mistakes that you should try to avoid. These mistakes may not

seem so awful, but making them can get you off to such a bad

start at a new job that they can affect your future at the

firm. Believe me, I know: I've made several of them myself. One of the worst mistakes I ever made at a new job was trying to find a best friend quickly. When I first met my co-workers, they smiled but they seemed very distant and unfriendly. So I attached myself to the first person who spoke kindly to me. I called her all the time, asking her for advice and gossip. Soon we were going to lunch together every day, and I started to dress like her and even to think like her. Unfortunately, all of our co-workers began treating me like they treated her, and that wasn't too good because they did not like or respect her very much. It took a great deal of effort on my part to detach myself from her and make friends with other co-workers. I'm glad that I did, though, because I got to see the company, and my job, from other perspectives. These new perspectives help me understand another major mistake I made that almost got me fired. This mistake involved not finding out the new company's goals and priorities. At my previous job, the company was obsessed with cost-efficiency. We were always asked to be aware of time and money and to figure out how to save both for the company. So when I started my new job, I instinctively tried to work quickly and cut costs. But these were not the priorities of the new company; instead, they valued service to customers. And after several clients complained about my attempts to speed up and save money, my boss told me to change my values or change my job.

Eleanor Mancho

When you finish paragraphing this piece of writing, discuss your answers to this question: How did you know where to begin and to end each paragraph?

THE TOPIC SENTENCE

Each paragraph in an academic essay should focus on a single point and should provide an explanation or an illustration of the point or evidence to support it. Teachers often tell students to begin each paragraph by stating the main point in a **topic sentence** (a sentence that states the main topic of the paragraph). The topic sentence lets readers know what to expect from the paragraph. It also serves as a focusing guide for writers: if you underline the key words in a topic sentence, you can check to make sure that all of the other sentences in the paragraph support the topic sentence.

GROUP WRITING ACTIVITY   **EXAMINING EXPECTATIONS ABOUT TOPIC SENTENCES AND PARAGRAPHS**

Get into a group with two or three other students, read the following student paragraph, then discuss the questions. Choose one group member to write down the responses of the entire group.

There are several reasons why I enjoy being a checker at Gristedes Supermarket. I like being able to go to school and work part-time and I make enough money to buy the things I need. Also, everyone agrees that I'm an excellent checker. I don't even have to look at the keys on my register. The store sells thousands of different items. The prices change every month, sometimes even every day. I have to be careful to watch for these price changes. I also have to watch for shoplifters. The store loses hundreds of dollars a day in stolen merchandise. Usually, this loss means that they have to charge shoppers more money in order to make a profit. I

```
look at people's clothing and pocketbooks to see if they have

any stolen stuff in them.  In addition, I've made some close

friends during the past five years that I've worked at

Gristedes.  My co-workers are nice to me and my boss is

terrific.  I guess the only thing I don't like about my job is

that if I make a mistake, they take it out of my pay.

Otherwise, it's a good job for me at this point in my life.

                                                  Mike Leung
```

1. Which sentence is the topic sentence?
2. Which words in this sentence limit what the writer can discuss in the paragraph?
3. After you read the topic sentence, what did you expect the paragraph to be about? What kinds of facts, observations, and experiences did you expect to see in the paragraph?
4. Which details do not seem related to the topic sentence? Why not?

PROBLEMS IN TOPIC SENTENCES

In the paragraph in the preceding exercise, Mike Leung's topic sentence is an effective one because it expresses an idea that can be explained or supported in one paragraph. If Mike crossed out the sentences that did not explain exactly why he enjoys his job, his paragraph would be clearer and more convincing.

Sometimes paragraph problems result from ineffective topic sentences. For instance, it is almost impossible to develop an effective paragraph about a topic sentence that is too narrow or that is simply a statement of fact. How much can you write about topic sentences such as, "I work as a manager in Gristedes Supermarket" or "There are three Gristedes Supermarkets in my city"?

A topic sentence that is too broad or too general is just as difficult to develop effectively as is one that is too narrow. For example, could you write a paragraph about topic sentences such as "Gristedes Supermarkets are having serious problems" or "Running a Gristedes Supermarket is a complicated business"? These topic sentences would probably require a multiparagraph essay (or a multi-essay report) to discuss all of the supporting points necessary to explain each in adequate detail.

EXERCISE **REVISING TOPIC SENTENCES**

The topic sentences below need to be revised. Decide why it would be difficult to write a paragraph about each one and then write a revised version of the sentence in the space below it. The first one has been done for you.

1. "Police are important to any community."
   What is the problem with this topic sentence?

   It's too broad – it doesn't help the writer limit his or her ideas.

   Your revision:

   The police in my community serve many important functions.

2. "I have been a policewoman for two years."
   What is the problem with this topic sentence?

   Your revision:

3. "Policemen and women often have to work ten hours a day."
   What is the problem with this topic sentence?

   Your revision:

4. "Policemen and women have problems just like the rest of us."
   What is the problem with this topic sentence?

   Your revision:

TOPIC SENTENCES AND SUPPORTING DETAILS

In Chapter 3, you practiced developing different types of supporting details—observations, experiences, and facts—for different purposes and audiences. Most topic sentences can be supported by a combination of facts, observations, and experiences. It is up to you to balance your purpose against the reader's needs and decide which type of details or which combination will work best for a particular topic sentence.

One way to make this decision is to consider whether you should support your topic sentence with **examples** or with **reasons**, or with a combination of examples *and* reasons. An **example** is a detail that answers the reader's question, "What do you mean by that statement?" Examples provide illustrations of your points—specific cases, objects, or instances. For instance, if you wanted to support the point that "being a housewife is a full-time job," you could provide examples of what you mean:

I cook three meals a day and clean the whole house.
I also have to do all the laundry and ironing.
Furthermore, I have to shop for the kids and help them prepare for all their daily activities.

A **reason** is a detail that answers the reader's question, "Why should I believe you?" Reasons provide explanations and justifications of your point—evidence that will convince readers that your argument makes sense. For instance, if you wanted to support the point that "housewives are the most unrewarded workers in this country," you could provide reasons why you think they are "unrewarded":

They work very hard twenty-four hours a day, but they receive no salary.
Their job doesn't give them any sick leave, vacation pay, or medical benefits.
When a housewife grows old, she has no pension to support her.

When you are asked to "describe," "illustrate," or "analyze" a topic, you are actually being asked to present **examples** as evidence that you understand the topic. When you are asked to "argue" or "evaluate" a topic, you are being asked to present **reasons** for your opinion about the topic. When you are asked to "discuss" a topic or to "explain" something, you should present *both* examples and reasons.

WRITING ACTIVITY   EVALUATING EXAMPLES IN A PARAGRAPH

After you read the paragraph below, use a separate piece of paper to answer the questions that follow the paragraph.

Being a housewife is a full-time job. My sister Dawn is up at 6:00 every morning, making breakfast for her husband and children and helping them prepare for their daily activities. Then she does laundry, ironing, and shopping, in addition to cleaning the whole house and cooking lunch and dinner. If one of her children gets sick, she must take him to the doctor, and she also has to take the dog to the vet for regular check-ups. Most afternoons, you can find Dawn helping with homework and preparing dinner. After everyone is finished eating, Dawn and her husband clean the kitchen and then she does some sewing. By the time she finally puts the children to bed, she often falls asleep herself, only to wake up the next morning and begin another "work" day.

Charles Restivo

1. Which words in the topic sentence limit what the writer can discuss in the paragraph?
2. How many examples did the writer provide to support the assertion in his topic sentence?
3. Which examples did you find most interesting? Why?

WRITING ACTIVITY   SUPPORTING TOPIC SENTENCES WITH EXAMPLES AND REASONS

Develop two different paragraphs about the same topic: a job that you had or currently have. This job can be one for which you were paid by an employer or one which you did for relatives or friends (such as babysitting for a younger sibling, mowing the lawn, or painting the apartment). After you have read the following directions, do some free-writing, brainstorming, and clustering about this job.

Paragraph 1

The first paragraph should describe the job. Use facts, experiences, and observations to develop **examples**, as in the student paragraph above, that will enable your classmates and teacher to get a clear sense of the job. What exactly was (or is) the job? What did you have to do? Where and when did you have to do it? For whom did you work? For how many days, months, or years did you do this job?

Paragraph 2

The second paragraph should evaluate the job much as Mike Leung's paragraph on page 70 does. Use facts, experiences, and observations to develop **reasons** that will help your readers understand why you liked or disliked this job. What were (or are) its good points and its bad points? Why did you like or dislike it?

LEVELS OF GENERALITY

Effective paragraphs consist of details that are **accurate** and **specific**. If your details are inaccurate, your reader will probably find it difficult to believe you. And if your details are very vague, your reader will not be able to understand you.

Usually the topic sentence is the most general idea in a paragraph. Each of the details that support it should be specific. However, no detail is completely general or completely specific: ideas are either more general or more specific than other ideas. For example, the statement "I have a job" is more general than the statement "I have a job in the health care profession." Here are some ideas arranged from most general to most specific.

1. I have a good job.
2. I have a good job as a nurse.
3. I have a good job as a baby nurse.
4. I am a baby nurse at Central General Hospital, and it is a good job.
5. I am a baby nurse at Central General Hospital, and I enjoy my job for many reasons.
6. I am a baby nurse at Central General Hospital, and I enjoy my job because I love babies and I make a good salary.
7. I am a baby nurse at Central General Hospital, and I enjoy my job because I love taking care of newborns and because I like making $35,000 a year.

Notice that each detail makes the idea above it more specific by providing more information about a key word or phrase. For example, sentence 4 gives more information about the word "nurse." It lets the reader know what kind of nurse the writer is and where she works. And sentence 6 is even more specific because it lets the reader know what the writer means by a "good" job that she "enjoys."

It is important to make your supporting details specific because in school or at work, your readers do not know you well enough to understand exactly what you mean when you use vague terms like "great" or "awful." What is "awful" to you might be wonderful to your readers. If you don't explain exactly what you mean—by giving specific examples—your readers may misunderstand you or get confused.

There are several ways to make supporting details more specific:

1. Give the exact names of things rather than writing about them in general terms. For example, how do these two pairs of sentences differ?
   a. She's a college teacher.
   b. Dr. Sanchez is a professor of computer science at Hunter College.

   c. Dr. Sanchez teaches several courses.
   d. Dr. Sanchez teaches Introductory Fortran, Advanced Cobol, and Integrated Systems.
2. Use concrete words that appeal to the reader's five senses—sight, hearing, touch, smell, and taste. How are these two pairs of sentences different?
   a. Dr. Sanchez doesn't look like a college professor.
   b. Dr. Sanchez is a tiny, slim woman with long, tawny red hair. Unlike my other female professors, she wears heavy makeup.

   c. Prof. Sanchez is usually very serious.
   d. Prof. Sanchez rarely smiles or laughs. She never makes jokes during a lesson, and she doesn't chat with students.

Notice that specific concrete details usually require more words or sentences to express them than do general abstract ideas. Also note that you cannot make an abstract idea more concrete or specific by explaining it with another abstract term:

Dr. Sanchez is very serious. She usually seems quite solemn and earnest.

"Solemn" and "earnest" are just as general as "serious." Neither expresses a sensory image that allows a reader to understand exactly what the writer means by "serious."

WRITING ACTIVITY **MAKING GENERAL IDEAS MORE SPECIFIC**

Each of the sentences below is too general to communicate a clear idea. Rewrite each sentence so that it has exact names and concrete sensory details (that you invent). You may have to write more than one sentence.

1. My boss is okay.

2. He hired me for the job.

3. He gives me a lot of responsibilities.

A third way of making your details more specific is to use vivid, descriptive verbs instead of ordinary, unclear ones. For example, compare the two descriptions of a baseball player below. The first is my paragraph, and the second is a poem by Robert Francis.

The runner is on first and he keeps moving off the base toward second. He goes a little way toward second and then gets nervous and runs back to first. He steps off the base again, and the pitcher watches him closely. He moves further and further away from the base. And then, as the pitcher throws the ball toward the batter, the runner runs to second base.

THE BASE STEALER

Poised between going and back, pulled
Both ways taut like a tightrope-walker,
Fingertips pointing the opposites,
Now bouncing tiptoe like a dropped ball

Or a kid skipping rope, come on, come on,
Running a scattering of steps sideways
How he teeters, skitters, tingles, teases
Taunts them, hovers like an ecstatic bird,
He's only flirting, crowd him, crowd him,
Delicate, delicate, delicate, delicate—now!

What impression do you get from the verbs in my paragraph? How is this different from the impression that you get from the verbs in the poem?

GROUP EXERCISE   **EXPERIENCING DESCRIPTIVE VERBS**

Do this exercise in a group in class or at home with your friends or family. Pick one of the sets of verbs below and act out each of the three verbs in the set. Ask the people watching you to guess each verb that you are performing and to discuss the differences in the set.

1. walk   stroll   strut
2. smile   grin   smirk
3. look   glance   glare

WRITING ACTIVITY   **MAKING DETAILS MORE SPECIFIC**

Below is a paragraph that is very vague and general. On a separate piece of paper, rewrite this paragraph by making up specific details to substitute for the underlined words. Try out the methods described earlier: use exact terms, concrete sensory words, and vivid verbs.

I work in a restaurant in my neighborhood. I'm going to quit soon because I don't like this job. The first reason why I don't like it is because I get paid so little. Also, the benefits are terrible. Secondly, the restaurant is really ugly. I want to work in a place that looks nice. Furthermore, the place smells. Sometimes, I get ill from the different smells in the kitchen. The only advantage of the job is that I get some meals there. And the food tastes pretty good. Since I'd like to make a lot of money and get free meals, I'm going to look for a job in a newer, cleaner place.

A STUDENT RESPONSE

Here are two uncorrected paragraphs that a college freshman wrote about her job.

On most afternoons, you can find me working hard at my job as a telephone solicitor for The Daily News. After my classes end, I ride the bus downtown, hop up to my desk on the fifth floor, and grab up the phone. Each day my supervisor hands me a new list of people's names, addresses, and phone numbers and I simply go down the list calling each one. I try to get people to subscribe to the paper by offering them discounts on home delivery or by telling them about the charity that part of their money will go to.

Telephone soliciting pays reasonably well ($5.50 an hour) and I receive some medical benefits. And the job is interesting. I don't have to worry about what to say because my speech is written down on a little card that I've almost memorized. Most of the people I call are happy to talk to me and many of them are willing to buy the subscriptions, especially if they know the money is going to a decent charity like Care or the March of Dimes. However, sometimes I get depressed when people hang up on me or when they get very nasty. The worst ones are the people who curse me. They make me feel like crying. Despite these ups and downs though, I enjoy my job and I'm lucky to have it.

Lisa Grant

<u>EXERCISE</u> **MAKING WRITING MORE SPECIFIC**

Reread Lisa Grant's paragraphs and write answers to these questions on a separate piece of paper.

1. Which examples or reasons help you to understand Grant's main points?
2. How could Grant's first paragraph be improved?
3. How could Grant's second paragraph be improved?

As discussed earlier, academic paragraphs often begin with a generalization—a topic sentence—that is followed by increasingly specific examples or reasons that clarify or explain the generalization. Lisa Grant's first paragraph illustrates this kind of ordering of details. Another typical pattern for organizing a paragraph is to develop specific details that lead up to a generalization. This method is illustrated by Grant's second paragraph.

OPTIONS FOR DEVELOPING PARAGRAPHS

Most inexperienced writers underestimate their readers' need for information; often, they do not provide enough examples and reasons to clarify the main point of each paragraph. Some strategies for developing these examples and reasons include narrating, describing, defining, comparing and contrasting, and analyzing. We all use these strategies when we think and speak. Indeed, we use them so naturally that most of us are not even conscious of them as techniques for organizing and communicating our ideas. The reason for studying these strategies is to learn to choose and to use them more effectively to support one's focus and purpose in writing. Each strategy is described and illustrated on the pages that follow.

Narration

One way to develop a topic sentence is to tell a story about it. Narrating an experience is an effective method for getting a reader's attention and for illustrating the point you are trying to make in a particular paragraph. In the student paragraph below, the writer uses narration to explain the anxiety produced by his first job interview.

I will always remember the morning that I had my first job interview. I woke up early because I was so nervous. My fingers shook as I was shaving, and I cut myself in several places. This made me even more nervous because I worried that the interviewer would think I was careless or clumsy. I dressed up in my best grey pin-stripe suit and I shined my wing-tip shoes till they gleamed. Then I became concerned that I was going to be late, so I ran to the bus. The bus ride seemed to stretch on forever. Finally, I arrived at the company office and gave the receptionist my name. My stomach was grumbling and I was sweating all over. I tried doing yoga breathing to calm down and finally my name was called and I walked in to the first interview of my life.

Paul Brasili

Ralph Abernathy's story about his mother, on page 39 in Chapter 2, offers another example of the way in which narrative details can be used to illustrate a main point.

WRITING ACTIVITY **DEVELOPING NARRATIVE PARAGRAPHS**

On a separate piece of paper, do some freewriting and some clustering for a discovery draft that narrates the morning of your first job interview, or your first day on a new job, or your first day at a new school. Invent an appropriate audience and purpose.

Description

You can help your reader understand the significance of a topic sentence by describing the point in vivid detail. Concrete impressions and observations help readers grasp your ideas and feelings about the topic. In the following student paragraph, the writer uses descriptive details to show his disgust with a particular job.

Last summer I drove a cab for a taxi company, and I never want to do that job again. Many of the cabs that are assigned to part-time drivers are wrecks that are falling apart. The outside of the cab that I was given to drive was all dented and rusted. Its windshield wipers were falling off, and its tires were dangerously bald. The old scratchy seats were falling apart with stuffing streaming out of every opening. And I always had trouble breathing in the cab. Since the ventilation openings were in the back of the cab, I was constantly breathing in fumes from my own engine. Furthermore, the brakes were low and most of the engine valves were leaky. Driving that cab made me really nervous.

Sal Beninotti

Another example of the use of descriptive details to support a main point is the paragraph by Charles Restivo on page 74 of this chapter.

WRITING ACTIVITY **DEVELOPING DESCRIPTIVE PARAGRAPHS**

On a separate piece of paper, do some freewriting and clustering for a discovery draft that describes a memorable job that you have or had. Include sensory details that will enable your reader to visualize the setting for the job. Help your reader "see," "hear," and "feel" the job's routines.

Definition

You can elaborate on your topic sentence with an explanation of a key word or concept. Define key terms by explaining their distinguishing characteristics and by giving examples of what you mean by these terms. The student paragraph that follows uses definition to clarify the writer's perception of his future profession.

```
      After college, I hope to be able to become an apprentice
manager in the telecommunications industry.
Telecommunications is the science of managing electronic
methods of communication.  A recent issue of an engineering
journal defined telecommunications as "the generic term for
whatever it takes to carry knowledge, information, sentiments,
or sensations across long distances."  Telecommunications
Managers install, operate, and direct electronic communications
systems.  While most of these systems use telephones, other
forms of telecommunication include radios, televisions,
telegraphs, computer terminals and facsimile (fax) machines.
                                                   Jack Keeler
```

The student paragraph on pages 155-156 of Chapter 6 illustrates the use of definition as supporting detail.

WRITING ACTIVITY   **DEVELOPING DEFINITION PARAGRAPHS**

On a separate piece of paper, do some freewriting and clustering for a discovery draft that defines the term "profession." Include the dictionary's definition of the term, but remember that a dictionary definition does not communicate to readers what this term means to *you*. Given your experiences and knowledge, what does a "profession" mean to you? Provide examples and illustrations that are appropriate for an audience of your classmates.

Comparison/Contrast

You can support your topic sentence by showing readers how your subject is similar to or different from something else. Explaining the similarities or differences between two or more people, things, events, or concepts enables readers to perceive them from your perspective. The student who wrote the following paragraph uses comparison and contrast to illustrate his dilemma in deciding what kind of company to work for after he graduates.

> Ever since the day I took apart and reassembled my parents' television set, I knew I wished to be an electronics engineer. Like doctors and lawyers, electronics engineers specialize in one of many areas, and I want to do aerospace research and rocket design. I have been thinking about the company that I want to eventually work for, and I'm having trouble making up my mind. Do I work for a giant corporation like Rockwell International in California or a small company like Rocket Research in Washington? They both design rocket engines and conduct applied aerospace research. But Rockwell is huge: it employs 95,000 people and offers many career opportunities. Rocket Research on the other hand has only 300 people and there isn't much room for advancement. But at Rocket, engineers are involved with all parts of systems design and application. At Rockwell, they only get to work on one small part of the project. I think I have to visit several more types of rocket research firms before I can make up my mind about the kind of place that's right for me.
>
> Isaac Stein

For another example of the use of comparison and contrast, see the student paragraph on page 51 of Chapter 3.

WRITING ACTIVITY **DEVELOPING COMPARISON/CONTRAST PARAGRAPHS**

On a separate piece of paper, do some freewriting and clustering for a discovery draft that compares or contrasts a "profession" with a "job." In what specific ways are a profession and a job similar? How exactly do they differ? Your audience for this draft is a group of high school students who are deciding whether they want to go to college for a profession or to end their education and work at a job.

Analysis

Another way to clarify your topic is by breaking it down into a sequence of steps or parts. When you analyze a process, you are helping readers to understand how it works or how it happens (or how to do it). When you analyze an action or an event, you are providing readers with your interpretation of its reasons, causes, or effects. In the two student paragraphs that follow, the writers use analysis to clarify and support their main points.

There are many myths about what it takes to get a good job in computer systems analysis. Most people think that you have to be excellent in math to design data processing systems. Others think that a systems analyst has to have a Ph.D. in computer science. In reality, neither belief is true. In order to become an effective systems analyst, people have to be logical thinkers and feel comfortable working with data. Since systems analysts have to work with programmers, they need to learn some programming basics, but they can learn these in computer courses in college. In addition, they can learn about hardware and software from the many books that are now available. Finally, they can get experience by entering a training program at a company that uses the kinds of data processing systems that interest them.

Bryan Turner

Working women, especially married working women, get
rewarded in many ways. All of my girlfriends work, and
although some of our husbands have had trouble adjusting, we
wouldn't give up our jobs for anything. Working outside the
home makes us more interesting people and more stimulating
wives. We have something to talk about besides shopping and
cleaning. We can share the struggles and the joys of trying
to achieve success and happiness. This makes many of us
better companions because we can be sympathetic to our
husbands' problems. Also, working outside the home lets women
meet all kinds of interesting people and go to different
places. This lets us make many more friends and business
acquaintances than if we just stayed home. But the best
reason for working is that women can earn a lot of money and
that makes a real difference to their families.

Jackie Nathanson

Additional examples of analysis paragraphs can be found in the student essay on learning disabilities on pages 160-162 of Chapter 6.

WRITING ACTIVITY **DEVELOPING ANALYSIS PARAGRAPHS**

On a separate piece of paper, do some freewriting, brainstorming,
and clustering for a discovery draft that (1) analyzes the reasons why
people go to college and (2) explains the process of applying for and
getting admitted to a college. Your audience is a group of high school
students.

WRITING ACTIVITY **ORDERING DETAILS FOR VARIED AUDIENCES AND PURPOSES**

For this activity, write two different paragraphs about the best
teacher you ever had (in school *or* out of school). For each paragraph,

do some prewriting and develop a discovery draft on a separate piece of paper. Decide on an appropriate order for developing your details. Use sensory language to let the reader see and hear this person in action.

Paragraph 1

The first paragraph should begin with a topic sentence that is followed by specific examples and reasons. The audience for this paragraph is a friend who is considering taking a course with this teacher next semester (or working with this person on a job next year). Your purpose is to convince this reader to study with this teacher.

Paragraph 2

The second paragraph should be composed of specific details leading up to your topic sentence. The audience for this paragraph is a supervisor who is deciding whether to rehire this teacher for the next three years. Your purpose is to convince this reader to rehire the teacher.

PARAGRAPHING WITH A WORD PROCESSOR

A word processor is the perfect tool for playing with paragraphs. If you are unsure whether your paragraphs are too long or too short, you can try out different paragraph breaks on the screen. As you examine each different paragraph division, you can decide which seem most sensible, in terms of your readers' need to understand your main point and supporting detail or their need to rest their eyes for a second.

In addition, a word processor enables you to examine each paragraph to determine if any details do not directly support the idea suggested by the topic sentence. You can temporarily OVERSTRIKE this material and then decide whether to delete it or to make it the focus of a separate paragraph. Here is an example of the various ways in which paragraphs can be broken up on SPLIT SCREENS.

```
FILE NAME:    My Profession Goals, Draft # 1

FILE DATE:    5/9/91


     The field that I am preparing for is nuclear medicine.

Nuclear medicine technologists (NMTs) use radioactive

materials to perform medical tests that produce diagnostic
```

```
information.  Some of the responsibilities of an NMT include
preparing and administering radio-drugs, using radioactive
equipment, and monitoring patients during treatments.  An
NMT does many things that are similar to the work of an
X-ray technologist; however, the sources of their treatments
differ.  X-rays are artificial

\-----+-----+-----+-----+-----+-----+-----+-----+----/
      Page: 1      Line: 2      Col: 4      Layout: 6
```

```
    The field that I am preparing for is nuclear medicine.

Nuclear medicine technologists (NMTs) use radioactive

materials to perform medical tests that produce diagnostic

information.  Some of the responsibilities of an NMT include

preparing and administering radio-drugs, using radioactive

equipment, and monitoring patients during treatments.

    An NMT does many things that are similar to the work of

an X-ray technologist; however, the sources of their

treatments differ. X-rays are artificial sources of

radiation, whereas

\-----+-----+-----+-----+-----+-----+-----+-----+----/
      Page: 1      Line: 2      Col: 4      Layout: 6
```

READ BEFORE YOU WRITE

Pages 89–90 contain two charts that present the results of a survey of American workers. The survey, entitled "Work in the 1980s and 1990s," was conducted by the Public Agenda Foundation. The first chart shows the ten job qualities that workers rated most important in terms of "motivation"—the qualities that would make them work harder. The second chart shows the ten job qualities that workers

The Top Ten Motivators

Managers and Professionals		Blue-Collar Workers		Clerical Workers
Men	Women	Men	Women	Women
A good chance for advancement (48%/29%)*	A good chance for advancement (47%/22%)*	Good pay (50%/22%)*	Good pay (44%/28%)*	A good chance for advancement (56%/19%)*
A great deal of responsibility (45/28)	A job that enables me to develop my abilities (44/18)*	A good chance for advancement (47/23)*	A good chance for advancement (42/17)*	A job that enables me to develop my abilities (52/24)
Recognition for good work (44/32)*	Recognition for good work (43/30)*	Pay tied to performance (47/28)*	Pay tied to performance (41/30)*	A challenging job (47/23)
A job where I can think for myself (44/29)	A great deal of responsibility (40/22)	Recognition for good work (42/37)*	A challenging job (37/23)	A job where I can think for myself (45/21)
A job that enables me to develop my abilities (42/28)*	A job where I can think for myself (38/33)	Interesting work (38/34)*	A job where I can think for myself (35/29)	A job that allows me to be creative (45/25)
A challenging job (42/29)	Good pay (37/30)*	See end results of my efforts (38/22)	Interesting work (35/28)*	See end results of my efforts (45/30)
A job that allows me to be creative (41/29)	Pay tied to performance (37/33)	A job that enables me to develop my abilities (36/29)	A job that enables me to develop my abilities (34/27)	Good pay (42/35)*
A job with pay tied to performance (40/39)*	A challenging job (35/25)	A challenging job (34/38)	See end results of my efforts (34/31)	A great deal of responsibility (42/37)
A say in important decisions (39/33)	A say in important decisions (32/33)	A job that allows me to be creative (34/34)	A job that allows me to be creative (33/33)	Recognition for good work (39/32)*
A place that does quality work (39/29)	A place that does quality work (32/32)	A job where I can think for myself (33/39)*	Recognition for good work (32/39)*	Interesting work (37/41)*

The first figure in parentheses is the percentage in the group that rated this factor a motivator; the second shows those who called it a satisfier.
*Items marked with an asterisk were on the list of the top-ten job features this group of workers most wanted more of (WORKING WOMAN, June 1983).

The Top Ten Satisfiers

Managers and Professionals		Blue-Collar Workers		Clerical Workers
Men	Women	Men	Women	Women
Job without too much rush and stress (71%/6%)	Job without too much rush and stress (57%/15%)	Job without too much rush and stress (57%/20%)	Job without too much rush and stress (55%/20%)	Convenient location (69%/13%)
Good working conditions (67/9)	People really care about me as a person (57/12)	Good working conditions (57/13)	Being informed about what goes on (55/10)	Working with people I like (69/8)
Convenient location (65/9)	Working with people I like (56/14)	Convenient location (53/10)	Getting along well with supervisor (51/17)	Job without too much rush and stress (66/12)
Being able to control work pace (61/9)	Convenient location (55/12)	Working with people I like (52/22)	Working with people I like (48/16)	Being able to control work pace (62/8)
Flexible working hours (61/15)	Getting along well with supervisor (54/17)	Getting along well with supervisor (52/20)	Flexible working hours (48/11)	Good working conditions (60/14)
Working with people I like (56/15)	Good fringe benefits (52/21)*	Being informed about what goes on (50/19)	Being able to control work pace (45/19)	Informal work environment (59/16)
Good fringe benefits (53/25)*	Job security, little chance of being laid off (52/27)	People who listen to your ideas (50/28)	People treat me with respect (45/17)*	All the tools I need to do my job (59/21)
Never asked to do anything improper or immoral (53/11)	Good working conditions (51/11)	Informal work environment (49/7)	Convenient location (44/14)	Efficient, effective managers (58/20)
Place I'm so proud of I want everyone to know I work there (53/20)	Never asked to do anything improper or immoral (50/15)	Being able to control work pace (47/29)	Good working conditions (44/14)	Fair treatment (54/15)*
Employer with good reputation (52/21)	Flexible working hours (48/19)	Fair treatment (46/26)	People who listen to your ideas (44/17)	Getting along well with supervisor (54/27)

The first figure in parentheses is the percentage of the group that rated this factor a satisfier; the second is the percentage that rated it a motivator.
*Items marked with an asterisk were on the list of the top-ten job features this group of workers most wanted more of (WORKING WOMAN, June 1983).

rated most important in terms of "satisfaction"—the qualities that would make them feel better at work. As you analyze the charts, consider the following questions:

1. What do the men and women surveyed need most to be satisfied with their jobs?

2. What job qualities most motivate these men and women to work hard at their jobs?

3. Why do you think the top "motivator" is so different from the top "satisfier"?

4. Which qualities on the list would motivate you most? Why?

5. Which qualities on the list would satisfy you most? Why?

The cartoon on p. 92 is about one woman's ideal job.

1. What do you think her chances of finding this job are?

2. What kinds of jobs might fulfill her needs?

WRITING ASSIGNMENT DEVELOPING FOUR PARAGRAPHS ABOUT AN IDEAL JOB

For this writing assignment, you will be developing several paragraphs about a job that you would consider ideal. Even if you have already chosen a career for which to prepare, speculate on the kind of job you would most like to do if you could have your choice of any job

"I'm hoping to find something in a meaningful, humanist, outreach kind of bag, with flexible hours, non-sexist bosses, and fabulous fringes."

in the world. Is there a job that you always dreamed of doing when you were younger? Imagine that you didn't have to worry about family responsibilities, or money, or location—what job would make you feel truly satisfied? Write a discovery draft of two paragraphs that describes this ideal job in detail. Then write a discovery draft of two more paragraphs that give specific reasons why this job would be ideal for you.

Prewriting Guidelines

Your first job is to specify your focus:

- What exactly are you describing?
- How much do you already know about this job?
- What else do you need to find out about it?

Next, determine your audience:

- Who might be interested in your ideal job?
- What do these readers know about the job?
- What do they need to know about it or about you?

Then, refine your purpose for writing this description. While your goal is to describe your ideal job and the reasons for your choice, you need to consider exactly what effect you want to have on your reader:

- How do you want your reader to see you?
- What do you want your reader to think about you?

Begin by using the techniques that you learned about in Chapter 2 to do prewriting: on a separate piece of paper, write down the job title and do some freewriting, brainstorming, and clustering about it. Turn these ideas into a discovery draft. When you are finished with each paragraph, circle the topic sentence, and underline all of the specific words and phrases and all of the vivid verbs. Then, get your classmates' responses to these drafts by following the guidelines on "How to Get Feedback about Your Discovery Draft" on pages 41–42. After you have received some responses to your discovery draft, use the following questions to determine whether it needs more specific supporting details:

Revising Questions

1. Who is my audience, and what else do they need to know about the job that I am describing?
2. What facts have I included about the job? What other facts could I state about this job that would reveal why it is ideal for me?
3. What observations have I included about this job? What other observations could I tell about this job that would reveal why it is ideal for me?
4. What experiences have I included about this job? What other experiences could I relate about this job that would reveal why it is ideal for me?
5. Which details in each paragraph are very specific? Which ones are too vague or general?
6. Which words in each paragraph are examples of sensory language? Where do I need more of these examples?

Revise your discovery draft based on your classmates' comments and on your answers to the Revising Questions above.

ADDITIONAL TOPICS TO WRITE ABOUT

Here are more topics to help you practice the skills that you learned in this chapter.

1. Narrate an experience that you had with a classmate or with a co-worker that made you feel very pleased with yourself.
2. Describe the nature of the work that people do in the job or profession for which you are preparing.
3. Define success: What does success mean to you (emotionally, socially, professionally, financially, athletically, or in other ways)?
4. Compare or contrast going to school with working at a job or profession: How are these two activities similar and/or different?
5. Analyze the steps or processes required to prepare for and to get a position in the job or profession in which you are interested.
6. Explain your viewpoint about sex discrimination in the workplace: Should women have equal opportunities to work at any job or profession that currently employs only men?

Reminders

Specify your focus:

- What points do you want to explain or describe?
- How much do you already know about your topic?
- What else do you need to find out about it?

Determine your audience:

- Who might be interested in reading your paragraph?
- What does this reader (or group of readers) already know about your topic?
- What else do they need or want to know about it or about you?

Refine your purpose:

- How do you want your reader to see you?
- What do you want your reader to think, feel, or do?

After you finish your discovery draft, get your classmates' responses by following the guidelines for "How to Get Feedback about Your Discovery Draft" previously discussed on pages 41–42.

ISSUES FOR YOUR JOURNAL

1. What did you learn from this chapter that you had not known before?

2. Reread your journal entries for the past month. Which ones had you forgotten? How does it make you feel to recover thoughts, observations, and feelings that you had forgotten about?
3. What does it mean to be a "man" or a "woman"? How does a child learn his or her sex role? How did you learn your sex role? Who or what taught you what it means to be a man or a woman?
4. Does pollution bother you? If so, what kind bothers you the most? Why? Do you think we are destroying our air and water? If so, what can the average citizen do about this environmental destruction?
5. How do you feel about space exploration? Our government spends millions of dollars on the research and development of space shuttles, space satellites, and space weapons. What is your opinion of this expenditure?

ADDITIONAL READING

The essay that follows appeared on the "opinion" page of a special issue of *Time* magazine. "Running Hard Just to Keep Up" was written by Sylvia Ann Hewlett, an economist who has written several books on the effects of the economy on the American family. In this essay, she describes the current burdens on working families. As you read each paragraph, think about the strategy that the writer used to develop her supporting details.

Faster and faster they go, harder and harder they push, but like hamsters on a wheel, America's working families are stuck at the bottom. Clobbered on two fronts, they must work twice as hard to stay even. On the income side, wages have gone down while taxes have risen. On the expenditure side, living costs have soared. Homes, health insurance, college education—the basic ingredients of the American Dream—are increasingly out of reach.

The crunch began with a dramatic falloff in earnings, particularly for blue-collar males. Between 1955 and 1973, the median wage of men leaped from $15,056 to $24,621. Then, quite suddenly, it started to drop. By 1987 the male wage, adjusted for inflation, was back down to $19,859, a 19% decline. To shore up family income, wives have flooded into the labor market, but their earning power is low. In 1988 the average family income was only 6% higher than in 1973, though almost twice as many wives were at work. In many households, one well-paid smokestack job with health insurance has been replaced by two service jobs without benefits. Burger King doesn't provide as well as Bethlehem Steel.

Higher taxes have tightened the pinch. The acclaimed Reagan tax cuts of 1986, which reduced marginal income taxes, merely shifted the burden to Social Security taxes, which fall heavily on low- and middle-income families. These payroll taxes were jacked up 24% during the 1980s. The true marginal tax rate is now higher for a couple making $14,000 a year than it is for a couple making $326,000 a year!

It doesn't help that over the past 25 years the cost of housing has jumped 56% and college tuitions have rocketed 87.9% in real dollars. Joseph Minarik, executive director of the congressional Joint Economic Committee estimates that the typical 30-year-old man buying a median-priced home in 1973 incurred carrying costs equal to 21% of his income. By 1987 this had risen to 40%. For the first time since World War II, home ownership among young families is declining. Complains Karen, a 26-year-old housewife in the Chicago area: "You either buy a home, both of you work and your kids suffer, or one of you works and you live in a rental. Paying rent feels like digging a hole and crawling right in."

This squeeze on families bodes ill for children. Twelve million youngsters have no medical coverage; 5 million teeter on the edge of homelessness. Because of poor prenatal care, a baby born in the shadow of the White House is now more likely to die in the first year of life than a baby born in Costa Rica.

But perhaps the resource in shortest supply to families is time together. The amount of "total contact time" between parents and children has dropped 40% over the past 25 years, says the Family Research Council in Washington. This is not good news. Researchers have uncovered ominous links between absentee parents and behavioral problems among children. A 1989 survey of 5,000 eighth-grade students in Southern California found, for instance, that latchkey children were twice as likely to use alcohol and drugs as were children supervised by adults after school.

How can this situation be remedied? Corporations should be encouraged to design a family-friendly workplace that gives parents the gift of time. Several U.S. firms have shown that it can be cost-effective to create a more fluid work environment. Government could encourage this by granting tax breaks to companies that offer flexible hours, part-time work with benefits, job sharing, parental leave and home-based employment opportunities.

To lighten the burden on working families, the tax system should be reconfigured so that relatively more is paid in income taxes and less in Social Security taxes. The government should also subsidize housing for a majority of young families with children. Rent vouchers in sufficient numbers would banish the specter of homelessness that haunts 10 million to 13 million low-income families. As for helping the middle class, the government should act as it did after World War II and offer low-interest mortgages to young families. Beginning in 1944, the Veterans Administration guaranteed 5 million home loans to ex-servicemen with no down payment required and a maximum interest rate of 4%. If something similar were done today, many more families could both buy a house and spend time with the kids. One Gallup poll shows that only 13% of working mothers want to work full time, although 52% of them do so. Often what keeps these mothers at work 40 hours a week is heavy mortgage payments.

The U.S. can and should bend its public policies to free time and resources for families with children. With male wages sagging and the divorce rate at 50%, it's hard to spin out a scenario in which large numbers of women have the option of staying home full time. The trick is to spread the burden around. Employers and government both have to pull their weight. This critical task of building strong families can no longer be defined as a private endeavor, least of all a private *female* endeavor. No society can afford to forget that on the backs of its children ride the future prosperity and integrity of the nation.

OPTIONAL WRITING ASSIGNMENT

Think about the career for which you are preparing. Write a discovery draft explaining how your career will enable you to balance the demands of your future job with your personal needs and your family's needs.

CHAPTER FIVE

WRITING ESSAYS

*Because there is no neat gradual way to learn
to write and because progress* seems *so
unpredictable and just plain slow, a major
part of learning to write is learning to put up
with this frustrating* process *itself.*

PETER ELBOW

*There is no muse whispering in your ear,
telling you what to say. You have to work at it.
Writing is a delicious agony.*

GWENDOLYN BROOKS

*The essay is a literary device for saying almost
everything about almost anything.*

ALDOUS HUXLEY

ESSAY DEVELOPMENT

Most of the writing that you have been doing for this book so far has taken the form of several long paragraphs. Often, however, your teachers or employers may ask you to write about topics that require you to develop your ideas in more detail than you could in one or two paragraphs. For these assignments, you need to write multiparagraph essays or reports. Although an essay is longer and more detailed than a paragraph, the method for developing both types of writing is essentially the same. Both forms—the paragraph and the essay—require writers to go through the following processes:

- focusing on a central idea for a clearly defined purpose and audience
- developing a main point with specific facts, observations, and experiences that can serve as convincing examples and reasons
- arranging details in a logical order
- writing an effective introduction and a conclusion

In an essay, the main point or the argument that the writer wants to make to the reader is his or her "thesis statement." The **thesis statement** of an essay, like the **topic sentence** of a paragraph, limits what can be discussed in the essay and acts as a focusing guide for the writer *and* for the reader. A thesis statement is usually more general than a topic sentence because it expresses the main point of the whole essay. Within the essay, each paragraph may have its own specific topic sentence. Since you have already practiced all the skills necessary for writing effective paragraphs, you should feel confident about writing effective essays.

GROUP WRITING TASK **LISTING THE DIFFERENCES BETWEEN PARAGRAPHS AND ESSAYS**

This writing task will help you explore some of the differences between a paragraph and an essay. Read the uncorrected paragraph and essay below and answer the questions that follow. Choose one person to record the group's answers.

```
DISCOVERY DRAFT OF A PARAGRAPH

ON THE EFFECTS OF TECHNOLOGY

America is slowly becoming a high-tech society.  New

technologies like computers and chemicals have changed the way
```

most of us live and work. While many people like the results
of these changes, many of us are suffering the consequences of
these changes. And the worst consequence is unemployment.
The millions of people out of work today think that it is due
to the recession. But it isn't. People have been put out of
work by robots, computers, and other kinds of machines that
can do the work that people used to do. These machines can do
work faster and more efficiently so many industries have fired
people and put in machines. And not only workers but
managers have also been affected by technology. Managers who
cannot adjust to computers are losing their jobs every day.
Technology may be improving our life but it is also taking
away our livelihood!

                                                    Robert Mason

              DISCOVERY DRAFT OF AN ESSAY ENTITLED
             "TECHNOLOGY'S IMPACT ON AMERICAN SOCIETY"
       America is slowly becoming a high-tech society. New
technologies like computers, robotics and chemical engineering
have changed the way most of us live and work. Life is
certainly easier now that we have new foods and drugs,
microwave ovens to cook in, computers to work on and new forms
of energy. However, while technology has made life easier, it
has had terrible consequences for many, many Americans.

       Many people are suffering the consequences of the changes
brought by technology. In my opinion, the worst consequence
of the new scientific technologies is unemployment. Millions

of people are out of work in America today, and many of them think that it is due to the recession. But it isn't. Many people have been put out of work by robots, computers, and other kinds of machines that can do the work that people used to do. The clearest example of this is the automotive industry, where robots have replaced human workers. These machines can do work faster and more efficiently, they can work twenty-four hours a day and they don't get sick or drunk. Thus hundreds of thousands of people who used to work on building cars no longer have jobs and may never get new ones.

In addition, workers are not the only people who are affected by technology. Managers who cannot adjust to computers and telecommunications systems are losing their jobs every day. And at the other end, secretaries who don't learn how to use computers may be fired or their jobs may be taken over by computers.

Thus we may have more food, better drugs, cheaper energy, and better communications. But we may lose our ability to pay for or use these things. Technology may be improving our lives, but it is also taking away our livelihoods!

Robert Mason

1. What is the topic sentence of the paragraph? What is the thesis statement in the essay? How do they differ?
2. What strategy did the writer use to develop the introduction of the essay? Is this introduction effective? Why or why not?
3. In what ways do the examples and the reasons in the paragraph differ from those in the essay?
4. Mark off the concluding sentence in the paragraph and the conclusion in the essay. In what ways do they differ?

THESIS STATEMENT AND TITLE

A thesis statement expresses the main idea that you want to develop in an essay. Often, the thesis statement also communicates your point of view about the essay's topic. Remember that the thesis is not simply a statement of an essay's topic. The topic is the subject that you have chosen to write about ("the effects of technology" or "the consequences of technology"); the thesis statement is a complete sentence that expresses your viewpoint about this topic ("While technology has made life easier, it has had terrible consequences for many, many people"). Although many professional authors do not write a thesis statement in their essays, writing one can help inexperienced writers narrow down their focus to the point that they want their essay to communicate.

Your thesis statement should be an assertion that you can develop or support in an essay of four to eight paragraphs. It should provide readers with a clear statement of the specific point that you want to make, yet it should also be general enough to cover all of the aspects of the topic that the essay will develop. If a thesis statement is too general, the writer can easily go off on tangents about the topic. In addition, an overly general thesis statement may confuse readers because it may lead them to expect the essay to develop ideas that the writer had not intended to discuss. For example, here is a thesis statement from an essay that a student wrote in response to the assignment at the end of the preceding chapter:

```
Nursing has many benefits.
```

This statement is so general that it is confusing: Will the essay be about the benefits of being a nurse or the benefits of having one? Also, it leads readers to expect an essay that describes all of the possible benefits that may be gained from nursing. Here is a revision:

```
Nursing is the ideal profession because it enables one to help

others while making an excellent salary.
```

This statement might be appropriate as a topic sentence for a paragraph, but it is too narrow for an essay. It limits the writer to describing only two reasons why nursing is the ideal job for him. Here is the writer's final revision of his thesis statement:

```
Nursing is an ideal career because it enables a person to

achieve many personal and professional goals.
```

This thesis statement gives the writer flexibility to develop the specific benefits of nursing that are important to him, and it lets readers know what to expect from the essay.

   A writer can put his or her thesis statement anywhere in an essay, but it is easier for the writer and for readers if the thesis statement is the final sentence of the essay's introduction. An essay's title and thesis statement focus the writer and the reader on the main points that will be developed in the paragraphs that follow. Since it is important that your title and thesis statement reflect exactly what your essay will discuss, you may want to write them both *after* you have written a discovery draft of your essay. For example, the original title of the first draft of Robert Mason's essay was "The Effects of Technology." In addition, the first draft of the essay did not have a clear thesis statement because he was not sure whether he wanted to prove a point about the effects of technology or just relate his observations about the topic. When he did some more brainstorming, he came up with more details and then he wrote another draft. Only then did he write a thesis statement: "While technology has made life easier, it has had terrible consequences for many, many Americans" and a new title: "Technology's Impact on American Society."

WRITING ACTIVITY **PREDICTING THE CONTENT OF ESSAYS FROM TITLES AND THESIS STATEMENTS**

   This activity is designed to show you how much readers rely on a clear, accurate title and thesis statement to get an overview of an essay. For each title and thesis statement below, write a brief description of the ideas that could be developed in an essay based on that title and thesis statement. The first one has been done for you as an example.

   1. Title: "The Benefits of Science"

   Thesis Statement: "During the past century, scientists and their practical partners—engineers—have worked together to solve some of humanity's worst problems and have improved the daily life of millions of people."

Ideas that this essay will probably develop:

The essay will probably give examples of the problems that scientists and engineers have worked together to solve.

2. Title: "The Case against Nuclear Energy"

Thesis Statement: "Those people who see nuclear energy as the clean, cost-efficient answer to America's ongoing energy crisis have somehow managed to ignore all of its hazards."

Ideas that this essay will probably develop:

3. Title: "Engineering for the Disabled"

Thesis Statement: "The artificial parts that bioengineers are developing are enhancing the lives of physically challenged people."

Ideas that this essay will probably develop:

4. Title: "Fable for Tomorrow"

Thesis Statement: "A grim specter has crept upon us almost unnoticed, and this imagined tragedy may easily become a stark reality we all shall know."

Ideas that this essay will probably develop:

A PROFESSIONAL RESPONSE

An essay by ecologist Rachel Carson entitled "A Fable for Tomorrow," has the same title and thesis statement as does #4 in the preceding writing activity. How accurate were your predictions of the ideas that would be developed in an essay with this title and thesis statement?

There was once a town in the heart of America where all life seemed to live in harmony with its surroundings. The town lay in the midst of a checkerboard of prosperous farms, with fields of grain and hillsides of orchards where, in spring, white clouds of bloom drifted above the green fields. In autumn, oak and maple and birch set up a blaze of color that flamed and flickered across a backdrop of pines. Then foxes barked in the hills and deer silently crossed the fields, half hidden in the mists of the fall mornings.

Along the roads, laurel, viburnum and alder, great ferns and wildflowers delighted the traveler's eye through much of the year. Even in winter the roadsides were places of beauty, where countless birds came to feed on the berries and on the seed heads of the dried weeds rising above the snow. The countryside was, in fact, famous for the abundance and variety of its bird life, and when the flood of migrants was pouring through in spring and fall people traveled from great distances to observe them. Others came to fish the streams, which flowed clear and cold out of the hills and contained shady pools where trout lay. So it had been from the days many years ago when the first settlers raised their houses, sank their wells, and built their barns.

Then a strange blight crept over the area and everything began to change. Some evil spell had settled on the community: mysterious maladies swept the flocks of chickens; the cattle and sheep sickened and died. Everywhere was a shadow of death. The farmers spoke of much illness among their families. In the town the doctors had become more and more puzzled by new kinds of sickness appearing among their patients. There had been several sudden and unexplained deaths, not only among adults but even among children, who would be stricken suddenly while at play and die within a few hours.

There was a strange stillness. The birds, for example— where had they gone? Many people spoke of them, puzzled and disturbed. The feeding stations in the backyards were deserted. The few birds seen anywhere were moribund; they trembled violently and could not fly. It was a spring without voices. On the mornings that had once throbbed with the dawn chorus of robins, catbirds, doves, jays, wrens, and scores of other bird voices there was now no sound; only silence lay over the fields and woods and marsh.

On the farms the hens brooded, but no chicks hatched. The farmers complained that they were unable to raise any pigs—the litters were small and the young survived only a few days. The apple trees were coming into bloom but no bees droned among the blossoms, so there was no pollination and there would be no fruit.

The roadsides, once so attractive, were now lined with browned and withered vegetation as though swept by fire. These, too, were silent, deserted by all living things. Even the streams were now lifeless. Anglers no longer visited them, for all the fish had died.

In the gutters under the eaves and between the shingles of the roofs, a white granular powder still showed a few patches; some weeks before it had fallen like snow upon the roofs and the lawns, the fields and streams.

No witchcraft, no enemy action had silenced the rebirth of new life in this stricken world. The people had done it themselves.

The town does not actually exist, but it might easily have a thousand counterparts in America or elsewhere in the world. I know of no community that has experienced all the misfortunes I describe. Yet every one of these disasters has actually happened somewhere, and many real communities have already suffered a substantial number of them. A grim specter has crept upon us almost unnoticed, and this imagined tragedy may easily become a stark reality we all shall know.

What has already silenced the voices of spring in countless towns in America?

EXERCISE **ANALYZING "A FABLE FOR TOMORROW"**

After reading the response above, consider the following questions:

1. A fable is a very short story that makes a cautionary point or that has a moral. What was the main point of this fable? What was the writer's purpose?
2. Why do you think the writer called this essay "A Fable for Tomorrow"?
3. Whom do you think the writer imagined as her audience?
4. How does the writer use comparisons and contrasts to develop her point?

5. This fable was written in 1962. How accurate was the writer in predicting the state of the earth today?

WRITING ACTIVITY EXPLORING IDEAS FOR AN ESSAY

Here are two topics for you to explore. You might want to develop one or both into a discovery draft.

1. What were your reactions to the preceding fable by Rachel Carson? Do you know a place that has changed because of the consequences of technology? For example, do you know an area that was polluted by chemicals or that was destroyed by commercial development? Describe the place before and after it changed. Also describe your reaction to the changes.
2. A fable often has two parts: a story that illustrates a moral and the moral itself. Write a fable about a moral that you believe in strongly.

EXERCISE WRITING THESIS STATEMENTS

Here are ten topics for essays. Choose *five* of them, and in the space below each of these five, write a thesis statement for an essay about the topic. Craft a sentence that states your viewpoint about the topic and that you could support in an essay of four to eight paragraphs.

1. the functions of religion

2. the effects of rock music

3. the problems of older students

4. the impact of television on children

5. the consequences of drinking and driving

6. racism on college campuses

7. government spending on space exploration

8. the hazards of modern pollutants

9. the uses of computers

10. the effects of gun control laws

OPTIONS FOR DEVELOPING ESSAYS

Writing an essay is similar to writing a paragraph. First you have to choose a topic that you feel comfortable writing about. If the topic has been assigned, you have to decide on a **focus** that is neither too broad nor too narrow. Next, you have to figure out what is your **purpose** and who is your actual or imaginary **audience**. Then, you should do some freewriting or brainstorming or clustering to develop the facts, observations, and experiences that will accomplish your purpose for this audience. The strategies for developing and organizing the details in an essay are the same ones that you practiced in Chapter 4 when you were developing different types of paragraphs: narrating, describing, defining, comparing, contrasting, and analyzing. These are simply the patterns of thinking that people use to sort out the events and experiences of their daily lives. A writer may use only one of these patterns to develop an essay or he or she may use a combination of these strategies. For example, if you were asked to write an essay on technology and science, you might decide to write an essay that was purely descriptive, with each supporting paragraph describing a different form of current technology. An outline of a draft of this essay might look like this:

- Paragraph 1—Introduction (with a "working" thesis statement)
- Paragraph 2—Description of one form of technology that has proven very valuable or useful
- Paragraph 3—Description of another form of helpful technology
- Paragraph 4—Conclusion

Depending on your purpose and audience, you could also have developed different details and used them to write an essay contrasting the advantages and the disadvantages of modern technology. Here is an outline of this essay:

- Paragraph 1—Introduction (including a "working" thesis statement about the impact of technology on people's lives)
- Paragraph 2—Description of one or two important recent technological breakthroughs
- Paragraph 3—Description of some of the advantages of these breakthroughs
- Paragraph 4—Description of some of the disadvantages of these breakthroughs
- Paragraph 5—Analysis of whether the benefits of the breakthroughs outweigh their disadvantages and problems
- Paragraph 6—Conclusion about the impact of technology

Note that while the essay outlined above is composed mostly of descriptive details, it ends with an analytic paragraph exploring the relative effects of the breakthroughs described in the preceding paragraphs.

How do writers decide which strategies to use to develop the body paragraphs of an essay? Experienced writers do not usually begin an essay by consciously deciding that it will be a "descriptive" essay or a "comparison/contrast" essay. Instead, they think about the purpose and audience for the essay and about the details that they have explored in their prewriting activities. As they develop these details to fit their purpose for writing, they use one or more of the strategies— deliberately or unconsciously—to shape their paragraphs.

Using two or more strategies within the same essay does not mean that the writer is confused or that the essay is disorganized; often, it indicates that the topic is complex and that the writer has thought of several ways of presenting his or her ideas. For example, here is another outline of a possible essay on the consequences of modern technology, one in which the writer uses a variety of strategies:

- Paragraph 1—Introduction (including a definition of a specific type of technology and a "working" thesis statement)
- Paragraph 2—Description of one problem created by this technology
- Paragraph 3—Narration of an incident related to the problem described in Paragraph 2
- Paragraph 4—Description of another problem
- Paragraph 5—Analysis of some of the causes of these problems
- Paragraph 6—Analysis of some reasons why it is important to rethink our attitude toward this technology
- Paragraph 7—Conclusion

There is no formula for determining the number of paragraphs an essay should have. An essay's paragraph development depends on the writer's purpose, thesis, and audience. Sometimes, thinking about the purpose and the audience helps writers realize that they need to do more brainstorming and clustering in order to generate new facts, observations, and experiences about the topic. These new details may suggest a pattern for a particular paragraph or for the entire essay.

WRITING ACTIVITY **ANALYZING AN ESSAY**

Below is a draft of an essay that a student wrote for her school newspaper. Her purpose was to convince other students that the chemical industry does not have adequate safety procedures. This essay is a persuasive one, but, as indicated, the writer used a combination of several types of paragraph patterns to make her point.

THIRD REVISION OF AN ESSAY

ON THE SAFETY OF CHEMICAL TECHNOLOGY

Introduction

1)   Recently, I was thinking about how "chemically dependent" all of us are. For example, each morning, I wake up and eat a breakfast composed of chemical preservatives and additives. Then I dress myself in clothes woven from chemical

Narration fibers and drive to school in a car that is built from
chemical compounds and that runs on other chemicals. I eat my
chemical lunch and drink a totally synthetic soda. If I'm not
feeling well, I take chemically-created pills or tablets. I
don't know how we would exist without all of these chemicals,
but I wonder if we are paying too high a price. Chemical
engineering is a dangerous industry, and we are all vulnerable
to chemical accidents.

Description 2)   The worst chemical accident in history, the release of
toxic gas in Bhopal, India, killed almost 10,000 people and
injured another 100,000. The chemical company responsible for
this accident was Union Carbide, the same company that
manufactures many of the additives in my food and the
synthetics in my clothes.

3)   When the Bhopal accident occurred, everybody said that it
was an isolated incident that could never occur in America
with all of its safety standards and checks. But it happened
again, this time in West Virginia, when another deadly

Comparison chemical seeped out of a Union Carbide plant. This accident
was similar to the one in Bhopal. Somehow aldicarb oxide, a
toxic chemical, leaked out of the plant. It was a miracle
that nobody died. Unlike in Bhopal, no one was killed, and

Contrast only 100 people were injured by the fumes. Clearly, however,
these kinds of accidents are happening more frequently than
anyone would have believed.

4)   What causes these kinds of chemical accidents? Union

Cause/effect
analysis

Carbide hasn't answered this question, but it seems that
safety procedures in many different chemical engineering
companies are unbelievably loose. People working in some
factories don't even know that they are working with toxic
chemicals nor do the people who live in the neighboring
communities. Safety drills aren't practiced regularly and
neighborhood evacuation plans don't exist or do not really
work. A repeat of the Bhopal nightmare could happen just
about anywhere near you or near me.

Argumentation
conclusion

5)   I know that many of the chemical manufacturers are now
developing policies about chemical accidents and are trying to
establish warning systems and evacuation plans. But I think
their efforts are too little and too late.

                                            Marla McWilliams

Write answers to the following questions:

1. What is the thesis statement of this essay?
2. What is the writer's purpose?
3. What kinds of readers do you think this writer was writing for?
4. How effective were the writer's details in supporting her thesis?
   Did she convince you of the dangers of chemical engineering?

ORDER IN AN ESSAY

The order of paragraphs in an essay (and of details in a paragraph) depends on the nature of the supporting details. If you are narrating a story or explaining a process, then the most natural order is a
chronological one in which details are organized as they occurred (or
would occur) in time. If your details lead you to describe, define, or analyze several factors, examples, reasons, causes, or effects, then the
most logical order is an emphatic one in which details are organized
from least important to most important.

Another ordering pattern that is often used in academic essays is
comparison/contrast. There are two strategies for ordering the details
in a comparison/contrast essay: *block* ordering and *alternating* ordering. In a block ordering pattern, you would discuss all of your information about one of the items that you are comparing or contrasting before going on to discuss the next item. In an alternating pattern, you
would first decide on the points of comparison or contrast, and then
develop the essay point by point, indicating how each point relates to
both of the items that you are comparing or contrasting.

Here is an outline of a comparison/contrast essay that has been
organized according to block order:

Introduction Thanks to bioengineering advances, childless couples can now

have the babies they long for. Women whose husbands are

infertile can become pregnant through artificial insemination

from a male donor. And men whose wives cannot have children

can hire surrogate mothers to conceive and bear their

children. While both of these processes enable infertile

couples to have children, surrogate motherhood causes many

more problems than does artificial insemination.

Paragraph 2 Artificial insemination produces a child that is genetically

linked to the wife in the childless couple. Artificial

insemination is legal. The male donor never sees the couple

or gets emotionally attached to the baby.

Paragraphs   Surrogate motherhood produces a child that is genetically

3 and 4   linked to the husband in the childless couple. Surrogate

motherhood is the target of many court cases and legal

controversies. Surrogate motherhood causes many emotional and

ethical problems because the surrogate mother carries and
bears the baby and then has to give it to the couple.

Here is an outline of the same essay reorganized by alternating order:

Paragraph 2   Both artificial insemination and surrogate motherhood produce
a child that is genetically linked to one member of the
childless couple.

Paragraph 3   Artificial insemination is legal; surrogate motherhood is the
target of many court cases and legal controversies.

Paragraph 4   The male donor in artificial insemination never knows the
couple or sees the baby; the surrogate mother carries and
bears the baby and has to give it to the couple (and this
causes many emotional and ethical problems).

EXERCISE   **DEVELOPING A COMPARISON OR A CONTRAST**

Think about two courses that you took recently in school and do
some brainstorming about the ways in which they were similar or different. Then decide on the important points that you want to compare
and contrast (for example, types of knowledge that you were expected
to learn, amount and difficulty of required reading and writing, and so
forth). Write a draft of an essay comparing and contrasting these two
courses using either block ordering or alternating ordering.

A PROFESSIONAL RESPONSE

Below is an essay from *Life Manipulation,* a book on bioengineering by David Lygre. Note that this author chose to make his thesis

statement the first sentence of the essay's conclusion. Read the essay carefully and underline the main point in each paragraph.

Reverence for life. Everyone I know believes in that. There's a mystery and wonder in life that fills us with awe and humility; it seems impossible that we could ever understand it all.

And yet, as we learn more about the mechanics of life, some of its secrets are disappearing. We're discovering how living creatures obey the same laws of nature as the rest of creation. Just as we are seizing control over our physical world, we are learning how to manipulate our biological world—to make "test-tube babies," to change our genetic makeup, to invent artificial body parts, to alter our brains, and to live longer. Indeed, we may even discover we can make life itself.

The revolution in biology could change not only our physical selves, but also the way we think of ourselves and others. The implications are truly stunning. As we put life under the microscope, carefully dissecting and analyzing each of its parts in the most exquisite detail, we may come to view life as a material, a lump of clay we can mold to our design. No longer will we accept the notion that a disease is incurable; no longer will we believe our bodies must eventually wear out and die; no longer will we accept whatever genetic features we happen to be born with. Indeed, we will no longer accept nature's way as inevitable, for we will wrest that power—and responsibility—from her.

Our technology promises to sweep us into a golden age, an age where we will control the mechanics of life. But our glittering new tools are only part of the story, for they are intertwined with the whole fabric of our society. Indeed, they create social, ethical, and legal dilemmas we have not faced before, problems we must resolve if our new age is to be a better one. For example, we have learned how to separate procreation from intercourse; now we can consider them separate matters as we seek moral guidelines for our behavior. With artificial insemination and "test-tube babies" at our disposal, we no longer must accept infertility as nature's final verdict; now we must decide how and when we should take matters into our own hands. When human cloning becomes a reality, we will have to decide when, if ever, to use it. As we learn how to diagnose more genetic diseases early in pregnancy, we will increasingly base our abortion decisions on the quality of our fetuses, including their sex. And as we learn how to control our genetic makeup directly, we will have even more power to choose what kinds of people we want. Who will we accept as "healthy" and "normal"? And since we will be able to keep people mechanically alive almost indefinitely, we will also have to decide when to let them die.

These and other issues . . . spring directly from our growing ability to manipulate life. The intrusion of this technology on our most intimate activities—having children, growing old, dying—forces us to respond. But what should we say? Should we say we will use these tools to benefit the largest number of people, or should our first priority be the dignity of each person? Whose rights are paramount—those of society as a whole, the prospective parents, the individual?

As the biorevolution speeds ahead, we find our legal, ethical, and social values lagging behind. It is hardly surprising. We pass new laws, for example, because of real problems, not hypothetical, pie-in-the-sky ones. The trouble is that some of these problems are not just hypothetical anymore. Our moral and social values also take time to change. Yet some of the questions we again face (What is life? When does life begin? When does it end? What is "meaningful" life? When should we "play God"?) are timeless, and it may be too much to expect that we will reach a consensus. Moreover, it is not at all clear how much our values should change just to accommodate our advancing technology. Indeed, science tells us what we *can* do; it does not tell us what we *should* do.

1. In your opinion, which details best support the writer's thesis statement?
2. How does the concluding sentence of this essay echo this thesis?
3. In the last two paragraphs of this essay, the writer asks several questions and does not answer them. Why do you think he did this?

WRITING ACTIVITY COMBINING PATTERNS TO DEVELOP AN ESSAY

How do you feel about the issues and questions raised in the previous essay, which describes several forms of bioengineering? Among the examples mentioned are techniques to help women get pregnant (through "test tube" fertilization), and surgery to transfer embryos to the womb of a surrogate mother. Other forms of bioengineering include synthetic genes that can be used to cure inherited diseases and cancer. Doctors have developed drugs and procedures to allow people to determine when and how they want to die. Finally, bioengineers have created artificial body parts (hands, legs, hip joints, and heart pacemakers) that can help people live longer and better lives.

The directions that follow will help you develop a discovery draft of an essay about your reaction to one of these forms or products of bioengineering.

1. Choose a topic on bioengineering. (It does not have to be one of the ones mentioned above.) Narrow down your focus for this topic (for example, "the consequences and problems of surrogate mothering").
2. Do at least ten minutes of freewriting about this topic and focus.
3. Decide for whom you are writing. What is this audience like? How familiar are they with the topic? How do they feel about it? Make a list of all the things that they will need or want to know about this topic.
4. Decide on your purpose. What exactly do you want to explain, describe, or prove? What do you want your audience to feel, think, or do?
5. On a separate piece of paper, do ten minutes of brainstorming on your focus. Circle the words or phrases that seem most important or useful and draw lines between the circles that seem related.
6. Take two of your circles from your brainstorming and do five minutes of clustering about them. Then, write a sentence that explains what your clustering is about.
7. Write a thesis statement about your focus.
8. Write four paragraphs that will support this thesis statement. Try to develop each paragraph with a different strategy.

When you are finished writing your discovery draft of these four paragraphs, follow the guidelines for "How to Get Feedback about Your Discovery Draft" discussed on pages 41-42.

A STUDENT RESPONSE

Here is an uncorrected student response to the preceding writing activity.

DISCOVERY DRAFT OF AN ESSAY ON BIOENGINEERING

I think that bacteria are the horses and cattle of the

future. Scientists will breed them and harness them to

provide us with food and energy just like horses and cattle

used to. And one day thanks to technology and the
bioengineering of bacteria, people on this planet will not go
hungry any more.

Millions of people around the world do not have enough to
eat and are malnourished. They don't eat a balanced diet and
they often get sick. Bioengineering can solve this problem.
Biochemists are now creating techniques for growing bacteria
that produce food. They can stimulate bacteria to act like
green plants and produce starch from carbon dioxide and
sunlight. If large quantities of this starch could be
produced cheaply then nobody would ever have to go hungry
again.

Also bioengineers are splicing genes in different
bacteria to make them produce things like vitamins and
antibiotics. If these things could be produced cheaply they
could be distributed all over the world. This would mean the
end of malnourishment and the diseases associated with it.
For example enough synthetic vitamins C and D are now
available to wipe out scurvy and pellegra. If other countries
could buy or develop these synthetic vitamins, these terrible
diseases would be wiped out.

Some people say that people should not tinker with nature
and that changing genes or bacteria is dangerous or has the
potential to be dangerous. But I think that anything we can
do to end the misery of hunger and starvation in this world
ought to be done. The benefits are worth the risk.

David McMahon

1. What is the writer's thesis?
2. Do his supporting details convince you of his thesis? Why or why not?
3. The writer used description and analysis to develop his paragraphs. What other strategies or details might he have included to support his point?

INTRODUCTIONS

The first paragraph of an essay is the most crucial one because it makes the reader decide whether or not to continue reading. In addition, the introductory paragraph usually states the writer's thesis and point of view so that the reader knows what to expect from the essay. Many experienced writers complete their introduction only *after* they have finished writing a draft of their body paragraphs and have a clear idea of what they wanted to show or to prove. In other words, they may write a one-sentence introduction and a one-sentence conclusion. Then, after they finish the first draft of the whole essay, they expand and revise their introductory and concluding sentences.

STRATEGIES FOR WRITING EFFECTIVE INTRODUCTIONS

1. Refer to a common condition that your thesis will discuss.

       Everyone is a born writer. Young children love to
   tell stories and young storytellers are thrilled when
   someone else can read their squiggles. But some of us
   lose our natural spontaneity as we grow up, and writing
   becomes more and more difficult to do.

2. Start with a direct quote that illustrates your thesis.

       "I can't write. I'm trying to begin, I can't think
   of anything to say," wrote Patricia Cummings in her essay
   on writing. Many students in our schools today feel
   similarly.

3. Use a brief story that illustrates your thesis.

```
    When my little brother Tommy was born, my life

changed.  When I first saw him, I knew something was

wrong with him, but I didn't know how much that something

was going to affect me.
```

4. Ask a question that will lead to your thesis.

```
    Everyone knows that women and men in America are not

treated as equals.  Women have less power and make less

money.  Why is this so?
```

5. Make sure that the approach you select for your introduction is appropriate for your topic, your purpose, and your audience.

PROBLEMS IN INTRODUCTIONS

An introduction provides readers with a first impression of the essay and with a sense of how interesting the essay will be. Thus, writers must make sure that their introductions don't bore or annoy readers. Here are some strategies that you should *avoid* when you write or revise introductions.

1. Do *not* apologize for your lack of knowledge or information about the essay's topic:

   ```
   "I really don't know too much about this subject."

   "Although I am not an expert about this, . . . ."
   ```

   Apologetic introductions make readers think that the writer doesn't know what he or she is talking about. If you genuinely do not know what you are discussing, find out more information. But don't advertise your ignorance to your readers.

2. Do *not* announce the content of the essay:

   ```
   "This essay will discuss . . ."

   "In this essay, I will explain . . ."
   ```

   An announcement of an essay's content is an admission by the writer that he or she is worried that readers will not understand an essay's purpose and ideas. If an essay is not clear and logical, an announcement about its purpose will not convince readers that the writer has achieved this purpose.

3. Do not use a boring introductory strategy, such as a dictionary definition, a familiar quotation, or a cliché:

```
"My dictionary describes 'sexism' as . . ."

"Intelligence makes a woman more attractive: 'If you've

got it, flaunt it'."
```

These introductions are so overused that they make readers feel that the writer didn't care enough about them to think up something original to say.

WRITING ACTIVITY   WRITING INTRODUCTIONS

Do *one* of the following activities:

1. Write an introduction for the four paragraphs that you wrote for the Writing Activity on bioengineering. Include your thesis statement in the introduction. Do not use any of the strategies discussed in the preceding section on problems in introductions.
2. Take out a discovery draft that you wrote for one of the assignments in this book. Write a new introduction for this draft, one that gets your readers' attention and makes them want to continue reading your essay.

PAIRED WRITING ACTIVITY   ANALYZING INTRODUCTIONS

Pair up with another student. Exchange the introductions that you wrote for the preceding Writing Activity. Answer the following questions about your classmate's introduction:

1. Which strategy did the writer use to develop the introduction?
2. How effective was this strategy in making you want to read the rest of the essay?
3. What are the characteristics of an effective introduction?

CONCLUSIONS

The closing paragraph of an essay is just as important as the opening one. If a conclusion is effectively written, it lets the reader know that the writer has supported his or her thesis, and it gives the essay an ending so the reader isn't left hanging. Just as there are several approaches to writing effective introductions, there are a variety of ways of writing interesting conclusions.

STRATEGIES FOR WRITING EFFECTIVE CONCLUSIONS

1. Briefly summarize the essay's main points.
2. Make an interesting analogy or comparison.
3. Suggest specific actions that the reader should take in light of your information.
4. Speculate about what your thesis implies for the future.
5. Make a brief remark that sums up your feelings.
6. Make sure that the approach you select for your conclusion is appropriate for your topic, purpose, and audience.

EXERCISE   **EVALUATING CONCLUSIONS**

   Read each of the five conclusions that follow. Decide which of the strategies above was used to write each conclusion. Be prepared to discuss why you think each conclusion sounds effective or ineffective.

   1.   I wish I could write as good as I run.

   2.   Thus, you can get ideas for writing simply by opening
        your eyes and your ears to what is going on inside of
        you and all around you.

   3.   Occasionally, I still long for a grandmother who rocks
        cozily in a rocking chair next to a warm fireplace,
        knitting afghans and feeding everyone chocolate chip
        cookies that she has baked herself. Then I think of my
        own version of a grandmother and burst with pride for
        her in spite of myself. Although it took many years for
        me to appreciate the wonder of having that very unique

and talented lady for my grandmother, I will never again
begrudge her chosen path in life. In fact, someday I
may follow in her dancing footsteps.

4. Despite these ups and downs, though, I enjoy my job and
    I'm lucky to have it.

5. Trying to begin is like being a little child who cannot
    write on unlined paper. I cannot write anything decent
    or interesting until after I have written something at
    least as long as the thing I want to end up with. I go
    back over it and cross it all out or throw it all away,
    but it operates as a set of lines that hold me up when I
    write, something to warm up the paper so my ink will
    "take," a security blanket. Producing writing, then,
    is not so much like filling a basin or a pool once, but
    rather getting water to keep flowing <u>through</u> till it
    finally runs clear.

WRITING ACTIVITY WRITING CONCLUSIONS

Read the following brief essay. It is an uncorrected revision of an
essay written by a college freshman in response to the topic "space
exploration." The concluding paragraph of this essay has been left off.
Write *two* different conclusions for this essay, using different methods.

Why do the mightiest nations of the world spend so much
energy and money on space exploration? Why are American
taxpayers willing to pay billions of dollars each year for the
construction of satellites and spaceships that explore barren

planets where nothing lives? Where and when is the pay-off?
I have wondered about these questions for the past decade.

Space enthusiasts say that our solar system has more
value for us than we can predict now. The different planets
and their moons may have chemicals that will improve our lives
and the weightlessness of space may allow us to create new and
valuable substances. And one day the planets and their moons
may serve as home to pioneers from the earth who can no longer
stand the overcrowded conditions on our planet. I don't agree
with people who say this. I think it's more important to use
what we have here on earth (including the millions of dollars
we spend on space flight) to feed, clothe and house all the
poor and the homeless.

Other people say that although we may not see immediate
benefits from space exploration, it satisfies our need to
explore. Humans have a craving to explore and they have
examined every inch of the earth. Space is the next frontier.
I don't know how to answer this defense of space except to say
that I think it's cruel and selfish to satisfy our need to
explore while we allow men, women and children to die from
exposure and hunger.

People in NASA and in the White House see space
exploration as a kind of steppingstone to future achievements
such as permanent space stations that could monitor our
weather and provide new sources of energy. They also see
space as the battlefield for World War III. The Star Wars
project that President Reagan asked our scientists to develop

is supposed to intercept and destroy nuclear weapons while
they are still in outer space. However, everything I have
read about this project leads me to believe that it is
impossible to build a protective shield against nuclear
missiles.

Your first conclusion:

Your second conclusion:

PAIRED WRITING ACTIVITY ANALYZING CONCLUSIONS

Pair up with another student. Exchange the conclusions that you wrote for the Writing Activity on pages 123-125. Answer the following questions for each of your classmate's conclusions:

1. Which strategy did he or she use to develop the conclusion?
2. How effective was this strategy? Why?
3. What are the characteristics of an effective conclusion?

PROBLEMS IN CONCLUSIONS

Just as there are introductions that annoy readers because they are so obvious or boring, there are conclusions that can irritate readers. Here are some strategies to *avoid* when you write or revise conclusions.

1. Do *not* summarize the entire essay:

   "This essay was about the problems experienced by very
   intelligent women. In this essay, I explained why
   professional women should not be afraid to flaunt their
   intellect and imagination."

2. Do *not* simply restate the thesis or the introduction in a conclusion:

   "As I said earlier, intelligence makes a woman more
   attractive. 'If you've got it flaunt it.' Executive women
   should not be afraid of their brains or of the impression
   that their intellect makes on those with whom they work."

3. Do *not* mention a new topic that has not been discussed in the essay:

   "Professional women should not be afraid to flaunt their
   intellect or their imagination. Nor should executive
   women be ashamed of their good looks. Although some
   beautiful career women may be discriminated against
   because of their appearance, they must strive to make
   others accept them as an equal. Good looks and a superior
   brain are a powerful combination for success in American
   society."

4. Do not announce that your conclusion is a "conclusion":

   "Thus, my conclusion is that professional women should
   use their intellect and their imagination to succeed."

WRITING ACTIVITY **WRITING INTRODUCTIONS AND CONCLUSIONS FOR ESSAYS**

Take out the discovery draft of an essay you wrote for one of the
writing activities you did earlier. On a separate piece of paper, write an

introduction and a conclusion for your essay. Then answer the following questions in the space provided:

1. Which approach did you use for your introduction? Why?

2. Which approach did you use for your conclusion? Why?

WRITING ACTIVITY ANALYZING AN ESSAY

Read the uncorrected student essay below. Then, on a separate piece of paper, answer the questions that follow the essay. Do this activity by yourself or with a classmate.

FORESTS AND FAST FOOD

Last night, I took my children to dinner at McDonald's. While they ate, I read the evening paper and my attention was caught by a headline that shouted "Forests Shrinking Across the World." Intrigued by this headline, I started reading the article. It began by offering information about the numbers of forests that are being cut down daily to provide wood and paper. As I read this, I thought to myself "So what? People all over the world need wood and paper." Then I put down the paper and watched my family eat.

My children were eating hamburgers that had been wrapped in thin yellow paper and inserted in a big styrofoam and paper box. Their french fries stuck out of oily paper bags, accompanied by small paper packages of salt and pepper. I was drinking coffee from a large white paper cup. In my coffee, I had mixed cream from a round paper container and sugar from a red paper package. Each of our meals was resting on a gray cardboard paper tray, covered by a white paper place mat. Ketchup had leaked over everything, so we had to use more than fifteen paper napkins to clean up our trays and ourselves. How many trees had been cut down and turned into the mess on our table?

I picked up the paper and read on. The article said that trees are not renewable and that we cannot plant them as fast as we cut them down. It also said that cutting down a forest destroys the soil and plants underneath and this destruction leads to the death of many animals and plants. Chopping down forests also affects the composition of the air we breathe because trees help change carbon dioxide into the oxygen we need to live. All this so that we can have cheap, throw-away fast food meals!

My family and I are never going to fast food restaurants again. And we are working hard at conserving paper in every area of our lives. However, we are just one family. We need families all over America to stop wasting paper. If they don't, the world's forests may not survive.

Mayumi Fujitsu

1. What is the writer's main point?
2. Did she write a thesis statement? If you think so, which sentence is the thesis? If you think not, then how do you know what her main point is?
3. What strategies and types of details did the writer use to develop and support her main point? How effective were these strategies and details?

4. How did the writer order the details in this essay?
5. How effective were the introduction and the conclusion?

DRAFTING WITH A WORD PROCESSOR

By now, you have written several discovery drafts of essays and collected ideas for new drafts. If you have word-processed this material, I hope that you have not "lost" any of it. I remember how I felt when I hit a combination of keys that accidentally erased my discovery draft of the second chapter of this book. I hope that you never experience what happened to me. Here are some precautions to take to make sure that you don't accidentally erase any part of your files:

1. Make a separate file—with a new FILE NAME—for each new piece of writing (so that you don't accidentally erase an old file by writing a new file on top of it). Give each file a NAME that clearly indicates the content of the file (for example, "Chap5.rev" reminds me that the file is my revision of Chapter 5).
2. SAVE your file to a back-up disk or drive every five or ten minutes (so that a power surge or drop doesn't destroy what you have written).
3. Make copies of all of your disks.
4. Print a HARD COPY of everything that you write (at the end of the day or, if necessary, at the end of every writing session).

When you develop a discovery draft of an essay on the computer screen, you may want to insert symbols and notes to yourself as you write. For example, if you run out of supporting details for a point that you have made or if you can't think of a specific word or phrase, insert a series of question marks or a note to yourself. Here is an example:

```
Some bioengineered miracles come back to haunt us.  For

example, the drug D.E.S. ??get real name?? was developed in

order to prevent miscarriages ??check facts??.  It did that,

but unfortunately is also caused genital cancer and ???? in

the daughters of mothers who took the drug when they were

pregnant with these daughters.
```

> Then when you are finished writing, use the SEARCH keys to find each set of question marks, so that you can erase them and type in the word or information that you needed.

READ BEFORE YOU WRITE

In this chapter, you have read about issues and problems in bioengineering and technology. Below are some related topics that you might want to select as a focus for an essay. Note that these are merely topics or subjects; none of them is a complete sentence or a thesis statement.

1. a bioengineering product or service that you consider unethical or unfair
2. a drug that has helped and/or harmed people
3. whether our government should increase or decrease funding for new weapons or weapon systems (and why)
4. whether our government should increase or decrease funding for space exploration (and why)
5. some hazards of current technology (for example, pollution or radioactive waste or fallout)

Here are some other topics that you might prefer to write about:

6. an old Nigerian proverb: "Treat the earth well. It was not given to you by your parents. It is loaned to you by your children."
7. something that you know how to do very well or something special that you know how to make (Assume that your audience knows nothing about your specialty and write an essay that explains how you do your specialty and why it is important.)
8. a serious problem in your community or country and some suggestions for solving it
9. a major decision that you made and its consequences for your life or family or friends
10. the "perfect" or ideal school or education (and why you think this school or type of education would be better than existing types)

WRITING ASSIGNMENT   DEVELOPING AN ESSAY

For this writing assignment, you will be developing an essay about one of the ten topics above. You may be wondering, "How many paragraphs should this essay be composed of?" My answer is: as many as it takes for you to illustrate or support your point. (If you're really concerned about the length of this particular essay, try to write a minimum of four paragraphs and a maximum of eight.) Begin with ten minutes of freewriting about your topic. Select a focus in your freewriting and do ten more minutes of brainstorming on this focus. Next, do five minutes of clustering about your focus to see if you have enough ideas to begin writing a discovery draft.

Prewriting Guidelines

Specify your focus:

- Which aspect, part, or characteristic of your topic are you going to focus on?
- How much do you already know about this focus?
- What else do you need to find out about it, and where will you look for this information?

Determine your audience:

- Who might be interested in knowing about the topic and focus that you have selected?
- What does this reader (or group of readers) already know about your topic and focus?
- What else might they need or want to know about this topic and focus?

Refine your purpose for writing this essay:

- What do you want your readers to understand about the topic and the focus that you have selected?
- What do you want your readers to think or to feel or to do when they are finished reading your essay?

Write a sentence that can serve as your working thesis statement. Then, reread your freewriting, brainstorming, and clustering and consider the way in which your details relate to your focus, audience, purpose, and working thesis statement. If you think you have enough examples or reasons to start writing a discovery draft, then start. If not, do some more thinking, brainstorming, and clustering. Then decide on the strategies that seem most appropriate for your purpose, your reader, and your details:

- Should you narrate a story or a sequence of events?
- Should you describe your observations about specific people, places, or things?
- Should you define your key terms and offer some examples of what you mean by them?

- Should you explain the similarities or differences between the things that you are discussing?
- Should you analyze the categories, the types, or the causes and results of specific events or behaviors?
- Should you evaluate the worth or importance of specific ideas or behaviors?

When you finish writing the discovery draft, write a title that sums up your topic or focus in a few words. Get responses to your discovery draft by following the guidelines for "How to Get Feedback about Your Discovery Draft" on pages 41–42. After you have received some responses to your discovery draft, answer the following questions to determine whether it needs more specific supporting details.

Revising Questions
1. What approach did I use for my introduction? How could I make my introduction more interesting?
2. How can I make my thesis statement clearer?
3. Who is my audience and what else do they need to know about my thesis?
4. What experiences have I included to support my point? What other experiences should I include?
5. What observations have I included to support my thesis and are there other observations I should include?
6. What facts have I included to support my thesis? What other facts should I consider?
7. Which words in each paragraph are examples of sensory language?
8. Which details in each paragraph are too general?
9. How are the details in each paragraph organized? If the logic breaks down, where does it do so and why?
10. Which approach did I use in my conclusion? How could I make my conclusion more effective?

Revise your discovery draft based on your classmates' comments and on your answers to these Revising Questions.

ADDITIONAL TOPICS TO WRITE ABOUT

Here are some more topics for you to write essays about using the various strategies that you practiced in this chapter.

1. A 1985 National Science Foundation poll found that "only one in fourteen Americans meets a minimal definition of scientific literacy" and that "40% of those polled believe in flying saucers, lucky numbers, and that rockets change the weather." In response to these findings, several scientists have proposed that elementary and secondary schools should have required courses in scientific and technological literacy. How do you feel about this proposal?

2. One of the worst side effects of recent advances in technology is pollution: Our air and water are being destroyed by pesticides, herbicides, synthetic plastics, aluminum, glass, and radioactive wastes. Barry Commoner feels that we are "destroying this planet as a suitable place for human habitation." What is your response to Commoner's assertion? What can or should American citizens do about technological pollution?

3. On January 28, 1986, six American astronauts and one civilian—teacher Christa McAuliffe—died in the explosion of the space shuttle *Challenger*. Polls taken after the tragedy (by the Roper Organization) indicated that most of the public felt that these deaths were "a price we must be willing to pay for the exploration and mastery of space." Do you agree or disagree? Why?

4. Statements made by several American presidents indicate that they think that a nuclear war could be limited and controlled. However, statements made by leaders of other countries make it clear that they intend to respond totally in the event of a nuclear attack. Should the United States continue to build offensive nuclear weapons or should it work toward negotiating nuclear arms control treaties—or should it do both?

5. Think up your own topic. Focus on an issue or a problem about which you feel strongly.

Reminders

Specify your focus:

- What points do you want to explain, describe, or defend?
- How much do you already know about your topic?
- What else do you need to find out about it?

Determine your audience:

- Who might be interested in reading your essay?
- What does this reader (or readers) already know about your topic? How do they feel about it?
- What else do they need or want to know about it?

Refine your purpose:

- What do you want your readers to think or feel or do?
- Which strategies will best accomplish this purpose (or these purposes)?

After you finish your discovery draft, get your classmates' responses by following the directions for "How to Get Feedback about Your Discovery Draft" on pages 41–42.

ISSUES FOR YOUR JOURNAL

1. What did the readings in this chapter make you wonder or worry about?
2. What have you been writing about for your other courses? What topics—in your reading and writing—have been particularly interesting?
3. How do you feel about the school you are currently attending? What are its good points? What are its bad points? How could it be improved?
4. Do you have a favorite television program? If so, what is it and why do you enjoy watching it? What do you learn about people or about life from it? How realistic is it? What kinds of stereotypes does it portray?
5. Look over your journal entries for the past two weeks. Which ones are particularly interesting? Why? Which ones might you want to develop into essays?

ADDITIONAL READING

"Magnitudes" is a poem about the consequences of environmental pollution. It was written by Howard Nemerov, the former poet laureate of the United States.

MAGNITUDES

Earth's wrath at our assaults is slow to come
But relentless when it does. It has to do
With catastrophic change, and with the limit
At which one order more of magnitude
Will bring us to a qualitative change
And disasters drastically different
From those we daily have to know about.

As with the speed of light, where speed itself
Becomes a limit and an absolute;
As with the splitting of the atom
And a little later of the nucleus;
As with the millions rising into billions—
The piker's kind in terms of money, yes,
But a million in terms of time and space
As the universe grew vast while the earth
Our habitat diminished to the size
Of a billiard ball, both relative
To the cosmos and to the numbers of ourselves,
The doubling numbers, the earth could accommodate.

We stand now in the place and limit of time
Where hardest knowledge is turning into dream,
And nightmares still confined in sleeping dark
Seem on the point of bringing into day
The sweating panic that starts the sleeper up.
One or another nightmare may come true,
And what to do then? What in the world to do?

OPTIONAL WRITING ASSIGNMENT

Think about some of the "assaults" upon the earth that Nemerov alludes to in his poem and about some of the "nightmares" that Nemerov fears. Do you think modern technology will lead to the future destruction of parts of our planet and of its inhabitants? Write an essay describing your vision of the future of our planet. Or write an essay explaining what we can do now to slow down or stop the destruction of our planet.

PART TWO

REVISING

REVISING IDEAS AND DETAILS

*Writing and rewriting are a constant search
for what it is one is saying.*

JOHN UPDIKE

*I have rewritten—often several times—every
word I have ever published. My pencils
outlast their erasers.*

VLADIMIR NABOKOV

THE IMPORTANCE OF REVISING

All writers need to revise. As they write a draft, they discover their ideas by making personal associations and private connections. These ideas may not make much sense to readers, so, like sculptors, they need to chisel and cut their material into a clearer, more precise form. Experienced writers know that revision is the *most important part* of the writing process: they write, then they revise, then write, then revise over and over again, producing numerous revised drafts. They do not stop revising until they feel that they have produced a piece of writing that is worth editing. But what exactly *is* revision? It is not editing, nor is it copying over a draft and fixing the mistakes. Revising is rethinking, reseeing, and reshaping—making a draft fit the writer's purposes and the intended reader's needs.

What should you revise first? Surveys of teachers and employers reveal that they consider problems in ideas and clarity the most serious flaws in papers. When teachers and employers are asked what they mean by "ideas" and "clarity," they usually take out essays and make comments like these:

"I don't understand what he's trying to prove in this essay."
"I read this report three times and I'm still not sure what her points are."
"I just can't follow his line of thought and logic."
"This paper is so vague that I don't believe one word."

You have already worked on revising the ideas and improving the clarity of your discovery drafts using the Revising Questions at the end of each chapter. This chapter and the two chapters that follow expand these revising activities by presenting strategies that you can incorporate into your own writing processes.

PAIRED WRITING TASK **DETERMINING REVISIONS IN EACH OTHER'S ESSAYS**

Do this writing task with a classmate. Take out a discovery draft of a piece of writing that you wrote for one of the assignments in this book (or for your teacher). Exchange papers with your classmate. After you have read your classmate's paper, write answers to the following questions (on a separate piece of paper). Do *not* discuss each other's papers until you are both finished writing your comments.

Your classmate's name: _____

1. What do you think was the writer's purpose here? What was he or she trying to say or to show?

2. Whom do you think the writer envisioned as the audience for this piece?
3. What is the writer's main point?
4. Which examples or reasons best support this main point?
5. Were there any places where you got confused? Why? Where did you need more information?
6. What else do you want to know about the topic that the writer is discussing? What else should the writer have included to make the piece more interesting?

HOW TO ACHIEVE SOME DISTANCE FROM YOUR WRITING

The first step in revising a draft is reading it again to examine what you have said about your topic and what else you still need to say or to explore. In order to do this, you have to gain some distance from your writing so that you can "re-see" it honestly and critically. Here are several strategies for helping you do this:

- Put the draft away for at least twenty-four hours (if possible). When you reread a draft after several hours or days, you may not remember everything that you were thinking when you wrote the draft. This makes it easier for you to read and evaluate what is actually on the page. Putting a draft aside for a while allows you to see where your ideas don't make sense and where the connections between the ideas are unclear.
- Pretend to be a reader who knows absolutely nothing about your topic. Think about what this reader would act like and think like; then read your draft from this reader's perspective and see if this reader would be confused by any parts of your draft.
- Read the draft out loud so that you can hear where it sounds strong or weak. Reading aloud also enables you to notice problems that you might not have noticed when you were reading silently. If you can, tape record yourself reading the draft aloud and then take notes on the problems in the draft as you play back the oral version.
- Ask classmates, friends, or relatives to read your draft and to tell you what they liked about it and what they thought was confusing or unclear.

You can turn to many people for responses to your drafts. Classmates, tutors, friends, and family can give you a general impression of a draft's strengths and weaknesses and can offer specific suggestions for revision. In order to benefit most from readers' responses to your drafts, keep these suggestions in mind:

1. Make your draft neat and legible and leave space for changes and notes.
2. Prepare questions to ask readers about specific aspects of the draft that trouble you.
3. Evaluate your readers' responses without becoming defensive. Readers are not criticizing you; they are trying to help you improve your writing.
4. Decide which of your readers' responses to follow and which to ignore.

GROUP EXERCISE REVISING COLLABORATIVELY

Get into a group with two or three classmates and ask one of them to help you revise a recent draft. After this person has read the draft, ask him or her to answer the questions in the Paired Writing Task on pages 140-141. Take notes as the person responds. Repeat this activity with another member of the group. Then, reconsider the purpose, focus, and audience for this draft and decide which of your readers' suggestions you should incorporate in your revision.

STRATEGIES FOR REVISING DISCOVERY DRAFTS

As you revise, remind yourself again that the ideas and details in your discovery draft are merely your initial thoughts. Don't feel committed to your first thoughts—new and better ideas will occur to you as you try to figure out exactly what it is that you want to say. Keep an open mind and be willing to cross out or change what you have already written. In addition, try using the following strategies to help you identify and revise problems in the content of *each* paragraph in your draft:

- Consider the extent to which your draft fulfills the requirements of the writing assignment *and* your own purpose(s) for writing the draft.
- Consider whether you tried to do too much or too little in this draft. Is the draft too broad and unfocused? Or is it too narrow and too limited in its scope?
- In the margin next to each paragraph, write one sentence explaining what the paragraph should make the reader think, feel, or do.

Make sure that every paragraph actually does what your marginal sentence says it should do. If it doesn't, rewrite it.

- Check to see if one of your supporting sentences is actually the main point that you want to make. If it is, rewrite the paragraph so it focuses on and supports this main point.
- Consider whether you have included enough observations, experiences, and facts to convince the specific reader for whom you are writing. If you haven't, add more.
- Make sure that your details are specific enough. Do they contain sensory words that let your reader see, hear, touch, and smell the subject of the paragraph? If not, cross out the general or vague words, and add descriptive words and lively, active verbs.
- Make sure that each observation, experience, or fact supports the main idea of the paragraph. If you are not sure whether one does, cross it out or rewrite it so that it is clearly related to the main point.
- Pinpoint the parts that sound good or that are particularly effective in order to get some clues about how to revise the weaker, confusing parts. Which details or words are particularly clear or interesting? Where is your voice especially strong and convincing?

WRITING ACTIVITY ANALYZING PROBLEMS IN SUPPORTING DETAILS

Identify the problems in the supporting details of this uncorrected paragraph by answering the eight questions that follow it.

Women who work get many rewards. For example I have many friends who work. Their husbands don't like it all that much, but they would never stop working (unless they became pregnant and were tired or wanted to stay home with their babies after they gave birth). Work is extremely important. It makes my friends and me more interesting because it gives us interesting things to do and to discuss, such as our problems, struggles and joy. And this makes us better girlfriends and wives. Also, working outside the home lets us meet more people than if we just stayed home. But the best reason for working is the money: it makes a real difference to our families.

1. What do you think this paragraph is supposed to make the reader think, feel, or do?
2. Does the paragraph accomplish this purpose? If not, what kinds of details should be added or changed?
3. Is one of the supporting sentences actually the main point? If so, underline it.
4. Does this paragraph have enough observations, experiences, and facts to be convincing? If not, what kinds of details does it need?
5. Does each observation, experience, or fact support the main idea of the paragraph? If any supporting detail does not do this, cross it out.
6. Are the observations and direct experiences believable? If not, which ones aren't and why aren't they believable?
7. Are the details specific enough and are there enough of them to convince you that "women who work get many rewards"?
8. The paragraph in this writing activity is actually the discovery draft of Jackie Nathanson's paragraph on page 86 of Chapter 4. What are some of the differences between the discovery draft (in this writing activity) and the revised version (in Chapter 4)?

A PROFESSIONAL RESPONSE

Below is a copy of my first draft for the beginning of Chapter 1 in this book. The comments and questions were written by one of the composition teachers who reviewed this book. (Before a textbook gets published, each chapter is reviewed seven or eight times by several expert teachers.) The handwritten revisions are mine. Compare the draft below to page 4 in this book. Note that the actual page of this text is different from the revised version below. This is because I revised almost every page in this book four or five additional times before my reviewers, my editor, and I were satisfied with it.

a born writer ?

These details seem connected. Can you make them more so?

Everybody is born with a desire to communicate. ~~As they~~ *Do you mean "communicate" or "write"? Clarify your meaning and strengthen this sentence*

~~learn to speak,~~ young children love to tell stories, and they

thrilled
are ~~so pleased~~ when other people understand these stories *and*

~~When they begin to write, they are just as thrilled when~~

~~people~~ read their writing. Some of us continue to ~~be thrilled~~ *preserve*

this sense of the magic of the written word as we
~~as~~ we grow up. Others of us ~~stop writing--or stop enjoying~~
Why? *lose touch with the magic*
~~it~~--because no one takes delight in our writing~~.~~ *or because*
of the criticisms that we receive

~~Some of us also stop writing for other reasons: parents~~

Too vague. What do you mean here?

~~or teachers criticize us or make us follow rules that don't~~
lose our spontaneity and we
~~make sense to us.~~ Gradually, we develop negative attitudes
How do you feel about writing? *influence*
toward writing. Attitudes are very important: They ~~determine~~
a writer's habits and processes *so*
~~our desire and our ability to do anything.~~ ~~Thus,~~ writers

These ideas are related; they should be in the same paragraph.

ought to understand their attitudes toward writing. One

attitude that many people have is that writing is easy and
can create perfect prose
that professional writers ~~write well~~ every time they write.

This is not true~~.~~*!* ~~Another attitude that interferes with~~

These ideas seem unrelated to the ones above. maybe you should put them in a different paragraph.

~~people's ability to write effectively is a belief that good~~

~~writers can write a piece of polished perfect prose in one~~

~~sitting. This is also untrue.~~

~~Most successful writers go through a complex process when~~

~~they write and they have many problems.~~

(moved to another section)

Which strikes you as being the most important revision that I made in my discovery draft of the opening page of this book?

HOW TO GENERATE NEW IDEAS FOR REVISING

As you reconsider your goals for a particular draft and your readers' responses to it, you will probably find paragraphs and sentences in the draft that are not relevant to the main idea or that need to be expressed more fully and more clearly. If you decide that your draft needs additional supporting details, you might want to use the techniques discussed in Chapter 2 to help you generate new material. Freewriting, brainstorming, and clustering are all activities that provide writers with new insights, ideas, and details.

A form of clustering called "branching" is a particularly productive technique for helping writers to evaluate the relevance of their supporting ideas and to generate new details for a discovery draft. To branch a cluster of a draft, do the following:

1. Write the main idea of the draft in a circle in the middle of a sheet of paper. Write each of your supporting points in its own circle and connect it to the main circle.
2. Next draw branches radiating from each supporting point and write in the observations, experiences, and facts that you used to make each supporting point specific and convincing.
3. Finally, evaluate your supporting points by asking yourself these questions:
   - Would one of the supporting points make a more effective main idea for the draft?
   - Is each supporting point relevant to the main idea? Should any be eliminated?
   - Which supporting points need more "branches"? Which ones do not have enough details to make them clear and specific? Should any branches be eliminated?

A STUDENT RESPONSE

Here is a branched cluster of Jackie Nathanson's paragraph on page 144 of this chapter. Look at the notes that she wrote in response to the cluster. How did her cluster and notes help her revise her paragraph into the final version that appears on page 86 of Chapter 4?

Don't underestimate the value of freewriting, brainstorming, and clustering in helping you to discover new insights into the ideas that you have written about in your draft. After you use these techniques to add new details to your draft, you will probably need to revise your draft again. As you reread your draft, ask yourself whether your writing communicates exactly what you meant to say. Will your readers understand your draft? Will they find your details logical and convincing?

If you decide that your draft needs more details, think about the reasons and examples that your instructor and classmates offer when they discuss a point in class. What kinds of evidence do they present as support for their assertions? What additional experiences, observations, and facts should you include to convince your instructor and classmates of the points that you have made in your draft?

As you consider these questions, you might decide that you need to get additional information from public sources for your draft. Much of the writing done in school and at work requires writers to present information beyond their personal experience, knowledge, and obser-

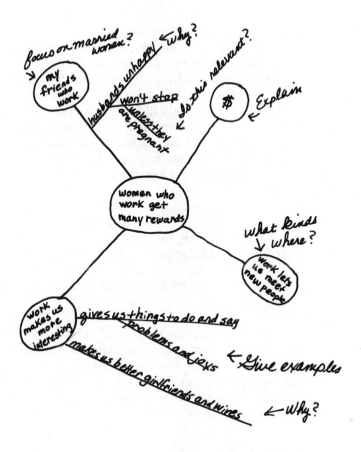

vations. Teachers and employers often expect students to be able to broaden their perspective and examine other people's viewpoints about a topic or a problem. One way to do this is to collect and analyze information about your topic from public sources (even if your draft is not a research paper). These sources include the following:

- people who know about the topic and can speak about it intelligently (including relatives, friends, classmates, teachers, employers, and other people who have information about your topic)
- articles in newspapers, magazines, and journals
- books, encyclopedias, and other reference works
- television and radio programs and movies

Public sources can provide you with additional observations and facts to include in your essays. When you consult people or read materials or watch programs about your topic, use the following techniques to help you record important information.

1. Prepare a list of questions about the main idea or thesis of your draft. What else do you want or need to find out about it? Use these questions to guide your readings.
2. If you are consulting a person, prepare specific questions in advance. Make sure that your questions are not "yes/no" questions but are ones that elicit the information that you need to know.
3. Take notes (when you talk to a person, when you consult reading material, and when you watch a program). Taking notes helps you remember information, and it enables you to record the ideas and questions that occur to you as you are listening, reading, or watching.
4. Identify the source at the top of the note. If the source is a person, write down her or his name, title, and relationship to you. If the source is reading material, give the author's name, the title, the publisher, the date published, the page numbers, and the library call number. Use a separate note card for each different source. (See Chapter 13 for further information on taking notes and working with sources.)

Consulting public sources of information helps you learn new ideas and facts, which can increase your understanding of your topic and can serve as the basis of new examples and reasons in your revisions. As you consider the viewpoints of other people, you may want to revise the thesis statement of your draft. This may lead you to write an entirely new discovery draft.

A STUDENT RESPONSE

Here is the original discovery draft of the comparison/contrast paragraph that Isaac Stein wrote for the activity on page 84 of Chapter 4. The draft is followed by his branched cluster of it.

DISCOVERY DRAFT

Ever since the day I took apart and reassembled my parent's television set, I knew I wished to be an electronics engineer. Like doctors and lawyers, electronics engineers specialize in one of many areas and I want to do aerospace research and rocket design. I have been thinking about the company that I want to eventually work for and I'm having

trouble making up my mind. Do I work for a giant corporation
like Rockwell International in California or a small company
like Rocket Research in Washington? Rockwell and Rocket
design rocket engines and conduct applied aerospace research.
Rockwell is huge: it employs 95,000 people and offers many
career opportunities. Rocket Research has only 300 people and
there isn't much room for advancement. At Rocket, engineers
are involved with all parts of systems design and application.
At Rockwell, they only get to work on one small part of a
project. I think I have to visit several more types of rocket
research firms before I can make up my mind about the kind of
place that's right for me.

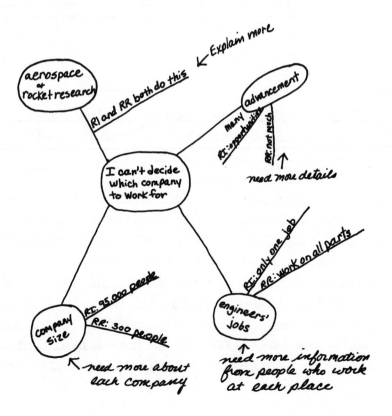

Call # 251.24   p 177 ("Employer Profiles")

Rocket Research Company, Redmont, WA
  Hires 1 business and 2 engineering majors
  per year. Starting Salary: $18,000
Tuition and fees reimbursed up to $500.
Summer Employment for College students

Rockwell International, El Segundo, CA

  Hires 200 business and 700 engineering
majors per year.
                Starting Salary: "competitive"

Interview with Chana Stein (cousin),
Electronics Technician at Rockwell International
El Segundo, California.

    Mrs. Stein doesn't mind the long
commute to Rockwell because the work is so
interesting — she gets to work on automotive,
aerospace, and telecommunications projects.
Also Rockwell is paying 100% of her
education for a PhD in electronics
engineering. And it offers her medical
and dental plans, a pension program,
and a recreational fitness program. She

Interview with Jack Irving (next door neighbor),
Senior Electronics Engineer at Royal Research, Inc.,
Eugene, Oregon.

Dr. Irving does the kind of work I want to
do: he designs airborne electronics systems
for use in rockets and space shuttles. He
wanted to be in a small firm because he
wanted to be in charge of the projects he
designs. Also he wants to work near
his home and not have a big commute.
He said small companies offer more
opportunities for promotion and

After Stein examined his cluster, he decided that he needed to consult several public sources to gather additional details for his draft. Here are examples of the 3″ × 5″ index cards that Stein wrote as he read an article and interviewed some people about the topic in a draft that he was trying to revise.

Here is Isaac Stein's first revision of his draft, in which he incorporated the information that he recorded from the sources that he consulted.

FIRST REVISION

Ever since the day I took apart and reassembled my

parent's television set, I knew I wished to be an electronics

engineer. Like doctors and lawyers, electronics engineers

specialize in one of many areas and I want to do aerospace

research and rocket design. I may have difficulty deciding on

the kind of company that I want to work for. Do I work for a

giant corporation like Rockwell International in California or a small company like Rocket Research in Washington? Rockwell and Rocket design rocket engines and conduct applied aerospace research. And they offer competitive entry level salaries and medical, dental, and pension plans.

They do have differences. Rockwell is huge: it employs 95,000 people and it hires 700 each year. Rocket has only 300 people and hires only two or three engineering majors each year. Rockwell pays for 100% of its employee's education expenses. Rocket only pays for $500. At Rocket, engineers are involved with all phases of systems design and application. At Rockwell, they only get to work on one small part of a project. Rocket is closer to my home. If I worked at Rockwell, I would have to move or have a big commute. My neighbor, Dr. Jack Irving who works at a small engineering company said that small firms like Rocket offer many more opportunities for promotion. I think I have to visit several more types of rocket research firms before I can make up my mind about the kind of place that's right for me.

A STUDENT RESPONSE

Here is the uncorrected discovery draft of two paragraphs that a student wrote about his ideal job. The handwritten comments were written by the writer's classmates.

DISCOVERY DRAFT

What's the job?

Ever since I was twelve years old, I wanted to be a *What do lawyers do*

lawyer. My uncle is a lawyer and he's terrific. He works for

The 2nd and 3rd sentences don't seem to belong here.

the District Attorney and he is the person I want to model myself on. My whole family has deep social concerns and I want to do something about this. Law is the answer. I want to be a civil liberties lawyer and handle discrimination cases. I know that being a lawyer involves a lot of hard work *Like what?* but I am looking forward to it.

Why?

I want to become a lawyer because it is the perfect *Why?* career for me. I enjoy helping people. And I think I have *What other skills do you have? What experiences have you had?* the right skills for this job. I like to have a lot of responsibilities and I don't mind working long hours. Money *What's okay?* doesn't mean that much to me but the salary is okay. I just *What does this have to do with being a lawyer?* have to be able to support myself. (I don't want to have to depend on my family and I don't want my future wife to work.) Thus, I think that being a lawyer will be a challenging and rewarding job.

Dear Shaun — I'm not clear about the main point of your first paragraph. And you need to provide more details Shaun Morrissey *about what civil liberties lawyers actually do. I like the second paragraph. It has more details. But you need to say more about why you want this career. —Irene*

After the writer read his classmates' comments and questions, he realized that he needed to consult other sources of information. He spoke to several relatives and teachers and read some magazine articles and books about his topic. His first uncorrected revision incorporates his new details.

FIRST REVISION

Ever since I was twelve years old, I wanted to be a lawyer. My whole family has deep social concerns and I want to do something about the injustice in our city and our community. Law is the answer, especially civil liberties law. A civil liberties lawyer protects the constitutional rights of minorities and of the poor and works on discrimination cases. They also interpret legal rulings and regulations for individuals and businesses who cannot afford their own private lawyers. This kind of work involves much reading, researching and writing but I am looking forward to doing these things. I want to be prepared so that I can win cases and help my clients.

Civil liberties law is the perfect career for me. I enjoy helping people and I despise discrimination. Also I think I have the right skills for this job. I am a volunteer worker at the Main Street Legal Aid Society and I help the lawyers conduct research and write briefs. I like to have a lot of different responsibilities and I don't mind working long hours. I know that civil liberties lawyers don't make as much money as other types of lawyers, but the $20,000-$30,000 a year is quite enough for me. And lawyers have good working conditions: offices and courtrooms are comfortable places to work. Thus, I think that being a civil liberties lawyer will make me very happy.

What are the most important differences between this writer's discovery draft and his first revision?

GROUP WRITING ACTIVITY REVISING IDEAS AND DETAILS IN A STUDENT'S ESSAY

This activity will help you broaden your perspective and practice the revising skills that you have learned so far in this chapter. Do this activity in a group. Select one person to record your group's comments, questions, and suggestions about the following draft of an essay on an ideal job. Consider what additional information should be added to make the essay clearer and more specific, and use the revising techniques discussed on pages 142–143 of this chapter to suggest revisions in this essay. It is double-spaced so that your group's suggested revisions can be written directly on the draft.

DISCOVERY DRAFT: INDUSTRIAL ENGINEERING

Very few engineers are women, but the opportunities for women engineers are terrific. There are more jobs at higher salaries available for women than in almost any other profession. However, because most engineers are traditionally men, most young women don't even consider a career in engineering.

I have wanted to be an engineer for a long time. In high school, I did well in science and math and my teachers encouraged me to think about a career in science. Most of them suggested that I go into nursing or become a science teacher. But I wanted to be able to design and to develop things. Now I am majoring in engineering and I think I want to be a mechanical engineer because I was always good with my hands and good at constructing things.

A mechanical engineer designs and develops machines that produce and that use power. She can change water and air power into electrical power. The specific work varies according to the field that you specialize in. But all mechanical engineers do research, design, and test work products. And not only do mechanical engineers design machines and tools, but they also design the factories that make this equipment.

> The thing that excites me most about being a mechanical engineer is that I will be designing and building machines that make life easier for people. Also I will be designing systems that can convert natural energy into electricity. Both of these activities will help our country in many ways. I will be making a contribution--as an engineer and as a woman.
>
> May Chang

HOW TO MAKE SUPPORTING DETAILS MORE CONVINCING

If you or some classmates read one of your discovery drafts and decide that it isn't believable, then you will have to add additional details and make your details more convincing. The previous section helped you learn how to develop new ideas and details, and this section will help you revise your details to make them more appropriate and more convincing. First, practice identifying problems in faulty reasoning. Here are eight details taken from different essays. Each illustrates a different type of unconvincing evidence, and each is followed by a suggestion for revision.

1. "Being a teacher isn't rewarding. My best friend makes only $15,000 and spends most of his time disciplining the children instead of teaching them."

   Problem: This writer provided **insufficient evidence**. One example doesn't prove anything. Readers might know many teachers who make much more money and who truly enjoy teaching.
   Solution: The writer should narrow his assertion and present more examples.

2. "I dream of becoming the president but I know I never will. There has never been a woman president and there never will be one."

   Problem: This writer has made a **hasty conclusion** that didn't follow from her evidence. Readers may think that there is an excellent possibility that a woman will become president in the future. Moreover, just because a pattern has existed in the past doesn't mean that it will go on forever.

Solution: The writer should think more carefully about the main point and examine the possibilities for change in American politics.

3. "I conducted an interview with my English professor, and he noted that the job outlook is best for computer systems analysts and technical engineers."

   Problem: This writer has cited a **false authority**. Why should readers believe that this English teacher is an expert on career options? Also, why should readers be convinced that this teacher's opinion is valid?

   Solution: The writer should interview experts on the topic and consult other sources of public information for new evidence.

4. "Racism and sexism are very injurious to our society. These attitudes are damaging because they hurt people."

   Problem: This writer has used **circular reasoning**—she has tried to prove her point by repeating it in different words. Readers often get bored or annoyed reading the same unsubstantiated assertions over and over again.

   Solution: The writer should provide specific facts, observations, and experiences that support the point.

5. "I doubt whether women will make it to the top executive levels of American corporations—most of them aren't ambitious or aggressive enough."

   Problem: This writer offered a **stereotype** that appeals to people's prejudices. This may antagonize readers who believe that women are just as qualified and as capable as men are. Furthermore, readers who know successful female corporate executives will find this stereotype unconvincing.

   Solution: The writer should examine the details to determine whether they are factual or simply reflect prejudices. Then, the writer should look for examples that can serve as convincing evidence.

6. "If a woman is going to have a family, then she doesn't need a long-term career. She can work until she has children and then give up her job and stay home."

   Problem: In addition to presenting a stereotype about women, this writer is using **either–or reasoning**. There are many alternatives that the writer has not considered. Readers may know women who have successful careers and happy families or women who work part-time and spend the remaining time with their children.

   Solution: The writer should interview people who are knowledgeable about the topic and consult sources of public information about it.

7. "More and more college graduates are preparing for careers in the computer field. Thus, I think it is the most promising field today."

Problem: This writer is using **majority rule reasoning**. She assumes that if most people are doing something, then it must be valid or right. However, readers may feel that an action or an idea is wrong or silly despite what the majority feels about it.
Solution: The writer should explore other reasons for the assertion. In this case, she should think of other reasons why the computer field seems promising.

8. "I have always wanted to be a surgeon because they have the most challenging jobs and they make much more money than other doctors do."

Problem: The writer has **overgeneralized**—he has turned one point into a broad conclusion about *all* surgeons. Readers may know surgeons who make less money than do other types of doctors, or they may know surgeons who are dissatisfied with their jobs.
Solution: The writer should qualify his assertions by using words like "most," "many," and "some" or by prefacing assertions with phrases like "In my experience" or "According to the doctors I know well."

Overgeneralizing is one of the most common problems for inexperienced writers. One simple technique for narrowing down generalizations is to find the indefinite pronouns in a discovery draft and substitute qualifiers for them. Here is a list of some indefinite pronouns and of qualifiers that can be substituted for them:

Indefinite Pronouns	*Qualifier Substitutes*
all, every, everybody	most, many, several, some
none, no one, nobody	almost none, almost nobody, very few
always	frequently, often, usually
never	almost never

EXERCISE **IDENTIFYING AND REVISING FAULTY REASONING**

Each sentence in the following paragraph is numbered, and these numbers correspond to the list below the paragraph. Read the paragraph. Then reread each sentence. If you think the reasoning is logical and convincing, write "OK" next to the corresponding number. If the reasoning is not logical or convincing, write a revision of it next to the corresponding number. The first one has been done for you as an example.

(1) Part-time work—working between fifteen and thirty hours a week—is better than working full-time. (2) Everybody I know works part-time and they think it's a terrific arrangement. (3) Part-time work is particularly good for women because once they have a family, they don't want to work full-time. (4) It's also good for senior citizens who do not want to work every day but who want the stimulation and the money they get from working. (5) Part-time employment is excellent; it really helps many people. (6) I work part-time at an art gallery and my employer thinks that part-time work is the answer to our city's unemployment problem. (7) In addition, part-time employment gives people experience and money while also allowing them to fulfill other needs in their lives or try out other career possibilities. (8) My best friend is a part-time waitress while she is studying acting, and she says that part-time employment is terrific. (9) I just might become a permanent part-timer!

1. Part-time work has several advantages over full-time work.

2. _____

3. _____

4. _____

5. _____

6. _____

7. _____

8. _____

9. _____

REVISING WITH A WORD PROCESSOR

Revising with a computerized word-processing program is easier than revising with a pen and paper or a typewriter. Every time you retrieve a draft from the computer's memory, it will appear on the screen—neat and legible—ready for you to move sentences and

paragraphs around or to delete words and type in new ones. Here
are some guidelines for revising the ideas and content of your word-
processed discovery drafts:

1. **BOLD** the thesis statement and the topic sentences so that they
   stand out from the rest of the text.
2. ~~OVERSTRIKE~~ all of the sentences that do not relate clearly and
   logically to the bold sentences.
3. BRACKET ([ ]) sentences or words that seem particularly effective
   in communicating your ideas.
4. Use the SEARCH FUNCTION to find key concepts and terms in
   the draft. Make sure each is explained in enough detail.
5. Add additional paragraphs, sentences, and words using the IN-
   SERT key or WINDOWS (if your program can create them).
6. Do *not* delete your original draft. Save it—and each revision—under a different name or under a coded title with the date of the
   text.
7. Print at least two copies of every revision to share with someone
   who is willing to help you do further revision.

READ BEFORE YOU WRITE

Here is a revision of a student essay that analyzes a process. The
writer is a college freshman with a learning disability. His purpose in
writing this essay was to explain to learning disabled high school seniors how to get ready to go to college.

```
HOW TO GET READY FOR COLLEGE IF YOU'RE LEARNING DISABLED

     Learning disabilities can make school very difficult.

Learning to read and write is not easy for students who have

visual perceptual problems or for those who find it difficult

to coordinate what they see with what they hear.  Some

learning disabled people have problems remembering

information, while others have trouble holding a pen and

writing notes with it.  Despite these problems, however,

learning disabled students can succeed.  Most of us are bright
```

and are willing to work hard and we are determined to get a
college degree. Indeed, I am in college now and I would like
to share with you the steps I took to prepare me to get ready
for this experience.

The first step that learning disabled (LD) students have
to take to go to college is to collect copies of all of their
test records so that they will have them ready to show to the
college's Director of Special Services. Next, they must make
an appointment to meet with this Director because he or she
will be one of the most important people in their academic
careers. When they have their conference with the Director,
LD students should bring a list of the special services and
tools that they have been using in high school or that they
want to use in college. LD students need to know whether the
college will supply them with these special tools (such as a
dictionary, calculator, tape recorder, and computer). In
addition, LD students need to request the special services and
accommodations that they are entitled to by law. These can
include tutoring in every subject, a writer to help them take
notes or take tests, extra time on tests, psychological
counseling, and a personal mentor. LD students have to ask
the Director for whatever they think they need.

Once students have a copy of their college's official
catalog, they should examine it carefully with their parents
or with a college counselor. This catalog will help them
understand all of the required courses that they must take and
the other requirements that they will need to fulfill to get

their degree. After they study the catalog, LD students should arrange for a special tour of the college campus, <u>before</u> the semester starts so that they can get familiar with all the buildings and offices. In addition, if the college offers a summer orientation program, LD students should definitely take it because it will help them get comfortable with the school and its policies.

Once LD students get to college, they should seek the support of other LD students and maybe even join a special support group or club. They should also set up study routines that will help them do their work. Finally, LD students should speak to their teachers about their disabilities and enlist their teachers' help in creating strategies to help them accomplish the work. I have done all of these things and they have proven very helpful in making me feel confident about my ability to succeed in and graduate from college.

James R. Lipton

WRITING ASSIGNMENT   WRITING AND REVISING AN ESSAY ABOUT A PROCESS

In the preceding essay, the writer analyzed a process: he explained the steps that learning disabled students should take in order to prepare themselves for college. This writing assignment asks you to use this "how to" strategy to develop a discovery draft of an essay. Choose a process about which you are an expert. Use freewriting, brainstorming, and clustering to develop a list of the steps that are required to complete the process successfully.

Prewriting Guidelines
Specify your focus:

- How much do you already know about the process you are explaining?

- What additional information do you need to find out, and how will you get this information?

  Determine your audience's needs:

- What do your readers already know about the process and what else do they need to know?
- How much background information do your readers need about the process before you explain its steps?
- How specific should your description of these steps be in order for your readers to understand them?

Revising Questions

1. What are the strengths of this essay? Which parts sound particularly forceful and convincing?
2. What is the point of each paragraph? In the margin next to each paragraph, write a sentence explaining what it should make the reader think, feel, or do. If the paragraph does not do what you intended it to do, add new ideas or rewrite the original ones.
3. Is one of your supporting sentences actually the main point that you want to make? If so, rewrite the essay so it focuses on and supports its new main point.
4. Do your examples and reasons accomplish your purpose in writing this draft? Are they appropriate for your intended readers? If not, revise them and add new details.
5. Are your details specific enough? Do they contain sensory details that let your reader see, hear, touch, smell, or taste the subject of each paragraph? Do the details convey clear pictures of how your subject looks and sounds to you? If not, cross out vague words and add descriptive words and active verbs.
6. Does each observation, experience, or fact support the main idea of each paragraph? If you are not sure whether it does, cross it out or rewrite it so that it is clearly related to the main point.
7. Do any paragraphs or sentences go off on tangents that are not directly related to your main idea? If so, cross them out.
8. Do you think your reader will believe your observations and experiences? If not, consult public sources and add facts and statistics and cite their sources (see pages 147–148 about how to cite references).
9. Does the introduction make your point(s) clear? Is it interesting? If not, use a different technique to develop a new introduction or make the original one clearer and more interesting. (See page 119 about introductions.)
10. Does the conclusion remind the reader of the main point(s) without using the same words you used in the introduction? Does it

stick to the point without bringing up new ideas? If not, make the conclusion clearer and more to the point or develop a new one using a different technique. (See page 122 about conclusions.)

ISSUES FOR YOUR JOURNAL

1. What strategies did you use to revise your most recent writing assignment? Which strategy was the most effective? Why? How did you decide when to stop revising and to hand in the final revision?
2. Complete this sentence: At this point in my life, I should be . . . What should you be now and why? What should your life be like now? Why?
3. According to statistics released by the Bureau of the Census in 1985, the median duration of marriage in America during the past half century was seven years. Why do you think this was so? What do you think happens to a relationship after seven years of marriage?
4. Have you ever been discriminated against? What happened? Why did it happen? How did it make you feel? What did you do about it? What could you have done about it? What will you do if it happens again in the future?
5. How do you feel about the proliferation of nuclear arms? Do nuclear weapons serve as a deterrent to war? What will happen if a country uses its nuclear weapons?

ADDITIONAL READING

The essay "Labels Like Learning Disabled Hinder Students' Development," appeared in a newspaper whose readers are mostly college and university teachers and administrators. The author, John Kelley, is Dean of Students at Kendall College in Illinois.

"You have a learning disability. That's why you have trouble with mathematics."

"Oh, so that's why; I have a learning disability. I can't do math."

"Learning disability" and other such labels may be useful for clinical diagnosis and treatment, but unfortunately, we have not left them in the clinic. We have taken them out into the street and into the classroom, where they have become a curse.

Some of us can remember a time when labeling hadn't yet achieved wide usage. For example, as a child engaged in a never-ending struggle to master spelling, I never knew I was cursed with a learning disability. The fact that words I had mastered one day were lost the next was simply another obstacle to be overcome. I learned to compensate, to use alternative words when writing, and to keep a dictionary constantly at my side. A dictionary still occupies a prominent place on my desk, and the miraculous speller in my computer is a godsend.

The psychologist Alfred Adler often talked about the ways people learn to compensate for their physical deficiencies. Adler apparently had not heard of the curse of learning disabilities; his concern was with treating the whole person. The compensation he observed is exactly what I, and countless others in my generation and before, used to combat difficulties we experienced in academic areas like spelling and arithmetic.

No more. We have developed labels and attached them to our students, who have become sophisticated at turning them to their own use. Not an academic quarter passes without at least one student (and usually several) coming into my office bemoaning the rigors of a course, saying "I can't do it. I have a learning disability." Sometimes the complaint will be altered slightly, with the student saying, "I'm only a C student." Sometimes other labels, such as "disadvantaged student," are substituted for learning disability. But the tenor of the lament is the same. One label or another always emerges at some point in the excuse. It is used as a justification for failure to perform, and it soon becomes a self-fulfilling prophecy.

One of my concerns as a dean of students is to find ways to motivate students. When they graduate, I would like them to be able to hold their heads high and say they gave their best shot in every course they took. I try to help them set goals toward that end and develop skills needed to attain them. I want students to believe, as I believe, that if they can honestly say they did their best, that's all anyone can ask.

Success, in my scheme of motivation, is precisely that: giving life one's best shot, regardless of how other people rate the outcome. The student who truly does his or her best and achieves a C is in my book a greater success than the one who just goes through the motions and comes out with a B, or even an A.

So when students give me a label as their excuse for inadequate performance, I begin to ask questions, particularly about the time they spend on homework. I understand the minimum college standard to be two hours of homework for each hour of class, which means that a course carrying four credit hours (the norm at our college) would require eight hours of homework each week. I ask students if they have put in that amount of work.

The responses are interesting. In all the times I have asked the question, not once has a "labeled" student said that he or she spent two hours on homework for each hour of class. They have already concluded that because they have a learning disability they cannot do the work or achieve higher than a C in the course.

I would prefer to say that such students may have courses in which they will need to devote more than the minimum time expected to their homework if they are going to give these courses their best shot. But it's a tough concept to get across. Having accepted the label we have placed on them, students believe in the curse.

The situation becomes even more ludicrous when such students do surpass their expected C grades. I remember one coming to tell me about the mistake his instructor had made. He laughed, saying the instructor had given him an A. The student said it was ridiculous, since he knew perfectly well that he never did better than C work.

Back in my own days of struggling through school, guidance counselors endeavored to ease my frustrations by trying to steer me into vocational courses. Fortunately, one of my teachers took time to explain to me about the bumblebee. The physical make-up of the bumblebee, it seems, is such that it is aerodynamically impossible for it to fly. Yet while we could label the bee "flying disabled," the bee doesn't know that, and so continues to fly, buzzing merrily on its way.

Not knowing I was under the curse of a learning disability, I resolved to be like the bumblebee. I ignored the advice of the well-meaning guidance counselors, passed up the opportunity for the vocational training our school system offered, and went on toward the world of higher education. Along the way I learned to compensate.

My purpose in giving these illustrations is not to focus unduly on students who have been marked "learning disabled." The label could just as well be "minority," "child of a broken home," "handicapped," or any number of others. The point is that our expectations, coupled with the students' self-image, frequently determine their performance. This is just as true in college as in primary or secondary school. Labels adopted by students and reinforced by the attitude of an instructor too often predict the academic outcome.

I often see the same students, resigned to failure in the classroom, putting forth amazing efforts in the quest of excellence on the basketball court or in the concert hall. I see them talking easily and endlessly in the dorm, when across the way in the academic buildings they are silent, convinced they cannot communicate.

When I talk with such students I point to those successes. I speak of the extra effort they gave to achieve excellence. I note that extra effort can also produce academic success. Helping students learn to translate extracurricular success to the classroom is the crucial task we face with many of our students. They can be taught to visualize themselves succeeding, to feel positively about themselves, to develop goals that make academic achievement something they want rather than something they have to do. Such inner motivation becomes a crucial factor in overcoming deficiencies.

Labels, even if clinically correct, only serve to hinder students' development. Hence we should begin by getting rid of them. Amazingly, when labels have been set aside, students are likely to discover the key to academic success: inner motivation coupled with the simple ingredient known as extra effort.

When I entered our computer lab to prepare the final draft of this paper, I discovered one of those previously "labeled" students sitting in front of a monitor, putting in extra time to learn the rudiments of computer operations. My heart soared as I watched; I knew he would succeed.

OPTIONAL WRITING ASSIGNMENT

Write an essay about a "label" that someone once attached to you. Describe how it helped or hindered your development or progress.

REVISING ORGANIZATION AND IMPROVING COHERENCE

To be a writer is to throw away a great deal,
not to be satisfied, to type again, and then
again, and once more, and over and over.
                                        JOHN HERSEY

Blot out, correct, insert, refine,
Enlarge, diminish, interline,
Be mindful, when invention fails,
To scratch your head, and bite your nails.
                                        JONATHAN SWIFT

METHODS OF REVISING ORGANIZATION AND COHERENCE

Organization refers to the arrangement of a series of ideas; **coherence** refers to the relationships between these ideas. Writers who don't revise have problems with the organization and the coherence of their material. This happens because of the nature of the writing process: writing stimulates thinking—new ideas occur to us as we write—and we have to rush to get these ideas down before they fade from memory. Frequently, the connections among these new ideas are in our heads but *not* on our papers. Thus, the organization of our discovery drafts may not be recognizable to our readers or may be inappropriate to the overall piece of writing. Most readers (except English teachers) simply are not willing to struggle to see connections that are not on the page.

In the previous chapter, you practiced revising the ideas and details in discovery drafts by adding and deleting material, expanding and elaborating on generalizations, spelling out the implications of ideas, and crossing out irrelevant details. When one revises organization and coherence, however, instead of adding and deleting, one tries to rearrange ideas in a clear and effective order and then to make them flow smoothly. Thus, revising organization often consists of "cutting and pasting": literally scissoring out each sentence and rearranging it in a new order with the other details in the draft. Revising coherence involves getting rid of distracting sentences and adding words and phrases that help readers recognize how each sentence is related to the sentences that come before and after it.

PAIRED WRITING TASK **DETERMINING REVISIONS**
IN ORGANIZATION AND COHERENCE

Work with a classmate. Take out a discovery draft of a piece of writing that you did for one of your assignments in this book or for your teacher. Exchange papers with your classmate. After you have read your classmate's paper, write answers to the questions below. Do *not* discuss each other's papers until you are both finished writing your comments.

1. What is the most important information in this draft? Does this information get highlighted—does it get enough attention? If not, where should this information be moved to?

2. Is the draft developed with a logical order? If so, what is this order?

3. Is there any place in the draft where you get lost or confused? Point out this place (or these places) to the writer and explain why the ideas do not seem to develop logically or clearly.

4. Put a star (*) next to each sentence that does not seem clearly related to the one before it or to the one that comes after it. Be prepared to discuss these sentences with the writer.

5. How else might this draft have been organized? Can any paragraphs or sentences be rearranged to make the draft more logical or more persuasive?

TECHNIQUES FOR REVISING ORGANIZATION

Before you examine the organization of your drafts, try to get some distance from your writing by using the techniques recommended on page 141 of Chapter 6. Then, look at the order you used to develop your details and think about whether readers will be able to follow the development of your ideas. Ask yourself the following questions:

- Is the order that I used recognizable to the readers for whom I am writing? Can they follow the development of my ideas without getting lost or confused?
- Is the order that I used the most appropriate and effective order for my details? Will my order help readers remember my most important points?

If you arranged the details in a discovery draft **chronologically,** check to see that each detail is described as it occurred in time. Make sure that you didn't jump back and forth in time, confusing your readers. If you arranged your details **spatially,** check to make sure that you used an obvious pattern of movement which a reader can follow (left to right, top to bottom, far to near, whole to parts). Finally, if you arranged your details **climactically,** check to make sure that you used a pattern that a reader can follow (least important to most important, least personal to most personal). Whatever pattern of organization you've used, consider whether another pattern might be clearer or more appropriate.

WRITING ACTIVITY   IDENTIFYING AND REVISING PROBLEMS IN ORGANIZATION

Here is the uncorrected discovery draft of two paragraphs that a student wrote based on the brainstorming list that was shown on page 31 of Chapter 2. He has already revised this essay for ideas and details—these changes are incorporated in the first revision below. Read the paragraphs and answer the questions that follow them.

FIRST REVISION: MY FAVORITE PLACE

My favorite place in the world is my car. It's the first car that I have ever owned and I really enjoy being in it. I like to sit inside and breathe the smell of leather and oil. The car is a 1989 Corvette and its previous owner took care of it. The blue paint gleams and the chrome sparkles. It's really smooth. The blue leather is worn but clean. And the stripes on the sides of the car really look fierce. Also there's a stereo radio and cassette with four speakers that can blast me to heaven.

I feel like this car is my real home. It's private. No one bothers me when I'm driving around or even sitting in the car. I can use it to go places that buses and trains just can't go. It's a terrific place to think and dream. Also, I like to race friends in the local drag strip. Even when I'm doing this, I feel alone and I love the feeling of space and

privacy. I zoom along feeling powerful and free. I also use
my car simply as a place to hang out, cruising the streets
with my girlfriend. And I enjoy being alone in the car. It's
my own space and my own machine and I love it.

Allen Brower

1. How is Brower's first paragraph organized? If you do not see a recognizable order or pattern, how would you suggest that he rearrange his details?

2. How is Brower's second paragraph organized? If you do not see a recognizable order or pattern, how would you suggest that he rearrange his details?

Here is the way the writer revised these paragraphs after his classmates commented on the problems in their organization:

SECOND REVISION: MY FAVORITE PLACE

My favorite place in the world is my car. It's the first
car that I have ever owned and I really enjoy it. The car is
a 1989 Corvette and its previous owner took good care of it.
The blue paint gleams and the chrome sparkles. And the
stripes on the sides of the car really look fierce. It is
sleek and smooth like a jet plane. The blue leather inside is
worn but clean. I like to sit inside and breathe the smell of
leather and oil. I also like to listen to the stereo radio
and cassette deck with four speakers that can blast me to
heaven.

Besides making me feel proud, my car has given me my
freedom. I can use it to go to places that buses and trains

```
just can't go.  Also, I like to get in it and race friends in

the local drag strip.  I zoom along feeling powerful and free.

Or I can use my car simply as a place to hang out, cruising

the streets with my girlfriend.  But most of all, I enjoy

being alone in the car.  It's private.  No one bothers me when

I'm driving or sitting in it.  It's a terrific place to

think and dream.  It's my own space and my own machine and I

love it.
```

Allen Brower

What are the most important differences between these two versions of Brower's piece?

A PROFESSIONAL RESPONSE

Here is a magazine article about the most promising careers for the next century. Read the article carefully in order to complete the exercise that follows.

CAREERS THAT PROMISE BIG PAYOFFS

The best preparation for a job in the year 2000 will be to master the tools required for advancement in almost any field: conceptual, reasoning and communication skills, as well as the ability to use a computer. But finding a promising career will also require an understanding of the future labor market. For example, accountants, doctors and lawyers will continue to thrive, but their fields won't grow as fast as those of, say, gerontologists or executive chefs.

Money's selections are based on forecasts by the Bureau of Labor Statistics and private experts on occupational trends. While the number of openings over the next 15 years can be projected for some careers, other jobs are too new for reliable estimates. Advanced degrees are important in research and academic jobs but often won't pay off as well as practical skills in other careers. The salaries listed are those currently earned by job-holders.

Artificial-intelligence specialist. Software experts who can program machines to mimic human thinking will be in the fore-front of computer research and applications. Openings: at least 50,000. Salary: $40,000 to $100,000 for corporate system developers. Master's and Ph.D. programs in artificial intelligence, help-ful for top jobs, are offered by Carnegie-Mellon University in Pittsburgh and Massachusetts Institute of Technology in Cambridge.

Data-base manager. A combination of computer expert, executive and librarian, this specialist will occupy a pivotal position at many corporations, controlling the creation and flow of information. Openings: 30,000 to 100,000 or more. Salary: $29,000 to $90,000. Graduate degree: computer science or business administration—or both—or library science. Two top library science schools: UCLA and the University of Michigan.

Environmental engineer. The federal government's toxic- and hazardous-waste cleanup program—the so-called super-fund—is likely to be renewed, providing an additional $7.5 billion for environmental projects by 1990. Corporate spending for waste disposal and recycling should also rise. The best jobs will go to engineers with environmental specialties. Openings: 20,000 immediately. Salary: $26,000 to $75,000 for a high-level manager. Schools with undergraduate programs include the University of Alabama, Michigan State University and Tulane University.

Executive chef. Jobs for all restaurant cooks will increase 42% by 2000, and executive chefs—graduates of well-known culinary schools with management skills—will be at the top of their trade. Openings: 50,000. Salary: $17,000 to $100,000. Among the best schools: Baltimore Institute of Culinary Arts, the Culinary Institute of America in Hyde Park, N.Y. and Johnson and Wales College in Providence, R.I.

Fiber-optics researcher. Optical fibers that transmit large amounts of information very quickly will be used in many industries. Openings: some 40,000 for fiber-optics researchers and technicians. Salary for researchers with master's degrees: $30,000 to $40,000. Graduate degrees in optics are offered at the University of Arizona and the University of Rochester.

Gerontologist. Specializing in the study of aging, these experts will find jobs ranging from managers of retirement facilities to researchers. Openings: 500,000 for nurses with geriatric training, 50,000 for researchers and therapists and 10,000 for physicians. Salary: $23,000 to $40,000 for specially trained nurse practitioners, $20,000 to $80,000 for researchers and as much as $125,000 for doctors. Schools with gerontology programs include Brandeis University, the University of Michigan and the University of Southern California.

Industrial psychologist. Specialists who study issues of the workplace are already being hired before they can complete their doctoral studies. Key areas range from personnel testing to redesigning corporate management hierarchies. Demand is expected to rise steeply over the next 15 years. Salary: holders of master's degrees earn $45,000 to $85,000. Some of the best programs are offered by the University of Maryland, Michigan State University and the University of Minnesota.

Skilled repairer. Computers still haven't learned how to fix themselves, and there will be no slackening in demand for mechanics, repairers and installers in other specialties ranging from air-conditioner installation to electronics. Openings: more than 1 million. The fastest growth will be in repair of desktop computers; some 55,000 technicians will be needed. Salary: $13,000 for newly minted vocational school graduates to $30,000 for experienced workers. Education required: high school, vocational school or junior college.

Teacher. A million more instructors will be needed, but the highest salaries will probably go to those who teach professional skills to corporate employees. Salary: $35,000 to $75,000. Premiums will be paid for teachers with specialties in computers and business management. Demand will also be strong for teachers of kindergarten through 12th grade, as well as vocational instructors at junior colleges. Top teaching programs include those at Columbia, Ohio State and Stanford universities.

Writer or entertainer. Expansion in the movie and television industries is expected to result in more than 100,000 new jobs for actors, musicians, scriptwriters and other artists. Salary: zero up to $350,000 a week for, say, a headliner in Las Vegas. Top acting schools include the Yale University School of Drama and the Juilliard School in New York City; universities with respected writing programs are the University of Iowa and Stanford University.

Writer: William C. Banks
Reporter associate: Kay Williams

EXERCISE **REORGANIZING SUPPORTING DETAILS**

Read this uncorrected revision of a paragraph that a student wrote summarizing the article above. Then answer the questions that follow the paragraph.

PROMISING CAREERS (FIRST REVISION)

Recently, Money magazine surveyed private experts and government sources to find out which careers will promise the biggest payoffs in the year 2000. Careers in the computer field seem to be thriving best particularly artificial-intelligence specialists and data-base managers. Money implied that a "promising career" is one that is growing quickly and one that offers high salaries. I want to be a marketing researcher even though Money didn't list this career as one of the most promising ones. Fiber-optics research and environmental engineering are promising careers. The careers that most people think of as the best and the highest-paying (careers in law, medicine, and accounting) are not growing as fast as some other fields. Other promising careers, according to Money, include gerontologists, executive chefs, and skilled repairers. Money notes that teaching is a promising career, but most teachers make very low salaries.

Elliot Carson

1. Can you recognize a logical order or development of ideas in this student's summary? If so, what is it? If not, where do you get lost or confused?
2. Which sentences don't seem to belong? Why not? Cross them out or draw an arrow pointing to the place where they might fit more logically.

WRITING ACTIVITY WRITING AND REVISING A BRIEF ESSAY

Reread the magazine article about promising careers on page 173. What is your reaction to the information presented in it? Here are some questions for you to consider:

- Does one of the careers strike you as particularly promising? Why?
- What do the ten careers all seem to have in common, if anything?
- The writer calls these careers "promising" because they have large numbers of job openings. Do you consider this the most important factor in selecting a career or are there other factors that are just as important (or even more important)?

Write a discovery draft of an essay about the career(s) that you consider most promising. You do *not* have to respond to any of the questions above. Begin by doing some freewriting, brainstorming, and clustering to find a purpose and an audience and to develop your examples and reasons. Revise the ideas and details in your discovery draft using the techniques that you have practiced in Chapter 6. Then, examine and revise the organization of your draft by answering the following questions:

1. What was my purpose in writing this essay? Did I accomplish this purpose?
2. Whom did I imagine as my audience when I wrote this paragraph? Will these readers recognize the order that I used? Can they follow the development of my ideas without getting lost or confused? If not, how can I rearrange my ideas so that they develop more logically?
3. How can I rearrange the details in each paragraph so that they develop more logically?
4. Is the order that I used for the entire essay and for each paragraph the most appropriate and effective order for my details? Will my order help readers remember my most important points? If not, how can I reorder my details so that they will develop my ideas logically and clearly?

Revise the organization of your draft based on your responses to these questions.

A PROFESSIONAL RESPONSE

Donald Murray is a famous English teacher who has written many books about teaching and learning writing. Here is a revision of the opening paragraph of the preface to one of his books. Note that he uses the word "title" instead of the book's actual title (*A Writer Teaches Writing*) because he did not write a title until after he had finished the book.

What kinds of revisions has Murray made?

PREFACE

[TITLE was ~~built~~ (written to give) ~~(from the experience of publishing writers~~ ~~and practicing teachers)~~ so that ~~(secondary school)~~ English teachers ~~would have a more~~ (will) an effective method of teaching composition, (based) (on) ~~The book reveals how the~~ professional writer[~~works and the~~ (book was tested by experienced teachers in 100's of classrooms to) ~~shows~~ how the steps ~~he~~ (the writer publishing writer) follows can be applied in ~~the~~ classroom.

This does ~~not~~ (not) mean that students will be trained to be professional writers. ~~It does mean that writing is a skill~~ ~~It does mean that~~ students will be ~~taught~~ (encouraged) (motivated) (to teach) (themselves) the lessons that professional writers have taught themselves.

~~The professional writer is not just the poet or~~ ~~journalist~~

(it does mean) (add transition]) ~~for~~ writing is ~~not a gift~~ (more) but (a skill), it is not (given) (than a gift,) so much as it is developed. This book will show the teacher how to help the student develop the ability to communicate in writing with others -- in a business letter, a poem, an engineering report, a news story, [etc.] -- whatever his ability and need.

— in school
test
scholarly
essay
paper
— afterschool

Need
Experience
(method book written)
How to use - variety
Acknowledgements

RETROSPECTIVE OUTLINES

Many teachers and textbook authors recommend that writers prepare outlines of their ideas and details in order to organize their material logically. While some writers use "scratch" outlines to see the logical relationships among their ideas, many others are uncomfortable preparing an outline before they have written a discovery draft. The reason for this is that in order to outline a piece of writing, a writer has to know, in some detail, what he or she wants to write about and how he or she plans to develop the ideas. Because almost all writers discover their ideas *as* they try to write about a topic, they may find it impossible to do any outlining until they are finished writing a draft. Another problem that can result from outlining ideas before exploring them in a discovery draft is that writers may feel that they have to stick to the outline and may not consider other more interesting or important ideas that aren't on their original outlines. If you do want to prepare an outline in advance, make sure that you don't get stuck on it. Be willing to include details that occur to you as you are writing.

A more productive way to use outlining is to outline a draft *after* you finish writing it. This is called a **retrospective outline** because retrospection means a review or a reexamination of things. A retrospective outline helps a writer see the places in a draft where supporting details are missing or are not logically organized. For example, below is the uncorrected discovery draft of Mayumi Fujitsu's essay on "Forests and Fast Food," the final version of which appears on pages 127–28 of Chapter 5. This draft is followed by her **retrospective outline**.

A STUDENT RESPONSE

Introduce scene/setting first —

FOREST AND FAST FOOD

My family and I are working hard at conserving paper in every area of our lives. However, we are just one family. We need families all over America to stop wasting paper. And last night, I discovered just how much paper families waste at fast food restaurants.

move this to the conclusion

Make this the introduction

took my children to

Last night, I ~~was reading the newspaper at~~ McDonald's.
I read the paper
While my kids ate dinner. My attention was caught by a
headline that shouted "Forests Shrinking Across the World."
Intrigued by this headline, I started reading the article. It
began by offering information about the numbers of forests
that are being cut down daily to provide wood and paper. As I
read this, I thought to myself "So what? People all over the
world need wood and paper." ¶My children were eating   *Needs a transition*
hamburgers that had been wrapped in thin yellow paper and
inserted in a big styrofoam and paper box. Their french fries
stuck out of oily paper bags, accompanied by small paper
packages of salt and pepper. I was drinking coffee from a   *Switch details around*
large white paper cup. In my coffee, I used cream from a
round paper container and sugar from a red paper package.
Each of our meals was resting on a gray cardboard paper tray,
covered by a white paper place-mat. Ketchup had leaked over
everything, so we had to use more than fifteen paper napkins
to clean up our trays and ourselves.

How many trees had been cut down and turned into the mess
on our table? I picked up the paper and read on. The article
said that trees are not renewable and that we cannot plant
them as fast as we cut them down. It also said that cutting
down a forest destroys the soil and plants underneath and this   *OK*
destruction leads to the death of many animals and plants.
Chopping down forest also affects the composition of the air
we breathe because trees help change carbon dioxide into the

oxygen we need to live. All this so that we can have cheap, throw-away fast food meals!

My family and I are never going to fast food restaurants again. ~~And families across our country should stop wasting paper. If they don't the world's forests may not survive~~.

More introductory statements here

Mayumi Fujitsu

RETROSPECTIVE OUTLINE OF MY DRAFT

I. Introduction and thesis statement: Families have to stop wasting paper, which I discovered by my own family's waste.

II. Supporting details (about the meal):

--everything on the table and on the meal was made from paper (from trees)

III. Supporting details (about the newspaper article):

--trees are not a renewable resource

--cutting down trees damages the ground and the air

IV. Conclusion: If we want forests to survive, my family and all families have to stop wasting paper.

After this student wrote her retrospective outline, she used it to reexamine her draft and to write the revision notes on it. Turn to pages 127–28 and reread her revision. How does this revision differ from the draft above?

TECHNIQUES FOR IMPROVING COHERENCE

Deciding on a logical organization for the details in your drafts is the first step toward communicating these ideas clearly and effectively to readers. The next step is making sure that your ideas develop smoothly—that they are not "choppy" or "jerky." The paragraphs and sentences in an essay should be revised so that they are linked to one another in ways that help readers follow them easily. The rest of this chapter will present a variety of strategies for achieving coherence, including ways to make a draft more unified, to add transitions, to use repetition, and to use pronouns.

Making Drafts More Unified

An essay or a paragraph cannot be cohesive if it is not unified. Unity is the quality of sticking to the main idea without going off into irrelevant details. As you reread a discovery draft, you may find that it is not unified at all, probably because your main concern was to write down ideas as you thought of them. One detail may have led you to an example or a reason that was not directly related to the focus of the paragraph or essay. When you revise your draft, you must find and delete all of the details that do not clearly develop the main idea of the paragraph and essay.

As a writer, I know how difficult it is to delete ideas and details in a discovery draft. After struggling, sometimes for hours, to get one's thoughts and feelings on the page, no one really wants to delete a single word. However, if writers want readers to follow their ideas, they must examine every sentence to see if it might lead readers astray. If you find a detail that isn't clearly related to the main idea or to the details before and after it, you should cross it out.

EXERCISE   **DELETING IDEAS FOR IMPROVED UNITY**

Here is an uncorrected paragraph from a discovery draft of a student's essay on the law of public education. Cross out any sentence that is not clearly related to the main point of the paragraph or that is not clearly related to the sentence before it.

FIRST REVISION: PRAYERS IN PUBLIC SCHOOL

(1) In 1963, the Supreme Court of the United States

decided that the reciting of prayers in public school violated

students' First Amendment right to freedom of religious

beliefs. (2) The First Amendment states, in part, that

"Congress shall make no law respecting an establishment of

religion, or prohibiting the free exercise thereof." (3)
There have been a number of cases involving church-state-
education relationships. (4) The Supreme Court has looked at
cases involving payments for children in parochial schools.
(5) Before 1963, the issue of the legality of prayers in
public schools was argued in many state and city courts with
differing results. (6) However, the 1963 Supreme Court
decision (which is still in effect) made it illegal for public
school teachers to refer to God or a supreme being and to read
from the Bible in religious exercises in class. (7) It also
made it illegal for public school teachers to wear religious
clothes in public school. (8) Currently, many religious
groups are questioning the 1963 ruling and trying to get the
Supreme Court to reconsider its decision.

Ruth Albert

Adding Transitions

Transitions are words and phrases that show the connections between ideas or between sentences. Experienced writers use transi-
tional words and phrases to bridge the gaps between ideas that may
seem unconnected to readers. Here are some commonly used transitions grouped according to the signal that they give and followed by examples of their use:

1. Transitions that signal an **additional** or a **similar** detail:
   furthermore   in addition   moreover
   also   similarly   likewise

   Example: In 1963, the Supreme Court of the United States decided
   that the recitation of prayers in public schools violated students'
   First Amendment right to freedom of religious beliefs. **Furthermore,** the Court prohibited public school teachers from discussing God as part of a class's opening exercise.

2. Transitions that signal a **contrasting** detail:
however   conversely   nevertheless
although   even though   on the other hand

   Example: In 1963, the Supreme Court of the United States decided that the recitation of prayers in public schools violated students' First Amendment right to freedom of religious beliefs. **However,** the Court allowed study of the Bible or religion when presented objectively as part of a program of literature or social studies.

3. Transitions that signal a **cause** or an **effect**:
consequently   as a result   therefore
thus   because   since

   Example: In 1963, the Supreme Court of the United States decided that the recitation of prayers in public schools violated students' First Amendment right to freedom of religious beliefs. **Consequently,** public school teachers have had to restrict most of their references to God while they are teaching.

4. Transitions that signal a **time-related** detail:
first   next   meanwhile
then   while   finally

   Example: In 1963, the Supreme Court of the United States decided that the recitation of prayers in public schools violated students' First Amendment right to freedom of religious beliefs. **Before** this decision, many public school students were required to recite the Lord's Prayer as part of every class's opening exercise.

5. Transitions that signal an **illustration**:
for example   such as   for instance
thus   in particular   in other words

   Example: In 1963, the Supreme Court of the United States decided that the recitation of prayers in public schools violated students' First Amendment right to freedom of religious beliefs. **In particular,** public school teachers were prohibited from requiring students to profess faith in God or to read the Bible in religious exercises in class.

6. Transitions that signal an **emphasis**:
indeed   in fact   most importantly
to repeat   again   truly

   Example: In 1963, the Supreme Court of the United States decided that the recitation of prayers in public schools violated students'

First Amendment right to freedom of religious beliefs. **In fact,** public school teachers were prohibited from even referring to God or to a supreme being in a religious manner in class.

EXERCISE   **USING TRANSITIONS**

Here is a paragraph that a student wrote in response to one of the writing activities in Chapter 4. Examine each blank space and decide if a transition is necessary to help readers understand the relationship between the ideas. If a transition is needed, fill in an appropriate one. Try not to repeat the same transition twice. If you do not think a transition is necessary, leave the space blank.

SECOND REVISION: NEGOTIATING A RAISE

There are several important steps that people have to consider when they try to negotiate a raise with their employers. _____ they have to decide how much they think their work is worth. _____ they have to decide exactly what they want in terms of money, benefits, and vacations. _____ they have to think about what their employers might be willing to pay and what they can realistically afford. _____ they have considered all of these things, people can sit down with their employers and reach agreements. _____ people have to realize that sometimes their employers cannot agree to the kind of raise that they want. _____ they have to be willing to compromise on some other things. _____ they might have to give up some fringe benefits or expense accounts. _____ the more they can understand their employers, the more successful people will be in negotiating raises.

Michael Fontaine

Using Repetition

Another way to achieve coherence is to repeat key words and phrases so that the main points keep echoing throughout a paragraph. If you don't want to repeat the exact word, you can use a synonym (a word or a phrase that has a similar meaning). For example, here is a draft of a paragraph that I wrote for page 181 of this section on coherence. Note that instead of simply repeating the words "coherent" and "coherently," I used other words and phrases to refer to these key terms.

Deciding on a logical order for the details in paragraphs is the first step toward communicating these ideas clearly and effectively to readers. The next step is making sure that these ideas develop smoothly--that they are not "choppy" or "jerky." The sentences and paragraphs in an essay should be revised so that they are linked to one another in ways that help readers follow them easily. Each detail must be coherent: it must be related in a recognizable way to the detail before and to the one after it.

EXERCISE ANALYZING REPETITION

Below is a paragraph from an essay entitled "Being a Man," by the writer Paul Theroux. Every time you see the word "man" or "manhood" in this paragraph, circle it. Also, circle every synonym for the words "man" or "manhood."

I have always disliked being a man. The whole idea of manhood in America is pitiful, in my opinion. This version of masculinity is a little like having to wear an ill-fitting coat for one's entire life (by contrast, I imagine femininity to be an oppressive sense of nakedness). Even the expression "Be a man!" strikes me as insulting and abusive. It means:

```
Be stupid, be unfeeling, obedient, soldierly and stop

thinking.   Man means "manly"--how can one think about men

without considering the terrible ambition of manliness?  And

yet it is part of every man's life.  It is a hideous and

crippling lie; it not only insists on difference and connives

at superiority, it is also by its very nature destructive--

emotionally damaging and socially harmful.
```

What is the effect of all of Theroux's repetition?

Using Pronouns

Pronouns are words that can be substituted for other words or phrases. Some examples of pronouns include *it, she, he, they, you, me, my, his, her, your, their, this, that, these, those, all, some, most, few, other, another.* Pronouns link details or sentences together by directing the reader's attention back to the words which they are replacing. Notice the use of the pronoun "it" in the sentences below.

Sexual discrimination is rampant at City College. *It* goes on in almost every class, and most students consider *it* a serious problem.

EXERCISE   IDENTIFYING PRONOUNS

Below is a student's uncorrected revision of a comparison paragraph. Circle each pronoun in the paragraph and draw an arrow back to the word it is replacing or referring to. The first one has been done as an example.

```
An "au pair" is a girl or woman who lives with a family

and takes care of (its) children and its housekeeping in

exchange for room and board and a small salary.  I have been

one here in America and in Denmark, and I have seen enormous

differences between the workload of American and foreign au

pairs.  In America, au pairs are really babysitters.  They
```

take care of the children all day. They are also expected to
do some cleaning and cook some meals. But after dinner, they
usually have their evenings to themselves, and they can go out
with their friends. Foreign au pairs, on the other hand, seem
to work much harder. They are babysitters <u>and</u> housekeepers
<u>and</u> maids. Most of the foreign au pairs I knew were expected
to care for the children, play with them, cook all of the
meals, clean the house, iron and shop. And in the evenings,
they were expected to babysit. I will never work overseas as
an au pair again!

A STUDENT RESPONSE

Here is the second uncorrected revision of the comparison/contrast paragraph that Isaac Stein wrote after he consulted several public sources of information. Note his revisions in the organization and coherence of his paper. Compare this version to his first draft on pages 148–49 of Chapter 6.

SECOND REVISION

Ever since the day I took apart and re-assembled my
parent's television set, I knew I wished to be an electronics
engineer. Like doctors and lawyers, electronics engineers ∧*also*
specialize in one of many areas and I want to do aerospace
                              However
research and rocket design. ∧ I am having difficulty deciding
on the kind of company that I want to work for. Do I work for
a giant corporation like Rockwell International in California
or a small company like Rocket Research in Washington?
They both
~~Rockwell and Rocket~~ design rocket engines and conduct applied

aerospace research. And, ~~they~~ [both of them] offer competitve entry level salaries and medical, dental, and pension plans. [However are very different] ~~They do have differences.~~ Rockwell is huge: it employs 95,000 people and it hires 700 each year. Rocket, [on the other hand] has only 300 people and hires only two or three engineering majors each year. Rockwell pays for 100% of its employee's education expenses, [but] Rocket only pays for $500. [However] At Rocket, engineers are involved with all phases of systems design and application. At Rockwell, they only get to work on one small part of a project. [Also] Rocket is closer to my home, [but] ~~If I work at~~ Rockwell [is not.] I would have to move or have a big commute. My neighbor, Dr. Jack Irving who works at a small engineering company said that small firms like Rocket offer many more opportunities for promotion. [He may be right but] I think I have to visit several more types of rocket research firms before I can make up my mind about the kind of place that's right for me.

In order to understand how Stein improved the coherence of his essay, follow the directions below:

1. Circle every transition in Stein's revision (the ones in the typed version *and* the handwritten ones).
2. Underline the key terms in each revised paragraph. Every time a key term is repeated, underline it. Also, underline every synonym that is used to replace these key terms.
3. Use a different color ink to circle every pronoun in the revision and to draw an arrow back to the word that it is replacing or referring to.

WRITING ACTIVITY IDENTIFYING AND REVISING PROBLEMS IN COHERENCE

Below is the uncorrected discovery draft of a paragraph that a student wrote for one of the writing activities in Chapter 4. Read it carefully. Then, follow these directions:

1. Delete any irrelevant sentences.
2. Add appropriate transitions wherever they seem necessary.
3. Repeat the key words or use synonyms to make the connections between the sentences clearer.
4. Substitute or add pronouns wherever they might be appropriate.

DISCOVERY DRAFT

After weighing all the factors relating to choosing a career, I have decided to go into the pharmaceuticals industry. The starting income for a salesman in the pharmaceuticals industry is $38,000. This salary is much better than the salary my brother makes as a teacher. This salary is reviewed semi-annually (with raises of $1,000-$3,000 possible at each review). The job has terrific benefits including pension, medical and dental policies and usually a free car. This job does involve a lot of traveling and the pressure is high. I cope well with pressure. The job offers excellent opportunities for promotion. A salesman or woman can become a sales manager after only five years and can make more than $45,000 a year. Women can be pharmaceutical salespeople too. I think pharmaceutical sales is a good career for me because I like doctors and nurses and these are the people who I would be meeting each day.

Ken Morris

REVISING WITH A WORD PROCESSOR

A word processor's SEARCH and REPLACE function keys make revising organization and coherence fun. Computerized "cutting and pasting" enables you to rearrange sentences in your paragraphs and paragraphs in your essay so as to improve the development, unity, and coherence of your writing. For example, you can delete details in a paragraph or reorder them to see what effect these changes have on the meaning and logical development of a draft. Or you can move examples and reasons from one paragraph to another if you think that they might be more effective in a different position. Here are some guidelines for revising the organization and coherence of your word-processed discovery drafts:

1. **BOLD** the thesis statement of the essay and the topic sentence of every paragraph so that they stand out from the rest of the text.
2. ~~OVERSTRIKE~~ all of the sentences that do not relate clearly and logically to the bold sentences.
3. BRACKET ([]) the key words or phrases in each paragraph to determine if you have used repetition effectively or if you need to add more repetition.
4. <u>UNDERLINE</u> the pronouns in each paragraph to determine if you have used pronouns effectively or if you need to change some nouns into pronouns.
5. Use the BLOCK and MOVE FUNCTIONS to move paragraphs around or to rearrange reasons and examples within a paragraph. If you want to compare your revision to your draft, put each paragraph into a WINDOW at the top of the screen and keep the revision on the bottom of the screen.
6. Do *not* delete your original draft. Save it—and each revision—under a different name or under a coded title with the date of the text.
7. Print at least two copies of every revision to share with someone who is willing to help you do further revision.

WRITING ASSIGNMENT WRITING AND REVISING AN ESSAY ABOUT A JOURNAL TOPIC

For this assignment, you will be writing a discovery draft of an essay and revising it twice: once for ideas and details and another time for organization and coherence. Begin by following the directions below:

1. Pick a topic that you have written about in your journal. Do ten minutes of freewriting about it. Then, do five minutes of brainstorming and five minutes of clustering to find a focus for a discovery draft of an essay about this topic.
2. Imagine that you know nothing about this topic and focus. Write down every question relating to this focus that you can think of. Then write down answers to each of your questions.

3. Narrow down your purpose for writing and write a brief description of the audience for whom you are writing.

4. Write a discovery draft of your essay.

5. Exchange discovery drafts with a classmate. Read your classmate's draft and write down questions about the information that you still need to know in order to understand your classmate's ideas. Also indicate any problems in the believability or the logic of your classmate's supporting details.

6. Outline your classmate's essay. Then, note any problems in organization and coherence. When you are finished, give the draft and your notes, outline, and comments back to the writer.

7. Revise the ideas and the details in your draft using your partner's comments and the techniques that you practiced in Chapter 6.

8. Use your partner's comments and the techniques that you practiced in this unit to revise the organization and coherence of your draft.

ISSUES FOR YOUR JOURNAL

1. Did you enjoy reading the student writing in this chapter (or in the previous chapters)? Why or why not?

2. What are you writing about in your other courses? Are you revising these pieces of writing? Why or why not?

3. How do you feel about marriage? If you are married, do you enjoy being married? Why or why not? If you aren't married, do you want to be? Why or why not?

4. What kind of music do you like best? Why? What does your preference for this type of music reveal about you?

5. Why is illegal drug use becoming an epidemic in our country? Do you know anyone who uses illicit drugs? Why do they do it? What needs does it fulfill? What are drugs doing to the people who take them?

ADDITIONAL READING

Here is the entire essay on "Being a Man," from which the paragraph on page 186 of this chapter was excerpted. In addition to writing many novels, the author—Paul Theroux— has written several nonfiction books that describe his travels across Europe, Latin America, and Asia.

BEING A MAN

There is a pathetic sentence in the chapter "Fetishism" in Dr. Norman Cameron's book *Personality Development and Psychopathology*. It goes, "Fetishists are nearly always men; and their commonest fetish is a woman's shoe." I cannot read that sentence without thinking that it is just one more awful thing about being a man—and perhaps it is an important thing to know about us.

I have always disliked being a man. The whole idea of manhood in America is pitiful, in my opinion. This version of masculinity is a little like having to wear an ill-fitting coat for one's entire life (by contrast, I imagine femininity to be an oppressive sense of nakedness). Even the expression "Be a man!" strikes me as insulting and abusive. It means: Be stupid, be unfeeling, obedient, soldierly and stop thinking. Man means "manly"—how can one think about men without considering the terrible ambition of manliness? And yet it is part of every man's life. It is a hideous and crippling lie; it not only insists on difference and connives at superiority, it is also by its very nature destructive—emotionally damaging and socially harmful.

The youth who is subverted, as most are, into believing in the masculine ideal is effectively separated from women and he spends the rest of his life finding women a riddle and a nuisance. Of course, there is a female version of this male affliction. It begins with mothers encouraging little girls to say (to other adults) "Do you like my new dress?" In a sense, little girls are traditionally urged to please adults with a kind of coquettishness, while boys are enjoined to behave like monkeys towards each other. The nine-year-old coquette proceeds to become womanish in a subtle power game in which she learns to be sexually indispensable, socially decorative and always alert to a man's sense of inadequacy.

Femininity—being lady-like—implies needing a man as witness and seducer; but masculinity celebrates the exclusive company of men. That is why it is so grotesque; and that is also why there is no manliness without inadequacy—because it denies men the natural friendship of women.

It is very hard to imagine any concept of manliness that does not belittle women, and it begins very early. At an age when I wanted to meet girls—let's say the treacherous years of thirteen to sixteen—I was told to take up a sport, get more fresh air, join the Boy Scouts, and I was urged not to read so much. It was the 1950s and if you asked too many questions about sex you were sent to camp—boy's camp, of course: the nightmare. Nothing is more unnatural or prison-like than a boy's camp, but if it were not for them we would have no Elks' Lodges, no pool rooms, no boxing matches, no Marines.

And perhaps no sports as we know them. Everyone is aware of how few in number are the athletes who behave like gentlemen. Just as high school basketball teaches you how to be a poor loser, the manly attitude towards sports seems to be little more than a recipe for creating bad marriages, social misfits, moral degenerates, sadists, latent rapists and just plain louts. I regard high school sports as a drug far worse than marijuana, and it is the reason that the average tennis champion, say, is a pathetic oaf.

Any objective study would find the quest for manliness essentially right-wing, puritanical, cowardly, neurotic and fueled largely by a fear of women. It is also certainly philistine. There is no book-hater like a Little League coach. But indeed all the creative arts are obnoxious to the manly ideal, because at their best the arts are pursued by uncompetitive and essentially solitary people. It makes it very hard for a creative youngster, for any boy who expresses the desire to be alone seems to be saying that there is something wrong with him.

It ought to be clear by now that I have something of an objection to the way we turn boys into men. It does not surprise me that when the President of the United States has his customary weekend off he dresses like a cowboy—it is both a measure of his insecurity and his willingness to please. In many ways, American culture does little more for a man than prepare him for modeling clothes in the L.L. Bean catalogue. I take this as a personal insult because for many years I found it impossible to admit to myself that I wanted to be a writer. It was my guilty secret, because being a writer was incompatible with being a man.

There are people who might deny this, but that is because the American writer, typically, has been so at pains to prove his manliness that we have come to see literariness and manliness as mingled qualities. But first there was a fear that writing was not a manly profession—indeed, not a profession at all. (The paradox in American letters is that it has always been easier for a woman to write and for a man to be published.) Growing up, I had thought of sports as wasteful and humiliating, and the idea of manliness was a bore. My wanting to become a writer was not a flight from that oppressive role-playing, but I quickly saw that it was at odds with it. Everything in stereotyped manliness goes against the life of the mind. The Hemingway personality is too tedious to go into here, and in any case his exertions are well-known, but certainly it was not until this aberrant behavior was examined by feminists in the

1960s that any male writer dared question the pugnacity in Hemingway's fiction. All the bullfighting and arm wrestling and elephant shooting diminished Hemingway as a writer, but it is consistent with a prevailing attitude in American writing: one cannot be a male writer without first proving that one is a man.

It is normal in America for a man to be dismissive or even somewhat apologetic about being a writer. Various factors make it easier. There is a heartiness about journalism that makes it acceptable—journalism is the manliest form of American writing and, therefore, the profession the most independent-minded women seek (yes, it is an illusion, but that is my point). Fiction-writing is equated with a kind of dispirited failure and is only manly when it produces wealth—money is masculinity. So is drinking. Being a drunkard is another assertion, if misplaced, of manliness. The American male writer is traditionally proud of his heavy drinking. But we are also a very literal-minded people. A man proves his manhood in America in old-fashioned ways. He kills lions, like Hemingway; or he hunts ducks, like Nathanael West; or he makes pronouncements like, "A man should carry enough knife to defend himself with," as James Jones once said to a *Life* interviewer. Or he says he can drink you under the table. But even tiny drunken William Faulkner loved to mount a horse and go fox hunting, and Jack Kerouac roistered up and down Manhattan in a lumberjack shirt (and spent every night of *The Subterraneans* with his mother in Queens). And we are familiar with the lengths to which Norman Mailer is prepared, in his endearing way, to prove that he is just as much a monster as the next man.

When the novelist John Irving was revealed as a wrestler, people took him to be a very serious writer; and even a bubble reputation like Eric (*Love Story*) Segal's was enhanced by the news that he ran the marathon in a respectable time. How surprised we would be if Joyce Carol Oates were revealed as a sumo wrestler or Joan Didion active in pumping iron. "Lives in New York City with her three children" is the typical woman writer's biographical note, for just as the male writer must prove he has achieved a sort of muscular manhood, the woman writer—or rather her publicists—must prove her motherhood.

There would be no point in saying any of this if it were not generally accepted that to be a man is somehow—even now in feminist-influenced America—a privilege. It is on the contrary an unmerciful and punishing burden. Being a man is bad enough; being manly is appalling (in this sense, women's lib has done much more for men than for women). It is the sinister silliness of men's fashions, and a clubby attitude in the arts. It is the subversion of good students. It is the so-called "Dress Code" of the Ritz-Carlton Hotel in Boston, and it is the institutionalized cheating in college sports. It is the most primitive insecurity.

And this is also why men often object to feminism but are afraid to explain why: of course women have a justified grievance, but most men believe—and with reason—that their lives are just as bad.

Paul Theroux

OPTIONAL WRITING ASSIGNMENT

Write an essay about what being a man or a woman means to you.

REVISING
SENTENCE STRUCTURE

To shift the structure of a sentence alters the meaning of that sentence, as definitely and as inflexibly as the position of a camera alters the meaning of the object being photographed. Many people know about camera angles now, but not so many know about sentences. The arrangement of the words matters, and the arrangement you want can be found in the picture in your mind.

JOAN DIDION

I am unlikely to trust a sentence that comes easily.

WILLIAM GASS

REASONS FOR REVISING SENTENCE STRUCTURE

In one of the epigraphs to this chapter, Joan Didion notes that shifting the structure of a sentence's parts alters the meaning of that sentence. Didion's point is that English sentences are very flexible—writers can move sentence parts around to express different ideas or emphases. However, as Didion warns, the arrangement of words in a sentence matters, and writers need to play with sentences until they find the arrangement that reflects the exact "picture in their mind." For instance, here are some ideas that I have in my mind right now as I am writing this chapter:

- I am struggling with this chapter.
- I am anxious.
- I hope that my revisions will improve this chapter.

Here are various arrangements of these ideas:

1. I am anxious while I am struggling with this chapter, and I hope that my revisions will improve it.
2. Anxiously, I am struggling with this chapter, hoping my revisions will improve it.
3. I am struggling with this chapter anxiously, hoping that my revisions will improve it.
4. As I struggle anxiously with this chapter, I hope that my revisions will improve it.
5. Hoping my revisions will improve this chapter, I struggle anxiously with it.

Which arrangement is "best"? The answer depends on the exact meaning that I want to express: Do I want to emphasize my anxiety (as sentences 1 and 2 do)? Do I want to focus on my struggle with this chapter (as 3 and 4 do)? Or do I want to point out my hope about my revisions (as 5 does)? As Didion says, I have to know the exact "picture in my mind"—my focus and my purpose—before I can decide which sentence structure conveys my precise meaning most accurately and clearly. Revising sentence structure involves adjusting words and sentences to make them more appropriate for one's purpose and audience. Usually, it is a waste of time to revise sentence structure before you revise your details, organization, and coherence. Too many students worry about changing sentences or words in a discovery draft, only to realize later that the whole sentence or paragraph is irrelevant and should be deleted.

PAIRED WRITING TASK REVISIONS IN SENTENCE STRUCTURE AND VOCABULARY

Work on this task with a classmate. Take out the discovery draft that you used for the Paired Writing Task on pages 169–170 of Chapter 7 or another discovery draft you have been working on. Exchange papers with your classmate, and write answers to the questions below. Do not discuss each other's papers until you are both finished writing your comments.

Your classmate's name:

1. How does your partner's sentence structure make him or her "sound"? (For example, does he or she sound uptight, formal, scientific, scholarly, informal, funny, or poetical?)
2. Which sentences are particularly interesting or sound particularly effective? Put a star next to them, and be prepared to tell your partner why you liked them.
3. Which sentences seem too short and simple?
4. Which sentences seem too long and confusing?
5. Point out the sentences that seem unclear and that need more details.

TECHNIQUES FOR REVISING SENTENCE STRUCTURE

There are three basic techniques for revising sentences so that they communicate your meaning more clearly and effectively: *expanding sentences by adding words and phrases, deleting unnecessary words*, and *combining sentences or parts of sentences*. The remainder of the chapter will discuss each strategy in detail.

ADDING WORDS TO SENTENCES

Expanding a sentence involves adding descriptive words and phrases to it. Examine each sentence in your draft and decide whether you need to add words to it to help your readers understand exactly what you mean. You can use the following questions to help you identify problems in sentences:

- Who or what is this sentence about? What details can I add to describe this subject more clearly or fully?
- What is this subject doing in this sentence? What details can I add to describe this action more specifically?

- What details can I add to describe where and when (or how long) the action in the sentence is taking place?
- What other words or phrases can I add to make this sentence clearer and more interesting?

As Joan Didion pointed out in the epigraph, English sentences are flexible: there are many different places in a sentence where descriptive words may be added. For example, here is an unclear sentence to which descriptive words have been added in several places:

1. Television has changed our definition of to be human.
2. Television has changed our definition of what it means to be human.
3. As the wheel and the alphabet did, television has changed our definition of what it means to be human.

The added words in sentence 2 help readers to understand exactly what the writer means. And the words that the writer added to the beginning of sentence 3 emphasize the importance of the changes that television has caused (i.e., changes as important as those brought about by the invention of the wheel and the alphabet).

PAIRED OR GROUP EXERCISE   **ADDING DESCRIPTIVE WORDS TO SENTENCES**

Work on this exercise with another student or with a group of classmates. Read each sentence below. In the space below each, revise the sentence by following the directions in parentheses. The first one has been done as an example.

1. Television has a̶n̶ *potent* effect on us, *and on their perception of reality* (Add descriptive words before "effect" and after "us.")

2. Interviews reveal that television has an effect on children. (Add descriptive words after "interviews," before "effect," and after "children.")

3. Children watch television. (Add descriptive words before "children," before "television," and after "television.")

4. By watching television, children learn things. (Add descriptive words before "television." Cross out "things" and substitute descriptive words for it.)

5. Television commercials teach children values. (Add descriptive words before "television," before "children," and before *or* after "values.")

Adding descriptive modifiers can also help you vary your sentence structures. Sentence variety is important for two reasons: (1) writers who consider several options for arranging the parts of a sentence have control over their writing and use language to express their exact meaning; and (2) varied sentence patterns are often more interesting to read than a series of sentences that all have the same structure. One simple way to achieve sentence variety is to add descriptive words to a sentence and then move them to the beginning or the end of the sentence. For example, look at the way the writer of the sentences below achieved some variety in his sentences:

- Television commercials sell products.
- Television commercials sell not only products but also values.
- Television commercials sell not only products but also values, by making us covet things that we never used to want.
- By making us covet things that we never used to want, television commercials sell not only products but also values.

WRITING ACTIVITY   **ADDING AND MOVING DESCRIPTIVE WORDS**

Go back to the exercise that you did on page 200. On a separate piece of paper, number from 1 to 5, and rewrite *each of your revised sentences*, moving some of the modifiers to the front of the sentences. Examples of possible revisions of the first sentence are below.

1. Television has an effect on us.

a. Television has a powerful effect on us without our being aware of it.
b. Without our being aware of it, television has a powerful effect on us.

<u>EXERCISE</u> **ANALYZING SENTENCE REVISIONS**

Here is Allen Brower's partially corrected revision of the first paragraph of his discovery draft, discussed in Chapter 7. Note his additional revisions in sentence structure.

```
        SECOND REVISION: MY FAVORITE PLACE

    My favorite place in the world is my car.  It's the first

car that I have ever owned and I really enjoy it.  The car is
                used
a⋀1989 Corvette and its previous owner took good care of it.
       midnite        like new   shiny           With silver
The⋀blue paint gleams⋀and the⋀chrome sparkles.  And the
                               it,             like a racer
stripes on the sides of⋀the car really look fierce.  It is

sleek and smooth like a jet plane.  the blue leather (Inside) is
      Sometimes                          heavy
worn but clean. ⋀ I like to sit inside and breathe the⋀smell of
                                   first-rate Akai
leather and oil.  I also like to listen to the⋀stereo radio

and cassette deck with four speakers that can blast me to

heaven.

                                                Allen Brower
```

Circle the descriptive words in Brower's revision that make it more interesting than the original.

When you revise your sentences, examine each one for vague or abstract words. Cross these out and substitute specific concrete and sensory words. For example, compare the original and revised versions of the fourth sentence in Allen Brower's paragraph in the preceding exercise:

Original: The blue paint gleams and the chrome sparkles.
Revision: The midnite blue paint gleams like new and the shiny
        chrome sparkles.

If you are not sure how to substitute specific details for vague or general ones, reread the section on "Levels of Generality" on pages 75–77 in Chapter 4. It describes several ways of making details more specific, such as:

- Give the exact names of things rather than writing about them in general terms.
- Replace general or abstract words with concrete sensory details. A concrete detail is one that can be perceived through the senses (it can be seen, heard, smelled, tasted, and/or touched).
- Use vivid, descriptive verbs instead of ordinary, vague ones.

WRITING ACTIVITY EXPANDING SENTENCES

The sentences below were taken from a student's discovery draft. Revise each sentence by substituting descriptive concrete words for the vague, abstract ones. Cross out the vague words and add details that make sense. Use exact terms, concrete sensory words, and vivid verbs. The first sentence has been done as an example.

1. Researchers have studied television and young people.

    During the past decade, many researchers have studied the effects of television programming on children aged three to fifteen.

2. Children start to watch TV when they are young.

3. These young kids have preferences based on their sex.

4. However, TV affects them all in many ways.

5. For example, children learn how to act by watching TV.

6. Some researchers believe that TV violence makes children violent.

7. Others believe it decreases violence.

8. It's hard to be sure because real-life violence is caused by many factors.

PROFESSIONAL RESPONSES

Here are some paragraphs written by people whose writing I admire. As you read each one, underline descriptive words that make each sentence convey the writer's thoughts and feelings.

Far out along the autumn plain, beneath the sloping light, an immense drove of cattle moved eastward. They went at a walk, not very fast, but faster than they could imaginably enjoy. Those in front were compelled by those behind; those at the rear, with few exceptions, did their best to keep up; those who were locked within the herd could no more help moving than the particles inside a falling rock.

James Agee
"A Mother's Tale"

I lay down on a solitary rock that was like an island in the bottom of the valley, and looked up. The grey sage-brush and the blue-grey rock around me were already in shadow, but high above me the canyon walls were dyed flame-colour with the sunset, and the Cliff City lay in a gold haze against its dark cavern. In a few minutes, it, too, was grey, and only the rim rock at the top held the red light. When that was gone, I could still see the copper glow in the piñons along the edge of the top ledges. The arc of sky over the canyon was silvery blue, with its pale yellow moon, and presently, stars shivered into it, like crystals dropped into perfectly clear water.

Willa Cather
The Professor's House

So Elvis Presley came, strumming a weird guitar and wagging his tail across the continent, ripping off fame and fortune as he scrunched his way, and, like a latter-day Johnny Appleseed, sowing seeds of a new rhythm and style in the white souls of the white youth of America, whose inner hunger and need was no longer satisfied with the antiseptic white shoes and whiter songs of Pat Boone. "You can do anything," sang Elvis to Pat Boone's white shoes, "but don't you step on my Blue Suede Shoes!"

Eldridge Cleaver
Soul on Ice

DELETING WORDS FROM SENTENCES

As you revise your writing, you will find many sentences that require additional descriptive words in order to communicate your thoughts more clearly and completely. You will also find many sentences that are too long, that are padded with unnecessary words. It is important to examine your sentences for "deadwood"—words that are not necessary to express your meaning or that distract readers from your meaning. You can use the list of "Wordy Phrases" on page 246 of Chapter 9 to help you identify some of these unnecessary words.

Sentence length is less important than sentence **economy**—the degree to which each word in a sentence contributes to the overall meaning of the sentence. Any word that isn't essential or that repeats the sense of another word in the sentence should be deleted. When experienced writers revise, they frequently add descriptive words to their sentences and then, on a later rereading, decide to delete some of these words. At this point, you may be asking yourself, "What's the point of adding a lot of words if I'm going to have to cross them out?" The answer is that revising is actually a form of experimentation: it's a process of adding and changing and deleting until each sentence says exactly what you want it to say.

Here is an example of a student writer's attempt to delete unnecessary words in her sentences:

~~In~~ Today~~'s society,~~ many parents ~~of children~~ use

television as a ~~tool to keep children busy.~~ *babysitter* However, ~~experts~~

~~who conduct research in this area~~ *researchers* have discovered that

children ~~of parents~~ who ~~let them~~ watch a lot of television

often ~~are becoming very lazy and don't want to do much.~~ *become passive.* These

researchers ~~place a great deal of emphasis on the fact~~ *emphasize* that

television may play a greater role in ~~developing the~~

~~socialization process of~~ *socializing* children than ~~the~~ parents ~~role.~~ *do.*

EXERCISE **DELETING AND SUBSTITUTING WORDS**

Look at the underlined phrases (groups of words) in each of the sentences in the following paragraph. For each underlined phrase, substitute a single verb that will express the meaning more effectively. The first one has been done as an example.

The woman was sitting by herself and was <u>deliberately not</u>
ignoring
<u>paying much attention</u> to her companions. She raised her head

and <u>slowly looked steadily</u> about her. Then, she got up and

<u>began to walk very slowly and carelessly</u> toward the river.

She saw one of her friends lying half asleep by the river's

edge, and something caused her to <u>turn her head rapidly toward</u>

him. She started <u>running as fast as a leopard</u> toward him.

When she reached him, she abruptly took his arm and <u>pulled</u>

<u>with a great effort on</u> it. She <u>moved him slowly</u> away from the

alligator's jaws just in time.

EXERCISE **DELETING UNNECESSARY WORDS AND PHRASES**

The uncorrected paragraph below was taken from a student's revision. Cross out all the words and phrases that you think are not essential to the meaning of each sentence. The first one has been done as an example.

~~There are~~ Many myths *exist* about women warriors, ~~and women who~~
but
~~fight fiercely.~~ However, most primitive and modern societies

do not arm their women and do not send them to armed combat.

In my opinion, women can be drafted. They can do non-combat

service. They don't take part in any combat that might be

dangerous or that might hurt them or kill them. However,

Konrad Lorenz has noted that among animals, it is the males

not the female animals that fight. When female animals do end

up fighting, they fight to the death. It seems that women

don't know the many different rituals and the rules of

fighting. Thus, women probably should not be allowed to

fight.

A STUDENT RESPONSE

Here is the student essay on which the preceding exercise was based. The author revised it by expanding her sentences and deleting unnecessary words.

```
              THIRD REVISION: WOMEN WARRIORS
                       ,the famous anthropologist,
    Margaret Mead was asked whether women should be permitted

to be combat soldiers.  She answered that they shouldn't.  She
                                      was intrigued by her answer,
said that they are "too fierce."  I am an anthropology major
 so I decided to do
here at Hunter College and I did some reading.  I wanted to

try and figure out what Mead meant.by her answer.
                                  historical and modern
    I discovered that there are many myths about women
                   in reality
warriors.  However, most primitive and modern societies do not

arm their women.  Women can be drafted.  They can do non-
 in offices. However    rarely                      or fight in
combat service, they don't take part in any real combat wars
 Still
   This doesn't prove that they are "too fierce" to do combat.
    Another notable anthropologist,
    Konrad Lorenz has pointed out that among animals, it is

the males that fight.  Not the females.  He also stated that
                      do    usually fight in defense of their babies and
when female animals fight, they fight to the death.  This may   they

be a clue into Mead's comment.  In addition, Lorenz noted that

throughout history, men and boys are the only ones who learn
```

the rituals and the rules of fighting. Maybe Mead means that

women don't know these rituals and rules. ~~Women don't know~~

~~how to play fair.~~ What would happen if women were ~~allowed to~~   *armed ?*

~~carry deadly weapons?~~ Maybe they would b~~low up the world.~~

~~They might~~ be too fierce. *Maybe* ∧ ~~T~~hey ~~might~~ *would* ∧ fight to the death of

the world.

Sonja Rossini

How do Rossini's handwritten revisions improve her essay?

COMBINING SENTENCES

A third technique that experienced writers use to improve their sentences is sentence combination. Writers can combine sentences or parts of sentences to clarify the relationships among their ideas and to highlight specific details. Combining sentences also enables writers to express ideas more clearly in fewer words. There are two basic ways to combine sentences:

1. by **coordinating** two or more complete sentences
2. by **subordinating** parts of sentences and joining these parts to other sentences

Coordination

The most common way to combine sentences is to coordinate them—to join them together with a comma and a **coordinator**. English has seven coordinators:

- **and** indicates that the second idea is in addition to the first idea: "I am writing Chapter 8, *and* I am also trying to revise Chapter 7."
- **but** and **yet** indicate that the second idea is in contrast to the first idea: "I am writing Chapter 8, *but (yet)* I know that I still have to revise Chapter 7."
- **for** indicates that the second idea explains the reason for the event in the first idea: "I can't stop working now, *for* I have two more chapters to finish by next month."

- **so** indicates that the events in the second idea are caused by the events in the first idea: "I must finish two more chapters soon, *so* I can't stop working now."
- **or** indicates that the second idea is an alternative to the first idea: "I can try to write Chapter 8, *or* I can work on revising Chapter 7."
- **nor** indicates that the second idea continues a negative statement begun in the first idea: "I am too tired to work on Chapter 8, *nor* do I feel like revising Chapter 7."

These coordinators are familiar to you; people use them all the time to connect their ideas in speaking and in writing. And I am also sure that at some point in your education, an English teacher told you never to do what I just did—begin a sentence with **and** or **but**. Technically, the coordinators are supposed to join two or more ideas into one complete sentence. But coordinators can be used to join ideas, even when the ideas that they link are separated by a period (as in the two ideas that I just wrote).

GROUP WRITING ACTIVITY **USING COORDINATORS**

Advertisers often use coordinators at the beginnings of sentences to link an idea to the one that came before it. Read the ad below and circle each coordinator. Why do you think the person who wrote this ad used coordinators to begin sentences instead of using them to combine two sentences into one?

It's the perfect marriage. Sony's new 8mm video phenomenon and your hand.

We call it the Handycam™ camera/recorder. It's so tiny it fits in one hand.

So anyone can use it anywhere, anytime.

Just point and shoot. And capture all the memories as they happen.

Then, with its handy companion deck, you can play your pictures back in full color and vivid sound, on any television.

Up to two hours of good times on a video tape no bigger than an audio cassette.

So bring your hand in to your local Sony dealer.

And try the Handycam on for size.

SONY.
THE ONE AND ONLY®

Get into a group of three students. On a separate piece of paper, revise this ad by combining some of the sentences. Try out different combinations and decide which ones express the writer's meaning most effectively.

Read the uncorrected student paragraph below, and decide which sentences might sound better if they were combined. Add a comma and a coordinator in the space between any sentences that you think ought to be joined, and delete any unnecessary words.

(1) Anthropology can be defined as the study of human behavior and culture. (2) Anthropologists can study biological objects. (3) They can study social patterns. (4) Their goal is to understand changes in people's physical and social development over time. (5) Anthropologists achieve this goal by examining the changes that have occurred as people adapted to new environments. (6) They dig up bone fossils. (7) They can compare the fossil forms to living ones. (8) Anthropologists make hypotheses about life in primitive cultures. (9) They cannot prove these hypotheses because the remains of these cultures are rare and in fragments. (10) Anthropologists cannot study early human life. (11) They can do research on ancient documents. (12) They can also study prehistoric artifacts. (13) These artifacts reveal how our human ancestors lived.

Subordination

To subordinate something means to treat it as less important than or dependent on something else. Writers can combine related ideas by subordinating one of them to the other with a **subordinator.** Here are two ideas that are joined first with a coordinator and then with a subordinator:

Idea 1: Anthropologists can make hypotheses.
Idea 2: Anthropologists cannot prove their hypotheses.

Coordination: Anthropologists can make hypotheses, *but* they cannot prove them.

Subordination: *Although* anthropologists can make hypotheses, they cannot prove them.

In the first sentence, the coordinator "but" joins two complete ideas, each of which receives equal emphasis. In the second sentence, the subordinator "although" indicates that the first idea is less important to the writer than the second idea. The subordinator also makes the first idea into an incomplete or dependent thought. The second idea ("they cannot prove them") does express a complete thought and, thus, gets more emphasis. If the writer had wanted to emphasize the *first* idea, he could have subordinated it:

Although they cannot prove their hypotheses, anthropologists can make them.

Subordinators are wonderful tools for revising sentences because they enable writers to show the relationships among their ideas and to emphasize different details. Here is a list of the most common subordinators, included in a chart that shows the three different ways of joining ideas in English. Note that English does not have subordinators that can be used to add on an additional or a similar idea. (The transitions in the third column of the chart should be familiar to you. In Chapter 7, you practiced using them at the beginnings of sentences to bridge the gap between two sentences that might seem unconnected to readers.)

Methods of Joining Related Ideas

Purpose	Coordinators	Subordinators	Transitions
To add an additional or similar idea	and		in addition furthermore moreover also
To add a contrasting idea	but yet whereas	although even though while	however nevertheless conversely
To add a cause or an effect	for so	because since if so that	therefore as a result consequently thus
To add a time-related idea or an alternative	or nor	once before during after when where	first today meanwhile then next last

Take another look at examples of each of these three ways of joining related ideas:

Coordination: Anthropologists can make hypotheses, *but* they cannot prove them.

Subordination: *Although* anthropologists can make hypotheses, they cannot prove them.

Transition: Anthropologists can make hypotheses. *However,* they cannot prove them.

How are the three sentences above different? All three indicate the same relationship between the same two ideas. However, the three statements differ in emphasis and pauses. The coordinator in the first sentence and the subordinator in the second sentence signal a close relationship between the two ideas in each sentence. (In the first, the related ideas are of equal importance. In the second, the second idea is more important.) The period and the transition in the third sentence stop the reader and indicate that the relationship between the two ideas is not close enough to justify combining them into one sentence.

Remember that these three different methods of joining related ideas create different types of sentences. A coordinator combines two complete sentences into one longer sentence. A subordinator also does this, but it makes one of the sentences into an incomplete idea. If you punctuate this incomplete idea as a sentence, you are making a sentence error called a *fragment*. Here are some common examples:

Anthropologists begin their research with a hypothesis. <u>Because this helps them decide exactly what to study. Once they have constructed a plausible hypothesis.</u> They can begin examining artifacts. <u>To see if these confirm their hypothesis.</u>

Don't punctuate a subordinated idea as a complete sentence. Combine it with the idea that it logically belongs with, in order to make one complete sentence. Here is the revision of the paragraph above:

Anthropologists begin their research with a hypothesis because this helps them decide exactly what to study. Once they have constructed a plausible hypothesis, they can begin examining artifacts to see if these confirm their hypothesis.

Furthermore, remember that a transition *cannot* be used to combine two sentences into one. Even though a transition sounds like a coordinator, it should not be punctuated like one. If you use a transition to combine two sentences into one, you are making a sentence error called a "run-on":

> Anthropologists have found that cultures vary independently, thus they know that no "race" can be better than any other.

If you want to combine two ideas into one sentence, use a coordinator or a subordinator:

> Anthropologists have found that cultures vary independently, *so* they know that no "race" can be better than any other.

> *Since* anthropologists have found that cultures vary independently, they know that no "race" can be better than any other.

If you want to keep the ideas in separate sentences, use a transition at the beginning of the second sentence to show the relationship between the two ideas:

> Anthropologists have found that cultures vary independently. *Thus*, they know that no "race" can be better than any other.

EXERCISE   **USING DIFFERENT METHODS TO JOIN IDEAS**

Here are five sets of related ideas taken from a student paragraph. In the space below, try joining each pair using *all three* methods discussed above. Use the chart on page 211 to help you select an appropriate coordinator, subordinator, and transition. The first one has been done as an example.

1. Anthropological research has shown that human behavior is very diverse. Human habits can vary endlessly.

Combined with a coordinator:

Anthropological research has shown that human behavior is very diverse, and human habits can vary endlessly.

Combined with a subordinator:

(This can't be done.)

Linked with a transition:

> *Anthropological research has shown that human behavior is very diverse. In addition, human habits can vary endlessly.*

2. Most animals reveal the same patterns of behavior within any given species. The human species has very few patterns that are shared by all people.

Combined with a coordinator:

Combined with a subordinator:

Linked with a transition:

3. All humans have similar physical and mental structures. One might expect all human behavior to be similar.

Combined with a coordinator:

Combined with a subordinator:

Linked with a transition:

4. Different societies differ in almost every aspect of their behavior. They speak very different languages.

Combined with a coordinator:

Combined with a subordinator:

Linked with a transition:

WRITING ACTIVITY **COORDINATING AND SUBORDINATING IDEAS**

Here is the paragraph from the exercise on page 210 of this chapter. Decide which sentences might sound better if they were combined with a coordinator *or* with a subordinator. Write your revision on a separate piece of paper.

(1) Anthropology can be defined as the study of human behavior and culture. (2) Anthropologists can study biological objects. (3) They can study social patterns. (4) Their goal is to understand changes in people's physical and social development over time. (5) Anthropologists achieve this goal by examining the changes that have occurred as people adapted to new environments. (6) They dig up bone fossils. (7) They can compare the fossil forms to living ones. (8) Anthropologists make hypotheses about life in primitive cultures. (9) They cannot prove these hypotheses because the remains of these cultures are rare and in fragments. (10) Anthropologists cannot study early human life. (11) They can do research on ancient documents. (12) They can also study prehistoric artifacts. (13) These artifacts reveal how our human ancestors lived.

A STUDENT RESPONSE

Here is the fourth version of Sonja Rossini's essay on "Women Warriors." The handwritten changes show the author's use of coordination *and* subordination.

FOURTH REVISION: WOMEN WARRIORS

Margaret Mead, the famous anthropologist, was once asked whether women should be permitted to be combat soldiers. She answered that they shouldn't*, because* ~~She said that~~ they are "too fierce." I was intrigued by her answer*, so* I decided to do some reading*, because* I wanted to figure out what Mead meant.

I discovered many historical and modern myths about women warriors. However, in reality, most primitive and modern societies do not arm their women. Women can be drafted *to* ~~They can~~ do non-combat service in offices*, but* ~~However,~~ they rarely take part in any real combat or fight in wars. ~~Still, this~~ *while most* ~~doesn't~~ prove that they are "too fierce" to do combat.

women do not fight, there is no proof

Another notable anthropologist, Konrad Lorenz has pointed out that among most species of animals, it is the males that fight. He also stated that when female animals do fight, ~~they~~ usually in defense of their babies, ~~and~~ they fight to the death. This may be a clue into Mead's comment: Women may be fiercer, deadlier fighters. In addition, Lorenz noted that throughout history, in all kinds of cultures and civilizations, men and boys are the only ones who learn the rituals and the rules of fighting. Maybe Mead means that *because* women don't know these rituals and rules, *they fight more "primitively."* ~~What would happen~~ If *they* ~~women~~ were armed? Maybe they would be ~~too~~ fierce, *so* ~~Maybe~~ *that* they would fight to the death of the world.

Sonja Rossini

Circle every coordinator and every subordinator that Rossini added. How is this revision different from the version on page 207?

A Special Case:
Subordination with Relative Pronouns

A **pronoun** is a word that can be used as a substitute for a noun or a noun phrase (for example, *he, him, your, mine, some,* and so forth). A relative pronoun is a special type of pronoun that is used simultaneously to replace a word or phrase *and* to connect a subordinate idea to another complete idea. The relative pronouns that are used to refer to people are *who, whom,* and *whose.* The relative pronouns that are used to refer to animals, objects, places, or ideas are *that* and *which.* Examples of the way each of these relative pronouns can be used to subordinate ideas follow.

- *who*
  Idea 1: Margaret Mead has written extensively on human relationships.
  Idea 2: Margaret Mead is a noted anthropologist.

  Margaret Mead, *who* is a noted anthropologist, has written extensively on human relationships (*or* Margaret Mead, *who* has written extensively on human relationships, is a noted anthropologist).

- *whom*
  Idea 1: Margaret Mead has written extensively on human relationships.
  Idea 2: I admire Margaret Mead greatly.

  Margaret Mead, *whom* I admire greatly, has written extensively on human relationships.

- *whose* (shows possession by people or objects)
  Idea 1: Margaret Mead has written extensively on human relationships.
  Idea 2: Margaret Mead's work earned her worldwide recognition.

  Margaret Mead, *whose* work earned her worldwide recognition, has written extensively on human relationships.

- *that*
  Idea 1: Margaret Mead's book is *Coming of Age in Samoa.*
  Idea 2: The book established her in the field.

  The book *that* established Margaret Mead in the field is *Coming of Age in Samoa.*

- *which*
Idea 1: Anthropology was Margaret Mead's passion.
Idea 2: Anthropology is the study of human culture and evolution.

Anthropology, *which* is the study of human culture and evolution, was Margaret Mead's passion.

Here are two easy guidelines for using *that* and *which*:

- When the idea that you want to subordinate is *needed by the reader to identify the subject of the main idea,* use *that* (or, if the subject is a person, use *who*), and don't put commas around the subordinated idea.

Mead's belief that nuclear warfare is insane has influenced a whole generation. (The subordinated idea is essential for letting the reader know which of Mead's beliefs has influenced a generation.)

- When the idea that you are subordinating *adds information that is not necessary for identifying the subject of the main idea,* use *which* or *who* and put a comma before and a comma after the subordinated idea. The commas indicate that the information between them is not essential for identifying the subject.

Mead's book on Samoa, which is still a classic in the field, influenced many anthropologists. (The subordinated idea is not needed by the reader to identify the book—the main idea makes that clear.)

EXERCISE   **SUBORDINATING WITH RELATIVE PRONOUNS**

Examine the following pairs of sentences. In the space below each pair, try to combine them by using a relative pronoun to subordinate the idea that you think should receive less emphasis. The first one has been done as an example.

1. a. Anthropologists have discovered something about human food habits.
   b. Human food habits vary endlessly.

   Anthropologists have discovered that human food habits vary endlessly.

2. a. Various researchers have seen some interesting food habits.
   b. Various researchers have observed almost every living society.

3. a. Eskimos eat meat and fish almost exclusively.
   b. Eskimos live in the Arctic.

4. a. Mexican Indians eat mostly grains and vegetables.
   b. Mexican Indians live in the plains.

5. a. Milk is drunk daily by East Africans.
   b. Milk is quite plentiful.

6. a. West Africans consider milk a luxury food.
   b. West Africans have few cows or goats.

The next four sets have three ideas in each set. Try to combine all three ideas into one sentence using the appropriate relative pronoun. The first one has been done as an example.

7. a. Some people are intrigued by the food habits of Mexican Indians.
   b. A favorite dish of Mexican Indians is dog meat.
   c. The dog meat has been aged.

Some people are intrigued by the food habits of Mexican Indians whose favorite dish is aged dog meat.

8. a. Some tribes in Syria regularly eat arsenic.
   b. Arsenic is a substance.
   c. Arsenic is extremely poisonous.

9. a. The Jappuras of India eat insects.
   b. The diet of the Jappuras of India is lacking in protein.
   c. The insects are crushed and cooked.

10. a. Clay is eaten by several Amazonian tribes.
    b. Clay is a source of minerals.
    c. Several Amazonian tribes soften the clay with water.

EXERCISE **COMBINING SENTENCES**

Below are some sentences about an archaeological finding in Lower Wadi Kubbaniya in Egypt. The people of Lower Wadi Kubbaniya lived and farmed there over 10,000 years ago. On a separate piece of paper, experiment with different ways of combining any sentences that might sound better combined. Try to use all of the strategies that you learned in this chapter.

1. Lower Wadi Kubbaniya must have been an unusually attractive environment.
2. It must have been an attractive place for the people.
3. The people were of the late Paleolithic era.
4. There were fish.
5. The fish were in the river.
6. There were ducks.
7. The ducks were in the marshlands.
8. There were trees and grasses.
9. The trees and grasses were fringing something.
10. The something was the water.
11. There were antelope and wild cattle.
12. The antelope and wild cattle roamed the vegetated area.
13. There was desert there then.
14. This desert was beyond a narrow band.

15. The narrow band was watered by the Nile.
16. There is desert there now.
17. We have found remains.
18. The remains are of ancient camps.
19. The remains are in several distinct places.
20. The remains are high up on the dunes.
21. The dunes are next to the floodplains.
22. The remains are also lower down on the ridges.
23. The ridges are between the swales.
24. The swales are in the embayment.
25. The swales are depressions in the ground.
26. We have found the remains in other places.
27. The other places are further down.
28. The other places are at the mouth of the wadi.
29. The mouth of the wadi empties into the channel.
30. The channel is part of the Nile.

When you are finished doing this exercise, turn to page 225 to see the original version of these paragraphs.

This chapter has provided you with many opportunities to combine sentences and parts of sentences in different ways. I hope that your efforts at sentence-combining have led you to see that there is no one right way to combine sentences or sentence parts. After you try out as many combinations as you can think of, you should evaluate them to determine which one—or ones—are most effective.

GUIDELINES FOR EVALUATING SENTENCE COMBINATIONS

- Which sentence combination communicates your meaning and your intended emphasis most clearly?
- Which combination sounds best?
- Is this combination appropriate for the purpose and context of the draft?
- Is this combination appropriate for your intended audience?

PAIRED EXERCISE **EVALUATING SENTENCE COMBINATIONS**

Work on this exercise with a classmate. Below is a set of sentences that can be combined. Immediately following this set are three revisions, each of which combines the sentences differently. Evaluate each revision with your partner and decide which one is best for *an academic essay on the effects of television.*

1. Television was created.
2. The creation took place fifty years ago.
3. Television has become ingrained.
4. It is ingrained deeply.
5. It is ingrained in American life.
6. Television is a necessity.
7. A person watches television.
8. The person is an average American.
9. The person watches about four hours a day.
10. He or she cannot imagine something.
11. The something is a day without television.

Revision A
Television was created fifty years ago. It has become deeply ingrained in American life. Television is a necessity. The average American watches television about four hours a day. He or she cannot imagine a day without television.

Revision B
Created fifty years ago, television has become deeply ingrained in American life. Television is a necessity. The average American watches television about four hours a day and he or she cannot imagine a day without television.

Revision C
Since the creation of television fifty years ago, it has become so deeply ingrained in American life that it is a necessity. The average American watches television about four hours a day and cannot imagine a day without it.

EXERCISE   **PLAYING WITH A WRITER'S SENTENCES**

Below are nine sentences that have been adapted from a passage in Eldridge Cleaver's *Soul on Ice* in which he writes about the importance of language and of writing. On a separate paper, combine them into as many variations as you can think of.

1. I lost my self-respect.
2. My pride dissolved.
3. My pride was in being a man.

4. My whole moral structure seemed to collapse.
5. My whole moral structure was shattered.
6. It was shattered completely.
7. I started to write because my pride dissolved.
8. I also started to write because my moral structure seemed to collapse.
9. I started to write to save myself.

When you finish this exercise, look at Cleaver's actual sentence, which can be found on page 267 of Chapter 10.

REVISING WITH A WORD PROCESSOR

Use your word processor's BLOCK and MOVE function keys to "cut and paste" sentences and parts of sentences when you are revising a draft for sentence effectiveness. Here are some guidelines for revising the sentence structure of your word-processed discovery drafts:

1. **BOLD** any descriptive words that you add to a sentence so that you can evaluate their impact on the way in which the sentence expresses your ideas.
2. DELETE all words in a sentence that do not relate clearly and logically to the sentence's idea or that may confuse or distract a reader.
3. BRACKET ([ ]) coordinators, and reread coordinated sentences to determine if they should be subordinated.
4. Put a paragraph from your draft into a WINDOW at the top of the screen. At the bottom of the screen, write as many combinations of sentences within the paragraph as you can think of. Compare these with each other and with the original sentences. Choose the combinations that you think sound best and are most appropriate for your purpose and readers.
5. Print a copy of your sentence combinations and revisions and ask a friend to help you evaluate their effectiveness.

WRITING ASSIGNMENT   WRITING AND REVISING AN ESSAY ABOUT THE IMPACT OF TELEVISION

Here is an excerpt from an essay by G. Comstock et al. that examines research on the impact of television on children and adults.

Goldbern and Gorn (1977) also exposed four- and five-year-olds either to a ten-minute program with no commercials, to the program with two commercials advertising a new version of a familiar toy, or to the program with two commercials on successive days (for a total of four exposures to the commercial). Children were then asked whether they would rather play with friends in the sandbox or with the advertised toy. Almost twice as many children who saw the program without the commercials opted for interaction with friends. Similarly, when faced with an option of playing with a "nice boy" without the toy or with a "not so nice boy" who had it, fewer than 35 percent of those who saw the commercials chose the toyless nice boy compared to 70 percent of those who did not see the commercials. A second set of questions addressed to the children concerned the impact of the commercials on parent–child relations. The children were told their mothers had expressed a preference for a tennis ball over the advertised toy. They were then asked which they liked best. Significantly more children from the control group followed their mother's judgment than did those exposed to the commercials. Moreover, when shown photographs of a father and son and told that the father denied the child's request for the advertised toy over 60 percent of the children who did not see the commercials felt the boy would still want to "play with his daddy," compared to fewer than 40 percent of those who saw the commercials. Finally, children who did not see the commercials were significantly more likely than children who did to state that a child who did not get the toy would remain happy. The authors interpret their results as indicating that television commercials encourage material as opposed to social orientation in children, that exposure to commercials may lead to parent–child conflict, and exposure can lead to disappointment and unhappiness when products are not obtained.

What is your reaction to this excerpt—in particular, to the last sentence of the excerpt? In your experience, do television programs or television commercials have negative effects on children? How should parents deal with their children's desire to watch television? Use the directions below to write a discovery draft about the impact of television on children.

1. Do five minutes of freewriting about the topic. Then, do five minutes of brainstorming and five minutes of clustering to find a focus.
2. Narrow down your purpose for writing and write a brief description of the audience for whom you are writing. Then, write a discovery draft of your essay.

3. Exchange discovery drafts with a classmate. Read your class-mate's draft and write down questions about the information that you still need to know in order to understand your classmate's ideas. Also indicate any problems in the believability or the logic of your classmate's supporting details and any problems in organization and coherence. When you are finished, give the draft and your notes back to the writer.

4. Revise the ideas, details, organization, and coherence of your draft using the techniques that you practiced in Chapters 6 and 7.

5. Examine each sentence in your revision. Add descriptive words in any places where they might make the sentence more interesting or informative. Then decide if any words or phrases should be moved to the front of some sentences. Move them.

6. Examine each sentence again, looking for vague or abstract terms. Circle each one and write in a more specific substitute. Use exact terms, sensory words, concrete terms, and vivid verbs wherever you can. Then, reexamine each sentence and delete any padding.

7. Identify sentences that might sound better combined. Experiment with different ways of combining them. Evaluate the combinations using the guidelines on page 221.

8. Rewrite your essay so that it incorporates all of your revisions in sentence structure.

Below is the paragraph that was adapted for the exercise on page 220.

Lower Wadi Kubbaniya must have been an unusually attractive environment for people of the late Paleolithic: fish in the river, ducks and geese in the marshlands, various bushes, trees and grasses fringing the water. Antelope and wild cattle roamed the vegetated area. Beyond the narrow band watered by the Nile, there was then, as now, desert. We have found the remains of ancient camps in several distinct places—high up on the dunes next to the floodplains, lower down on the ridges between the swales, or depressions, in the embayment, and still farther down at the mouth of the wadi where it empties into the Nile channel.

ISSUES FOR YOUR JOURNAL

1. Do you watch much television? Why? How does it affect your life or your values?

2. What kinds of writing are you doing for your other courses? How can you use your journal to help you explore material from these courses?
3. How are different groups of people portrayed on television? How do television programs or commercials create or uphold stereotypes?
4. What is "sexist language"? Do you find it offensive? Why or why not?
5. Does your state have a "seat belt" law, a law that requires drivers and passengers to wear their seat belts? If it does have one, how do you feel about it? If not, should it have one? Why or why not?

ADDITIONAL READING

Several of the exercises in this chapter were based on material from the field of anthropology. The essay that follows, "Correcting the Neanderthal Stereotype," is about some of the stereotypes that have evolved from anthropological research. The author, Betty McCollister, is a freelance writer interested in evolution.

CORRECTING THE NEANDERTAL STEREOTYPE

If we have progressed at all in the twentieth century, it's because we have managed to correct unfair and derogatory stereotypes of our fellow humans and replace them with the salutary and enriching reality. Discovering that groups once contemptuously dismissed as "wops," "hunkies," "chinks," "kikes," "niggers," or whatever are in reality multidimensional, worthwhile, interesting members of the human community has made us all better people.

We could profit even more by doing the same for our long-extinct neandertal cousins. Cartoons regularly depict a neandertal male, club in hand, dragging his female by the hair. Critics of anachronistic attitudes, especially toward women, call them *neandertal*. Yet, no evidence supports the idea that these people—supposedly crude, misshapen, and savage—were anything of the sort; in fact, more and more material has come to light suggesting the opposite. The stereotype may be as wildly off the mark as the idiotic comic strips in which humans and dinosaurs coexist—an idea wrong by about sixty million years.

Many questions remain, of course. How could they not, concerning creatures who vanished thirty-five thousand to forty thousand years ago? One question is: how closely are we and they related? A few anthropologists speculate that Cro-Magnon invaders from the south lived for a period with neandertals who had ventured north thousands of years earlier and eventually absorbed them. In that case, a few neandertal genes survive to this day in our genetic heritage. Most investigators divide the two types into subspecies and infer that, while they could have interbred—leaving skulls which display traits of both subspecies—their hybrid offspring would have been sterile, and the earlier subspecies became extinct.

Neandertals roamed Europe and Asia for at least fifty thousand years, perhaps 150,000 or more. When they disappeared, they left the planet much as it had been before they arrived—which is more than can be said for us. They were neither misshapen nor deformed. The error arose when the first attempt to flesh out a neandertal male was made with a skeleton which at the time, in the absence of other skeletons, was thought to be typical. It wasn't; it was that of a severely crippled elderly male. The neandertal men and women stood fully upright. They were shorter and stockier than their successors, with heavier bones and more powerful muscles. The average skull was slightly larger than that of *Homo sapiens sapiens* and differently shaped—longer, with sloping brow and receding chin.

They were religious. Their burial sites unmistakably proclaim their belief in life after death. One site in particular indicates a love of beauty: fifty thousand years ago, a tribe placed a corpse, presumably of an important and beloved person, on a bier of white, yellow, and blue flowers atop dark green branches.

Studies of hunting-gathering societies today, combined with deductions from abundant discoveries of ancient sites and artifacts, allow educated guesses about tribal behavior, including the status of women within the tribe. The brutish male who clubs and drags his mate to the cave, far from being primitive reality, is a projection of contemporary male wishful thinking. In the hunting-gathering way of life, which over hundreds of thousands of years allowed us to evolve, women were partners. Their gathering was more dependable than the men's hunting, making their contribution vital. It wasn't until the agricultural revolution a mere few thousand years ago, when possessing replaced sharing, that women were reduced to chattel.

Does it matter that our stereotype of our long-gone cousins is hopelessly skewed? It does. It matters a great deal. We cannot even begin to tackle constructively the multiple, interlocking problems which threaten our species and our planet today without some grasp of who and what we are, how we got that way, and what does or does not work for us.

We got here—from *Homo habilis* two million years ago or (if you like) *Australopithecus afarensis*, little Lucy, three and half million years ago—as members of small, cohesive tribes. Although we cannot observe them directly, we can use common sense to figure out what kinds of behavior would have been useful or counterproductive in that milieu. Across the long marches of millennia and in the tribes surviving at present, love and loyalty, trust and sharing, agreement on the rules, and a strong sense of belonging are what worked. The greed, exploitation, selfishness, callousness, and aggression which propel current movers and shakers would have been suicidal in a tribal context. For that matter, they are today in the long run, though they work for the few at the expense of the many in the short run.

A century ago, the phrase *survival of the fittest* was misinterpreted by the misguided Herbert Spencer and some of his coterie to mean ruthlessness and oppression. Strenuously disowned by the kindly Darwin and long outdated, the concept that might makes right persists among persons who don't understand evolution. Actually, qualities such as altruism, integrity, loyalty, reverence for the human spirit, and nurturing were important in the ancestral survival kit. Kinder, gentler tribes would tend to outlive, outbreed, and outadapt those without a social glue to bind them together.

The tribal life which until recently (a geological eye-blink in time, actually) wired us to require love, nurture, family, and belonging has largely disappeared. We can't bring it back. But we can find clues to our current alienation and malaise, once we understand what we have lost and why that loss is wreaking havoc on us and on the mother planet that birthed us.

Anthropologists who could travel back in time to a neandertal settlement of fifty thousand years ago would almost certainly meet a more hospitable reception and face less danger than they would in any large American city's slums. They might well find the tribe observing winter solstice or vernal equinox with prayer, music and dance, feasts and gifts. Their biggest culture-shock would probably be in discovering strong human affinities rather than differences.

On the other hand, the culture-shock experienced by neandertals transported to the late twentieth century would be violent indeed. They would be horrified by the noise, filth, squalor, suffering, cruelty, exploitation, alienation, and other pathological aberrations of modern life, especially as it is lived amidst roads and vehicles and buildings constructed of dead and soulless materials, spirit-deadeners inflicted on us by the Frankenstein's monster of technology.

Correcting the neandertal stereotype would enable us to learn—humbly and to our benefit—that those ancient cousins, like our own ancestors, knew a few basic things about life and living that we have forgotten and will have to relearn if we and our planet are to have any future at all, let alone one which could allow us to evolve further and realize our as yet undreamed of human potential.

Betty McCollister

OPTIONAL WRITING ASSIGNMENT

The author of "Correcting the Neandertal Stereotype" argues that modern-day men and women have much to learn from accurate interpretations of the lives of primitive people. Write an essay explaining your point of view about the author's assertion.

_____ CHAPTER NINE_____

REVISING DICTION

*"When I use a word," Humpty Dumpty said,
in rather a scornful tone, "it means just what
I choose it to mean—neither more nor less."*

*"The question is," said Alice, "whether
you can make words mean so many different
things."*

*"The question is," said Humpty
Dumpty, "which is to be master—that's all."*

LEWIS CARROLL

*The difference between the right word and
the almost right word is the difference
between lightning and the lightning bug.*

MARK TWAIN

METHODS OF REVISING DICTION

Like Humpty Dumpty, people often assume that their words mean exactly what they choose them to mean. For example, writers often use words like "great," "terrible," "few," "a lot," and "thing" without stopping to consider whether their readers know exactly what they mean by these terms. How carefully do you choose your words when you are writing? Communication begins with words, and the aim of this chapter is to help you choose and use words more effectively. Your diction (choice of words) reveals your thoughts and attitudes as clearly as your behavior does. For instance, if you label one friend as "cheap" and another as "economical," your label indicates a difference in your attitude toward these friends. In addition, changing one word in a sentence can dramatically change the sentence's emotional impact:

My friend stared at the strangers.
My friend glared at the strangers.

The first statement is neutral; the second implies an opinion about the friend's feelings. When you edit your diction, you must make sure that the words you have selected express the meaning *and* the attitudes that you intended.

A writer's ability to revise diction depends on his or her vocabulary; one cannot choose words one doesn't know. Thus, one of the skills involved in selecting words effectively is building a bigger vocabulary. People have three vocabularies: one for speaking, one for writing, and one for reading. When they write, people often use more precise language than they do when they speak. And when they read, they can understand many words that they might never use when speaking or writing. For example, do you know what the word "incarcerated" means? If you do, did you ever use it when you were speaking to someone? Did you ever use it in your writing? If you aren't familiar with this word, can you figure out what it means when you read it in the context of a sentence such as the following?

After the prisoner had been incarcerated for twenty years, the parole board finally decided to examine his appeal for freedom.

Since each type of vocabulary affects the other types, the more you read, the larger your writing and speaking vocabularies will grow. The more attention you pay to learning unfamiliar words in the material you read, the more words you will have at your command to convey ideas effectively to your readers.

PAIRED WRITING TASK **IDENTIFYING PROBLEMS IN DICTION**

Work with a classmate on this task. Examine a revision that you wrote for one of the assignments in this book or for your teacher. Exchange papers with your classmate. After you read your partner's paper, write answers to the questions below. Do *not* discuss each other's papers until you are both finished writing your comments.

Your partner's name:

1. What do you think the writer was trying to say or to show you in this paper?

2. Which words don't seem to make much sense? List them in the space below.

3. Which words seem vague, unclear, or too general? List them below.

4. Which words don't seem appropriate for the topic or for the purpose of the essay? Which words are too formal or too informal (or sound like slang)? List them below.

When you are finished answering the questions above, return the essay to your partner and discuss it. Suggest alternate words for any of the words that you listed above.

INACCURACY AND INAPPROPRIATENESS

When they revise their diction, experienced writers make sure that the words they have used are **accurate** and are **appropriate** for their purpose and readers. Accuracy is extremely important: if writers use words incorrectly or if they use vague words, their writing will be confusing or unintentionally humorous. Here is an example of a sentence with words that are vague and misused:

> The Lakers' loss was not such a big deal and I hope that they don't succor to the Celtics next week.

I have no idea what this writer means by the phrase "such a big deal." And I'm sure that he didn't want me to giggle at his misuse of "succor." If this writer had checked his diction, he would have looked up the word "succor" in a dictionary and discovered that it didn't communicate the point he was trying to make (that the Lakers shouldn't yield to the Celtics). Or he might have used a *thesaurus* (a dictionary of synonyms) to look up the word "succor." If he had, he would have found the following entry:

> Succor, v.   1. Aid, assist, help, relieve
> 2. Cherish, foster, encourage, comfort
> n.   Relief, aid, assistance, help

The writer would have seen that he had misused "succor" and he might have realized that the word that he meant was "succumb" (which means "yield" or "give in"). Looking up a word to make sure that you are using it correctly or to find a better synonym is one of the best ways of increasing your vocabulary. Unfortunately, many writing textbooks warn students not to use "big words" or synonyms that they haven't used before because they might use them incorrectly. I think these warnings are counterproductive. How can you learn the precise meaning of a word unless you try it out in a sentence and see how your reader reacts to it? Furthermore, if you always play it safe as a writer—using simple words whose meanings you are sure of—your writing will be technically correct but monotonous. Thus, my advice is to learn and to use as many new words and synonyms as you can. Just make sure that you edit them for accuracy and appropriateness *before* you hand in a piece of writing to a teacher or an employer.

INAPPROPRIATE CONNOTATIONS

Why do so many textbook writers warn inexperienced writers against using synonyms that they have looked up in a dictionary or in a thesaurus? Because words have different **denotative** and **connotative** meanings. A dictionary lists the denotations of a word: the objective, literal meanings of the word at the particular point in time that the dictionary was written. Many words also have connotations: emotional associations and personal meanings that individuals attach to the word.

For example, here are one dictionary's denotations of the word "thin":

thin, adj.   1. having relatively little depth
2. having little fat or flesh; lean; gaunt

The denotation of the word "thin" is neutral, but each person's connotation of this word differs, depending on the person's sex, experiences, and opinions. For some people the connotation will be neutral: "Everyone in my family tends to be thin." For others, the word "thin" may have a positive connotation: "My sister is so thin that she looks stunning in this year's fashions. She could be a model." And for others, the word carries a negative connotation: "My sister is so thin that she looks sick. She should get some meat on her bones."

Although connotations are often private and individual, many words carry universal connotations that writers can use to create different impressions. For instance, here are three descriptions of a person:

1. James is an overweight, shy man who is firm about his beliefs.
2. James is a fat, withdrawn man who is rigid about his beliefs.
3. James is a well-nourished, reserved man who is resolute about his beliefs.

The adjectives in the first description ("overweight," "shy," "firm") are neutral. The adjectives in the second and the third descriptions have the same denotations as the adjectives in the first, but their connotations are quite different! Revising diction involves examining the connotations of the words you have written and deciding whether they carry the emotional shades of meaning that you intended them to convey. Two words may be synonymous, but no two words have exactly the same connotations.

Try to be sensitive to the connotations of words when you are writing *and* when you are reading, because the more you understand the emotional power of connotations, the less you will be manipulated by words. For instance, advertisers sell their products by exploiting the connotative power of words: everything is either *new, improved,* or *revolutionary*—words that connote desirable qualities for most Americans. Here are some more examples of this manipulative use of the connotations of words:

1. (about a motorcycle) "It's a mean marauder, tough, maneuverable. It makes you feel good and look bad."
2. (about a cigarette) "Alive with pleasure. Light, cool, refreshingly smooth."

Using connotations in this manner is a form of dishonest, manipulative writing. Be aware of it, and revise any such uses in your writing.

EXERCISE CHOOSING AN APPROPRIATE LEVEL OF DICTION

Below are two versions of an evaluation of the movie *Shoah*. The first is a letter to a friend; the second is a movie review for an English class. These evaluations have been adapted so that you can choose the most appropriate word or phrase in each sentence. Examine each set of choices and circle the word whose connotations are most appropriate for the purpose and the audience. If you are not sure of the meaning of a word, look it up in your dictionary.

January 2

Dear Alex:

When you (arrive, get, come) here next week, you must see

Shoah. This (film, documentary, movie) is about the (killing,

mass murder, extermination) of the Jews in Germany in the

Holocaust. I thought it was (superb, great, excellent) and

movie critics have (hailed it as, called it, said it's)

a masterpiece. It's ten hours long, and it's (exhibited,

displayed, on) in two parts.

When I first (ascertained, found out, discovered) how

(lengthy, long, prolonged) the movie was, I didn't think I

could (handle, bear, take) ten hours of watching people being

(killed, wiped out, butchered) and (corpses, dead bodies,

carcasses) being shoveled into graves. But <u>Shoah</u> doesn't have
even one of these types of (<u>visions</u>, <u>images</u>, <u>sights</u>). The
whole movie is about the people who (<u>were part of</u>, <u>were</u>
<u>involved in</u>, <u>assumed a role in</u>) the Holocaust. It's got
stories from the (<u>Jews</u>, <u>martyrs</u>, <u>victims</u>) and from (<u>murderers</u>,
<u>bad guys</u>, <u>killers</u>).

I think I'm going to see it again with you because I was
really (<u>stunned</u>, <u>surprised</u>, <u>shook up</u>) and moved by it.
Anyway, I've got (<u>various</u>, <u>a lot of</u>, <u>numerous</u>) other things
planned for us to do. See you soon.

Love,

Amy

A REVIEW OF SHOAH

The word "Shoah" is the Hebrew word for "annihilation,"
and this (<u>flick</u>, <u>documentary</u>, <u>movie</u>) is about the (<u>killing</u>,
<u>mass murder</u>, <u>extermination</u>) of the Jews in Germany in the
Holocaust. It was written and directed by Claude Lanzmann and
movie critics have (<u>called it</u>, <u>hailed it as</u>, <u>said it's</u>)
a masterpiece. Almost ten hours long, it is (<u>exhibited</u>, <u>on</u>,
<u>displayed</u>) in two parts.

When I first (<u>ascertained</u>, <u>found out</u>, <u>discovered</u>) how
(<u>lengthy</u>, <u>long</u>, <u>prolonged</u>) the movie was, I wondered how I
would be able to sit through ten hours of watching people
being (<u>killed</u>, <u>wiped out</u>, <u>butchered</u>) and (<u>corpses</u>, <u>dead</u>
<u>bodies</u>, <u>carcasses</u>) being shoveled into graves. But <u>Shoah</u>
doesn't have even one of these types of (<u>visions</u>, <u>images</u>,

sights). Instead the whole movie is about the people who
(were part of, were involved in, assumed a role in) the
Holocaust. We hear stories from the (Jews, martyrs, victims)
and from (murderers, bad guys, killers) and we see the
concentration camps as they are today--(beautiful, nice,
glorious) villages.

I am not Jewish but I was (stunned, surprised, shook up)
and moved by this (impassioned, strong, totally awesome)
movie. It taught me important lessons about people's
inhumanity.

Amy White

VAGUE TERMS

In addition to examining the denotations and connotations of
words, another way to ensure that you are using accurate diction is to
revise your writing to eliminate vague, general words. Some writers
use a kind of shorthand language in their discovery drafts and even in
their initial revisions. They know what they mean by their vague terms
and they expect their readers to know too. However, most readers have
no interest in trying to guess at a writer's meaning. Here are some of
these vague "all-purpose" terms that can ruin the precision of your
writing:

- great, good, fine, nice, okay, all right
- terrible, awful, bad
- big, huge, gigantic
- funny, strange, interesting
- a lot, lots, many, plenty
- things, aspects, factors, stuff
- kind of, sort of

These words could have so many different meanings that they
don't communicate anything clearly. For instance, if someone told you
that she had read *a lot* of books for her sociology course, how many

books would you assume she read? Five? Ten? Twenty? If the same person then told you that she learned important *things* from these books, what would you assume that she learned? Facts? Stories? Observations? Lessons? When you revise your diction, check for these all-purpose words and substitute more specific terms.

EXERCISE   **REVISING ALL-PURPOSE WORDS**

Here is an uncorrected paragraph that has been adapted from a student essay. Circle every vague word and write in a more precise substitute.

Why do the superpowers spend a lot of money on weapons and so little on their people? I think that the arms race is a bad thing. The superpowers have a lot of weapons. They could blow up the earth many times. It's so strange that they continue to build more. And the really bad thing is that while Russia and the U.S. spend lots of money on weapons, children are starving or dying from awful things. Supporters of nuclear weapons say that there are many factors affecting the buildup of weapons. They worry that if Russia has more or better weapons than us, it will attack us or our friends. This means that the U.S. and Russia have to build up arms at the same rate. This idea was okay for many years, but now other countries have nuclear weapons. This is terrible because a nut might bomb us without caring about the consequences. I think the arms race is really bad.

CLICHÉS

Another form of shorthand language that all writers should eliminate from the final revisions of their writing is the **cliché** (pronounced "klee-shay"). A cliché is a phrase that has been used so often that it no longer means much, and readers don't pay much attention to it. Expressions such as "pretty as a picture," "apple of my eye," and "worked like a dog" give readers the impression that the writer is too lazy or too dull to think of an interesting way of saying something. Because clichés come to mind so easily, people frequently include them in their discovery drafts. However, experienced writers always look for them and replace them when they are revising their diction.

EXERCISE **REWRITING CLICHÉS**

Rewrite each of the underlined clichés in the following paragraph. On a separate piece of paper, rewrite the entire paragraph, *substituting* a new expression or phrase in place of every cliché.

My mom is <u>second to none</u>. She's as <u>pretty as a picture</u> and as <u>sweet as honey</u>. I know <u>beyond a shadow of a doubt</u> that I am my mom's <u>pride and joy</u>, and her love has always kept me <u>safe and sound</u>. My mom works hard for <u>the finer things in life</u>, and she's usually as <u>busy as a bee</u>. But she always has time for me and lends me <u>a helping hand</u>, especially when I'm <u>down and out</u>. In <u>this day and age</u>, teenagers often put their parents down, but not me. My mom is <u>one in a million</u>. I want to <u>follow in her footsteps</u>.

Many clichés are based on comparisons between two dissimilar things: "pretty as a picture," "happy as a lark," "smart as a whip," "proud as a peacock." Because clichéd comparisons are used so often, they lose their originality and their meaning. Instead of falling back on clichés, writers should try to develop their own fresh, interesting comparisons that can capture their readers' attention and imagination. Comparisons that include the words *like* or *as* are called **similes**, and similes can help readers see things in new ways:

An hour after the bomb was dropped, Hiroshima looked like an oozing wound.

The image "an oozing wound" stirs readers' imaginations and enables them to understand how the writer feels about this topic. Metaphors—

implied comparisons that do not use *like* or *as*—also have this emotional power:

Hiroshima was no longer a city but a decaying barren riverbed.

The writer of this metaphor invites readers to see a once bustling city as a riverbed that is rotting away from the effects of the atomic bomb. When you revise your diction, try to include similes and metaphors that are rich in sensory details. Try to think of fresh, original details that will capture your ideas exactly.

EXERCISE   **WRITING SIMILES**

Use your imagination to finish each of the following comparisons with a fresh, vivid image:

1. This classroom looks like

2. Going to school is like

3. Brainstorming is like

4. Revising an essay is like

INAPPROPRIATE LEVEL OF USAGE

Usages are customary ways of speaking and writing. In Chapter 1, you read about some of the conventions of Standard Written English (SWE) usage. SWE is a dialect, and like all spoken and written dialects, it has at least two different usage levels: **formal** and **informal**. Usage levels are always linked to social situations and are affected by the age, sex, race, and social background of the speaker/writer and of the audience. The ability to change one's usage level to fit the situation and the audience is a survival skill needed in school and at work. You know intuitively that the language you use with your best friend is often inappropriate for your teacher or your employer. For instance, think about the consequences of using slang or obscene words with some of your teachers or employers.

The ability to choose appropriate words for different writing contexts develops with practice. Students who have not received much feedback on their writing often try to make their writing sound more "academic" by selecting words that are too formal for their purposes and readers. Instead of impressing readers, they often confuse readers or unintentionally amuse them. Here is an example of overly formal diction:

I have perused the essay and found the author's protestations to be preposterous.

The language is pretentious and exaggerated. If the diction in the previous sentence were less formal, it would be easier to read:

I have read the essay and found the author's assertions to be unreasonable.

The most difficult part of revising one's diction for academic writing is finding a balance between extreme informality and extreme formality. This is not easy to do, particularly for writers who have not done much academic reading and writing or who have not worked at building their vocabulary. If you learn a new word and try it out in a sentence, you run the risk of its being inappropriate in the particular sentence or essay. However, I always advise students to take this risk.

EXERCISE **EXAMINING CONNOTATIONS AND LEVELS OF FORMALITY**

Work with a classmate on this exercise. Below are five sets of synonyms. (1) Arrange the words in each set according to their usage levels—from most formal to most informal. (2) Then, choose *two* words in each set and write a sentence for each that clearly indicates the differences in the connotations of these two words.

1. kill, murder, wipe out, slay
   Most Formal   Most Informal

   slay, murder, kill, wipe out

   a. *The thief felt no remorse about slaying his victim.*

   b. *Afraid of being caught, the kid thought about wiping out the cop.*

2. silly, nonsensical, nutty, preposterous
   Most Formal   Most Informal

   a.

   b.

3. quickly, fast, rapidly, expeditiously
Most Formal   Most Informal

a.

b.

4. know-how, aptitude, smarts, skill
Most Formal   Most Informal

a.

b.

5. examine, scrutinize, check out, investigate
Most Formal   Most Informal

a.

b.

EXERCISE   **CHOOSING APPROPRIATE DICTION FOR DIFFERENT CONTEXTS**

Here are two versions of a statement made by Harold M. Agnew, a nuclear physicist who worked on the atomic bomb that the United States dropped on Hiroshima in 1945. I have made adaptations of his statement for different purposes and readers. In each version, examine each set of choices and choose the most appropriate word or phrase.

Assume that Agnew wrote the following paragraph in a letter to his wife. In this letter he was trying to justify his current work on nuclear arms.

(I've, I have) always felt that science and the military
(are obligated to, should, have to) work together. And they
have, from (the beginning, Day One, the outset), whether it was
Leonardo da Vinci or Michelangelo or whoever. They were
always (making, concocting, designing) things for the people
in charge. . . . War is too (outrageous, important,
momentous) to be left to (the rising generation, the young,
kids). The young people who go around yelling "(Get rid of,
dismantle, destroy) the Bomb!" ought to be careful, (because,
'cause, for the reason that) the politicians might put a bow
and arrow in their hands and make the (young people, kids,
youths) (go, sally forth, rush out) again, knowing that
nothing is going to happen to them [the politicians]. With
the (progressive growth, development, proliferation) of
nuclear weapons, the (man, guy, chap) who says "Go fight a
war" is talking to himself.

Now assume that Agnew wrote the following paragraph in a press
release for reporters who wanted to interview him about his views on
nuclear weapons.

(I've, I have) always felt that science and the military
(are obligated to, should, have to) work together. And they
have, from (the beginning, Day One, the outset), whether it was
Leonardo da Vinci or Michelangelo or whoever. They were
always (making, concocting, designing) things for the people
in charge. . . . War is too (outrageous, important,
momentous) to be left to (the rising generation, the young,
kids). The young people who go around yelling "(Get rid of,

dismantle, destroy) the Bomb!" ought to be careful, (because,

'cause, for the reason that) the politicians might put a bow

and arrow in their hands and make the (young people, kids,

youths) (go, sally forth, rush out) again, knowing that

nothing is going to happen to them [the politicians]. With

the (progressive growth, development, proliferation) of

nuclear weapons, the (man, guy, chap) who says "Go fight a

war" is talking to himself.

When you have finished this exercise, turn to page 253 of this chapter to see Agnew's actual statement.

THE AUTHORIAL "I"

Student writers are often puzzled by the recommendation made by many teachers and textbooks that they should "avoid the frequent use of the first-person pronouns *I* and *we* and the second-person pronoun *you*." There are two reasons behind this advice: (1) these pronouns make a piece of writing sound informal, as if the writer knows the reader well, and (2) if many sentences include *I* and *we*, the piece of writing seems focused on the writer rather than on the topic. For instance, read the two paragraphs that follow. How do they differ in tone?

I think the arms race is terribly destructive: we have enough weapons to blow each other up six times. You may say that building our nuclear defenses is a protective device, but I think that we cannot protect ourselves against maniacs who might decide to bomb us without caring about the results.

The arms race is terribly destructive: the United States and Russia have enough weapons to blow each other up six times. Supporters of nuclear weapons believe that building America's nuclear defenses is a protective device, but the United States cannot protect itself against maniacs who might decide to bomb an American city without caring about the results.

In the second paragraph, the writer has substituted clear, specific nouns for the vague *we, you, I,* and *us,* and she has deleted the unnecessary introducer "I think." This makes the second paragraph sound more objective and more focused on the arms race (rather than on the writer). For many types of academic writing, a conversational tone like the one used in the first paragraph is inappropriate since it gives the impression that the writer is relying solely on her personal experience for support rather than on objective evidence. However, first- and second-person pronouns may be absolutely appropriate for some types of academic writing, particularly if the assignment asks writers to share their experiences or their reactions to something. In addition, writers should use *I* if avoiding it would make their writing sound awkward. For example, here are two sentences in which the writer's avoidance of *I* sounds silly:

> When considering the personal consequences of nuclear war, this writer gets quite worried. It is believed that atomic war will devastate life on this planet.

Contrast these sentences with the following one:

> I am quite worried about the consequences of nuclear war since I believe that atomic war will devastate life on this planet.

You have to make a decision about how you want to sound.

WRITING ACTIVITY   CHANGING USAGE LEVELS FOR DIFFERENT AUDIENCES

The focus of this activity is a movie that you recently saw or a book that you recently read. Think about your responses to this movie or book and consider why you would or would not recommend it to others. Then write *two* reviews of the movie or book: one review should take the form of a letter to your best friend; the other should be an essay for your school's newspaper.

Remember, a movie or book review is not merely a description of the plot and characters. A review should express the writer's overall judgment about the worth of the work and it should support that judgment with direct references to specific features of the work (such as the ideas, the characters, the action, the setting, the acting, the language, and the style).

Write the letter to your friend first. Then, adapt the details, vocabulary, and sentence structure of your letter to change it into a formal review essay that would be appropriate for a newspaper. When you are finished writing both versions, examine and revise each one so that it is appropriate for your purpose and your reader.

WORDINESS

Wordiness—the use of several words instead of a single word—often results when writers strain to make their diction sound academic or overly formal. For instance, a writer who thinks that a wordy phrase is more forceful than a single word will write that his essay "concerns the subject of . . ." or "pertains to the topic of . . ." instead of writing that it is "about" the issue. Inexperienced writers may think that wordy phrases make their writing more impressive; experienced writers know that excess words slow sentences down, obscure meaning, and bore readers. Here are a few comments about wordiness by some famous writers:

If it is possible to cut a word out, always cut it out. *George Orwell*

Clutter is the disease of American writing. We are a society strangling in unnecessary words, circular constructions, pompous frills, and meaningless jargon. *William Zinsser*

To write simply is as difficult as to be good. *Somerset Maugham*

Striking a balance between sketchiness and wordiness, like finding the appropriate word for a context, is a difficult skill that develops with practice. One trick for editing wordiness is to identify and eliminate the following common wordy phrases and to substitute their single-word alternatives.

Wordy Phrases and Their Alternatives	
the fact that phrases	
due to the fact that	because
regardless of the fact that	although
in view of the fact that	since
in light of the fact that	because
aware of the fact that	know
in spite of the fact that	despite
that phrases	
for the reason that	because
it is important that	should
in the event that	if
on the condition that	if
of phrases	
on the subject of	about
pertaining to the matter of	about
on the basis of	because
by means of	by

EXERCISE   **REVISING WORDINESS**

Examine an essay that you wrote for an assignment in this book or for your teacher. Underline every wordy phrase that you find and substitute a single-word or phrase alternative for it. Be ruthless: cross out every word that isn't absolutely necessary for expressing your meaning.

SEXIST LANGUAGE

Gender-specific words refer to a particular sex: "fireman," "stewardess," "his," or "her." When gender-specific words are used to refer to people of both sexes, these words become sexist and offensive to many people. Sexist language is often in the eye of the beholder. For example, what is your reaction to the gender-specific words in the following sentence?

In the future, the department chairman will run the meetings, and his secretary will keep minutes and transcribe her minutes for the record.

Many people would find the sentence above offensive because it implies that all of the chairs of departments are men and all of the secretaries are women. Moreover, unless this sex-based division of labor is a fact, this sentence is inaccurate: some chairs may be female and some secretaries may be male. Here is a revision of the sentence that is more accurate and less offensive:

In the future, the department chair will run the meetings, and the secretary will keep minutes and transcribe the minutes for the record.

Sexist language often results from the fact that English does not have gender-neutral pronouns and the tradition is to use the male pronoun for everyone. However, this tradition often results in offensive and inaccurate language. For example, can you find inaccuracies in the following sentence?

The typical student at my college is trying hard to improve his communication skills. Also, everyone in my English class is concerned about his writing.

Both uses of the pronoun "his" are probably inaccurate: few American colleges admit males only, so the typical student in most colleges could be male or female. Similarly, English classes are composed of male and female students. These sexist inaccuracies are just as incorrect as are other types of pronoun errors. For example, the pronoun agreement error in the following sentence is similar to the errors in the sentences above:

> The typical student at my college is trying hard to improve their life.

The correct pronoun to refer to one student whose gender is unidentified is "his or her," *not* "their." You can turn to pages 307–311 of Chapter 11 for additional information about pronoun reference and agreement. Here are some guidelines for you to follow for sentences in which you have used a pronoun to refer back to a noun that is singular and not necessarily male (such as "the typical student").

GUIDELINES FOR NONSEXIST DICTION

1. Use a gender-neutral term instead of a gender-specific one:
   > That rule was voted on by a majority of the members of Congress (instead of *Congressmen*).
   > Several police officers were needed to subdue the criminal (instead of *policemen*).
2. Use plural nouns instead of singular ones:
   > Most students at Hunter College are trying hard to improve their lives.
3. Use *he or she*, *his or her*, and *him or her* to refer to indefinite pronouns:
   > Everyone in Professor Greenberg's class is concerned about his or her writing.

   Note: Use this alternative sparingly because it gets tiresome to read. If you think you are using it too often, convert the indefinite pronoun into a plural noun:
   > All of the students in Professor Greenberg's class are concerned about their writing.
4. Use the indefinite pronoun *one:*
   > One should try hard to improve one's writing.
5. Omit unnecessary pronouns wherever you can:
   > Each student should hand in the essay next week (instead of *his essay* or *his or her essay*).

> 6. Use *Ms.* instead of *Mrs.* or *Miss* (unless you are writing a letter to a woman who has a professional title—like *Dr.*—or who has requested that you use *Mrs.* or *Miss*):
>
> Ms. Williams is planning on becoming a lawyer.

Unfortunately, sexism, like racism and ageism, won't disappear from our language as long as it exists in our lives. Nevertheless, as an educated, intelligent member of our society, you have an obligation to use language impartially and accurately.

PAIRED EXERCISE **REVISING SEXIST LANGUAGE**

Work with a classmate on this exercise. Revise the sexist language in the sentences below. The first one has been done as an example.

1. The ~~foreman~~ *supervisor* on this job must check his *or her* list to determine if ~~he has~~ *there are* enough ~~manpower~~ *people* to complete the job.

2. Any student in this class who uses sexist language must revise his paper.

3. Miss Klein is the best lady lawyer in the firm.

4. Everyone in the class handed in his assignment on the future of mankind.

5. If a person has a problem on the flight, he should ring for the stewardess and she will inform the captain.

6. At this company, each businessman will require his administrative assistant to draft his weekly schedule.

7. The chairman of each company is responsible for verifying the quality of all man-made materials that his company exports.

EXERCISE **FINDING SEXIST LANGUAGE**

Take out an essay that you wrote for an assignment in this book or for your teacher. Circle every instance of sexist language and rewrite the essay, using nonsexist diction.

DICTION AND DICTIONARIES

A dictionary is a valuable learning tool: in addition to giving the spelling, the meaning, and the pronunciation of words, a good college dictionary also presents information about the history of each word, about its modern usage, and about its synonyms and their connotations. While I am not recommending that you take up dictionary-reading as a new pastime, I do advocate the regular use of a standard college dictionary as an excellent way to learn new words, to check the accuracy of one's diction, and to improve one's spelling. Do not waste your money on a pocket dictionary: it doesn't include as many words or as much information about each word as does a college dictionary. Here are four standard college dictionaries:

- *The American Heritage Dictionary of the English Language* (Boston: Houghton Mifflin)
- *Funk & Wagnalls Standard College Dictionary* (New York: Harcourt Brace Jovanovich)
- *The Random House College Dictionary* (New York: Random House)
- *Webster's New World Dictionary of American English, Third College Edition* (Cleveland and New York: Simon & Schuster)

Here is an entry for the word "remunerate" from the 1966 edition of *Webster's Third New International Dictionary:*

re·mu·ner·ate \rə'myünə,rāt, rē'-, *usu* -ād·+V\ *vt* -ED/-ING/-S [L *remuneratus,* past part. of *remunerare* to recompense, reward, fr. *re-* + *munerare* to give, present, fr. *muner-, munus* gift — more at MEAN] **1 :** to pay an equivalent for (as a service, loss, expense) **2 :** to pay an equivalent to (a person) for a service, loss, or expense **:** RECOMPENSE, COMPENSATE **syn** see PAY

1. correct spelling of the word with dots indicating the separate syllables
2. pronunciation key
3. part of speech (v.t.=**transitive** verb or a verb that needs an object)
4. correct spelling of the past tense ending (which is the same as the past participle ending for this verb)
5. correct spelling of the "ing" ending for this verb
6. correct spelling of the third person present tense ending
7. derivation of the word (L=Latin)
8. definitions of the word
9. synonyms

Be aware that different dictionaries offer different information. Each dictionary represents the judgments of the group of people who wrote it, and these judgments mirror the constantly changing nature of language itself. Finally, no matter which dictionary you buy, it won't help you make decisions about diction if it sits on your shelf. Read the introductory material so you know how to use the dictionary properly, and then USE IT.

EXERCISE **USING THE DICTIONARY**

Get a copy of a standard college dictionary and follow the directions below:

1. Look up the word *compound.*
   a. How do you spell each of the syllables that make up this word?

   b. What are the different ways of pronouncing this word?

   c. What language did this word come from, and what did it mean in that language?

   d. What part of speech is this word defined as *first?*

   e. What other part of speech can this word be?

   f. How many definitions are given for this word and what are they?

g. How many synonyms are given for this word, and what are they?

h. Write two sentences: In one, use this word as one part of speech; in the other, use the word as the other part of speech.

2. Look up the verb *lie*.
   a. What language did this word come from, and what did it mean in this language?

   b. What are the definitions of the verb *lie*?

   c. What words does your dictionary give as synonyms for *lie* (as a verb)?

   d. Look up each synonym and explain how the connotation of each one differs slightly from the connotation of *lie*.

   e. Write a sentence using the verb *lie*. Then, write a sentence for each of the synonyms for this verb.

A PROFESSIONAL RESPONSE

Here is the statement by Harold Agnew that was adapted earlier in this chapter. Compare the words and phrases that he used with the choices that you selected in the exercise.

A NEW WORLD, A MYSTIC WORLD

I have always felt that science and the military *should* work together. And they have, from *Day One*, whether it was Leonardo da Vinci or Michelangelo or whoever. They were always *designing* things for the people in charge. . . . War is too *important* to be left to *the young*. The young people who go around yelling *"Get rid* of the Bomb!"* ought to be careful, *'cause* the politicians might put a bow and arrow in their hands and make the *kids sally forth* again, knowing that nothing is going to happen to them [the politicians]. With the *development* of nuclear weapons, the guy who says "Go fight a war" is talking to himself.

Harold Agnew

The actual context of this statement was an interview between Agnew and a reporter for *Time* magazine on the fortieth anniversary of the bombing of Hiroshima. Is Agnew's vocabulary appropriate for this context? Why or why not?

REVISING WITH A WORD PROCESSOR

Here are some guidelines for revising the diction of your word-processed discovery drafts:

1. If your word processor has a built-in THESAURUS, use it to find a synonym for any word in your draft that seems vague, unclear, or inappropriate for your purpose and audience.
2. Use the SEARCH function key to find the vague or trite expressions that you have a habit of using. Substitute a more concrete or clearer synonym for each.
3. Use the SEARCH function key to find wordy expressions (such as "the fact that" and "at this point in time") and replace them with a single word or phrase.
4. Use the SEARCH function key to find sexist language: search for every use of the word "man," "men," and "his." Substitute gender-neutral terms wherever they would be more accurate and appropriate.
5. Use a STYLE CHECKER program to print out the frequency of words in your drafts. If you discover that you have used many of the same words over and over, SEARCH for these words and substitute appropriate synonyms.
6. Print a copy of your revision and ask a friend to help you evaluate your diction.

WRITING ASSIGNMENT **WRITING AND REVISING AN ESSAY ABOUT NUCLEAR WEAPONS**

Here is an essay on nuclear war by Theo Sommer, the editor of *Die Zeit*, a weekly magazine published in Hamburg, Germany. It was written on the fortieth anniversary of America's bombing of Hiroshima.

A NEW ERA
from Hiroshima to a Balance of Terror

The nuclear age began in the early hours of Aug. 6, 1945, when the bomb bay of the *Enola Gay* opened and the first atomic bomb used in anger was dropped. It weighed about four tons and had a destructive power equivalent to that of 20,000 tons of conventional explosive. It exploded forty-three seconds later above Hiroshima.

Virtually nothing was left of the city. Tens of thousands died instantly, as they would three days later in Nagasaki—killed by radiation, burned to a cinder, or torn apart by the shock wave. There were probably 200,000 dead in two cities.

"My God, what have we done?" the copilot asked when the *Enola Gay* turned to steer clear of the mushroom cloud. This question has preoccupied humanity ever since, and the answers have differed.

As the streets of Hiroshima and Nagasaki still lay in ruins a thirty-six-year-old Yale professor, Bernard Brodie, wrote a book, *The Absolute Weapon—Atomic Power and the World Order*. His basic tenet was that "hitherto the aim of the military has been to win wars. From now on its main aim must be to prevent them." Deterrent strategy was born.

The diametrically opposite conclusion was reached, at the same time and also at Yale, by a twenty-five-year-old law student, William Borden, who had served in World War II as a bomber pilot. His book, *There Will Be No Time—The Revolution in Strategy*, was based on the assumption that America's enemies would soon have atomic weapons. An armed peace could not last forever. He advised the U.S. to prepare for a nuclear war so that it could win if necessary.

These two viewpoints have held sway in the debate on war and peace in the nuclear age. In practice they often have merged.

If deterrence is to work, the argument runs, the opponent must be told repeatedly that should it fail, the other side would be well able to wage and even win a nuclear war. The contradiction thus arose between a proclaimed strategy of nuclear deterrence and an actual strategy of nuclear war.

Several U.S. presidents have been tempted to resort to a nuclear strike to gain an advantage—in Korea and Indochina, and during the Berlin and Cuban crises. Nikita Khrushchev played nuclear poker in the Caribbean, and Leonid Brezhnev did so in the Yom Kippur War. Yet in the end world leaders realized that to use nuclear weapons was a risk they could not afford.

But can we rely on the common sense of world leaders in years to come? Does the fact that the balance of terror has kept the peace for decades insure that it will continue to do so?

The nuclear powers have increased in number. There are five: the U.S., the Soviet Union, Britain, France, and China. Several others have the technological capability to manufacture nuclear weapons, including Israel, India, Pakistan, and South Africa. The larger the number of nuclear powers, the greater the risk.

The nuclear powers' stockpiles now amount to a staggering 50,000 warheads, whereas two years after Hiroshima the Americans had a mere thirteen devices, and the Soviets had none. Moreover, the explosive power of nuclear warheads has been increased to an incredible degree. There has yet to be an answer to former U.S. Defense Secretary Robert S. McNamara's question, "How much is enough?"

A final alarming fact is that the superpowers have not conducted serious disarmament and arms control negotiations for six years. Meanwhile, nuclear stockpiles grow. Bids to control the arms race are weaker than the inclination to boost it in exotic ways.

The idea of a nuclear holocaust by no means appalls only people inclined to hysteria. It also causes gooseflesh among many who are aware of the deterrent system's advantages.

At a gathering of scientists who built the first atomic bomb forty years ago, Nobel Laureate Isidor Isaac Rabi made a frightening comment. The nations of the world, he said, were like people lining up in front of the gas chambers at Auschwitz while scientists were busy perfecting the gas chambers.

Statesmen must take heart if there is to be any change. That is the only possible lesson on the 40th anniversary of Hiroshima.

Theo Sommer

After you finish reading the essay, do some prewriting for an essay about nuclear weapons or about nuclear war. Think about the two different viewpoints that were described in the essay (the viewpoints of Bernard Brodie and of William Borden). Which viewpoint do you share? How do you feel about the possibility of a nuclear war? Should our country prepare for a nuclear war? Is a nuclear war "winnable" or "survivable"? Can anything be done to prevent a nuclear war?

If you cannot think of anything to say about this topic, do some research: read magazines, journals, and books that discuss this topic and take notes. Do some freewriting, brainstorming, and clustering about the topic. Then write a discovery draft of an essay that describes your view about the nuclear arms race or that describes your reaction to living with the threat of nuclear war. When you are finished writing your discovery draft of this essay, revise it using the techniques that you practiced in Chapters 6, 7, and 8. Next, revise your diction using the methods that you learned in this chapter.

Exchange essays with a classmate. After you read your classmate's essay, revise its sentence structure *and* diction. Circle every problem that you find. Return the essays and discuss them.

ISSUES FOR YOUR JOURNAL

1. Were you ever in a situation in which you were aware that people spoke "differently" from you (much more formally or informally)? How did it make you feel?
2. Write a description of a situation in which you deliberately adapted your spoken diction to fit an audience whom you wanted to impress. What did you do? Why? What were the results? What might have happened if you had not changed your diction?
3. How has your education changed your diction? Do you use different words (or do you use words differently) than do relatives or friends who have not had as much schooling as you? How do these differences make you feel?
4. Look back over your journal entries. Has your diction changed at all? If so, in what ways? If not, select a journal entry and rewrite it using more specific or more formal language. Then compare it to the original entry.
5. What are some of the advantages and disadvantages of computers? How can computers help people? How will the increasing use of computers hurt some people?

ADDITIONAL READING

The essay that follows, "A Question of Language," was written by Gloria Naylor, the award-winning novelist and English professor. One of her novels, *The Women of Brewster Place*, was serialized on national television.

A QUESTION OF LANGUAGE

Language is the subject. It is the written form with which I've managed to keep the wolf away from the door and, in diaries, to keep my sanity. In spite of this, I consider the written word inferior to the spoken, and much of the frustration experienced by novelists is the awareness that whatever we manage to capture in even the most transcendent passages falls far short of the richness of life. Dialogue achieves its power in the dynamics of a fleeting moment of sight, sound, smell, and touch.

I'm not going to enter the debate here about whether it is language that shapes reality or vice versa. That battle is doomed to be waged whenever we seek intermittent reprieve from the chicken and egg dispute. I will simply take the position that the spoken word, like the written word, amounts to a nonsensical arrangement of sounds or letters without a consensus that assigns "meaning." And building from the meanings of what we hear, we order reality. Words themselves are innocuous; it is the consensus that gives them true power.

I remember the first time I heard the word *nigger*. In my third-grade class, our math tests were being passed down the rows, and as I handed the papers to a little boy in back of me, I remarked that once again he had received a much lower mark than I did. He snatched his test from me and spit out that word. Had he called me a nymphomaniac or a necrophiliac, I couldn't have been more puzzled. I didn't know what a nigger was, but I knew that whatever it meant, it was something he shouldn't have called me. This was verified when I raised my hand, and in a loud voice repeated what he had said and watched the teacher scold him for using a "bad" word. I was later to go home and ask the inevitable question that every black parent must face—"Mommy, what does 'nigger' mean?"

And what exactly did it mean? Thinking back, I realize that this could not have been the first time the word was used in my presence. I was part of a large extended family that had migrated from the rural South after World War II and formed a close-knit network that gravitated around my maternal grandparents. Their ground-floor apartment in one of the buildings they owned in Harlem was a weekend mecca for my immediate family, along with countless aunts, uncles, and cousins who brought along assorted friends. It was a bustling and open house with assorted neighbors and tenants popping in and out to exchange bits of gossip, pick up an old quarrel or referee the ongoing checkers game in which my grandmother cheated shamelessly. They were all there to let down their hair and put up their feet after a week of labor in the factories, laundries, and shipyards of New York.

Amid the clamor, which could reach deafening proportions—two or three conversations going on simultaneously, punctuated by the sound of a baby's crying somewhere in the back rooms or out on the street—there was still a rigid set of rules about what was said and how. Older children were sent out of the living room when it was time to get into the juicy details about "you-know-who" up on the third floor who had gone and gotten herself "p-r-e-g-n-a-n-t!" But my parents, knowing that I could spell well beyond my years, always demanded that I follow the others out to play. Beyond sexual misconduct and death, everything else was considered harmless for our young ears. And so among the anecdotes of the triumphs and disappointments in the various workings of their lives, the word *nigger* was used in my presence, but it was set within contexts and inflections that caused it to register in my mind as something else.

In the singular, the word was always applied to a man who had distinguished himself in some situation that brought their approval for his strength, intelligence, or drive:

"Did Johnny really do that?"

"I'm telling you, that nigger pulled in $6,000 of overtime last year. Said he got enough for a down payment on a house."

When used with a possessive adjective by a woman—"my nigger"—it became a term of endearment for husband or boyfriend. But it could be more than just a term applied to a man. In their mouths it became the pure essence of manhood—a disembodied force that channeled their past history of struggle and present survival against the odds into a victorious statement of being: "Yeah, that old foreman found out quick enough—you don't mess with a nigger."

In the plural, it became a description of some group within the community that had overstepped the bounds of decency as my family defined it: Parents who neglected their children, a drunken couple who fought in public, people who simply refused to look for work, those with excessively dirty mouths or unkempt households were all "trifling niggers." This particular circle could forgive hard times, unemployment, the occasional bout of depression—they had gone through all of that themselves—but the unforgivable sin was lack of self-respect.

A woman could never be a *nigger* in the singular, with its connotation of confirming worth. The noun *girl* was its closest equivalent in that sense, but only when used in direct address and regardless of the gender doing the addressing. *Girl* was a token of respect for a woman. The one-syllable word was drawn out to sound like three in recognition of the extra ounce of wit, nerve or daring that the woman had shown in the situation under discussion.

"G-i-r-l, stop. You mean you said that to his face?"

But if the word was used in a third-person reference or shortened so that it almost snapped out of the mouth, it always involved some element of communal disapproval. And age became an important factor in these exchanges. It was only between individuals of the same generation, or from the older person to a younger (but never the other way around), that "girl" would be considered a compliment.

I don't agree with the argument that use of the word *nigger* at this social stratum of the black community was an internalization of racism. The dynamics were the exact opposite: the people in my grandmother's living room took a word that whites used to signify worthlessness or degradation and rendered it impotent. Gathering there together, they transformed *nigger* to signify the varied and complex human beings they knew themselves to be. If the word was to disappear totally from the mouths of even the most liberal of white society, no one in that room was naïve enough to believe it would disappear from white minds. Meeting the word head-on, they proved it had absolutely nothing to do with the way they were determined to live their lives.

So there must have been dozens of times that the word *nigger* was spoken in front of me before I reached the third grade. But I didn't "hear" it until it was said by a small pair of lips that had already learned it could be a way to humiliate me. That was the word I went home and asked my mother about. And since she knew that I had to grow up in America, she took me in her lap and explained.

Gloria Naylor

OPTIONAL WRITING ASSIGNMENT

Using Naylor's essay as a model, write a draft about a word that has a special meaning in your life. Describe how you came to understand the word's denotation and connotations.

PART THREE

EDITING

CHAPTER TEN

EDITING
SENTENCE STRUCTURE

*A sentence should read as if its author, had he
held a plough instead of a pen, could have
drawn a furrow deep and straight to the end.*

HENRY DAVID THOREAU

*A story can be wrecked by a faulty rhythm in
a sentence—especially if it occurs toward the
end.*

TRUMAN CAPOTE

THE IMPORTANCE OF EDITING

Editing is the process of identifying and correcting errors and unconventional forms in a piece of writing. When writers edit, they make their writing conform to certain academic, professional, technical, or business conventions. These conventions are simply customs or practices agreed upon by the people acknowledged as experts in the field. All of us follow conventions every day, and these conventions vary in different places or languages. For example, in English, written material is read and written from left to right; in certain other languages it is written from right to left; and in some languages it is written from top to bottom. Writing from left to right is not inherently better or more logical than writing from right to left or from top to bottom; it is simply a convention that has to be followed in many countries if the writer wants to be understood.

Academic writing has its own set of conventions—of sentence structure, grammar, punctuation, and spelling—that readers expect will be followed. There are two fundamental reasons why all writers should edit their writing: (1) nonstandard forms interfere with a reader's interpretation of the writer's meaning, and (2) errors are annoying and distracting to most readers. For instance, what is your reaction to this uncorrected paragraph from a student's essay for a sociology course?

The nature/nurture contraversy goes on century after century despite all the research on the effects of genetic inheritance versus the effects of environmental experiences. Studies of identicle twin show that biological heredity is more important for some trates than for others. For example, intelligence and socialability. However, all personality traits are shaped by experience, in fact some researchers claim that individual difference in ability and achievement are almost entirely environmental.

The content, organization, and coherence of this paragraph are fine, but the errors violate our expectations of academic writing, making it difficult to understand what the writer is trying to say. Because readers expect to see Standard Written English in academic essays, this writer's use of unconventional sentence structure, grammar, and spelling is very distracting. Moreover, his errors give the impression that he doesn't care too much about the reader or the topic. If *you* care about your topic and your reader, you should edit your writing.

PAIRED WRITING TASK   EDITING EACH OTHER'S ESSAYS

With a classmate, examine a final revision of a piece of writing that you did for one of the assignments in this book or for your teacher. Exchange papers with your classmate. After you have read your classmate's paper, write answers to the questions below. Do *not* discuss each other's papers until you are both finished writing your comments.

Your classmate's name:

1. What do you think the writer was trying to say or to show you in this paper?

2. Which sentences have problems, errors, or seem wrong? Which sentences don't seem to make sense? Put a star next to each one and be prepared to discuss it.
3. Which verbs seem incorrect? Which verb or noun endings seem incorrect? Circle each one, and be prepared to discuss it.
4. Which words don't seem to make sense? Underline each one, and be prepared to discuss it.
5. What errors in spelling and punctuation appear in your partner's piece? Be prepared to point each one out to your partner.

EDITING TECHNIQUES AND PROOFREADING

Editing is the final step of the writing process. At some point in the development of a piece of writing, writers stop revising and say, "Enough!" They decide that the piece is as clear, logical, and well-organized as they can make it, given the circumstances in which they are writing it and the deadline for submitting it. Then, they stop revising and start editing. They examine each sentence and each word, slowly and objectively, looking for sources of confusion and ways of improving clarity and correctness. Editing involves identifying and correcting errors in sentence structure, grammar, spelling, and punctuation. Editing is not an easy task. Many writers are so close to their writing that they are unable to see the errors on the page. All writers need to get some distance from their work in order to proofread objectively. You can get some distance from your writing by following the methods that were discussed on pages 141–42 of Chapter 6. Below are some additional techniques that experienced writers use to identify errors and nonstandard forms in their work.

- Read the piece *aloud slowly*, one word at a time, to another person or into a tape recorder. Reading aloud slowly helps you see errors that you cannot catch when you read silently.
- Place a ruler or a sheet of paper under each line of your writing in order to force your eyes to move more slowly over each line.
- Read your writing from the end to the beginning, one sentence at a time (read the last sentence, then the next to the last, and so forth). Reading each sentence out of its context helps you judge whether it is a complete sentence.
- Every time your teacher returns a paper to you, write down his or her comments related to editing in the Writing Progress Log in this book's appendix. This will help you track your progress in eliminating errors from your writing.

For example, here is an entry from the Writing Progress Log of one student:

Date ___11/5/91___ Course ___Sociology 101___
Title of Paper Reaction to First Set of Readings

Strengths:

Clear analysis of the issues
Effective use of details from the
readings

Problems and Errors:

Word ending errors: twins, differences

Sentence structure errors: 1 fragment and 1 run-on

The appendix of this book also has a Spelling Log to help you keep track of words that you usually misspell. Here is an entry from this student's Spelling Log:

Problem Word	Misspelling	Cause
controversy	*contraversy*	*mixed up a and o*
inheritance	*inheratance*	*mixed up a and i*
environmental	*enviromental*	*forgot the n*
identical	*identicle*	*spelled cal as cle*

STANDARD WRITTEN ENGLISH (SWE) SENTENCE STRUCTURE

This chapter presents several methods for correcting or eliminating different types of sentence structure errors. However, remember that the rules and conventions of SWE vary, depending on the purpose and on the reader. Many professional writers break the formal rules of SWE all the time. For example, many English handbooks advise writers not to begin sentences with "and" or "but" because these coordinators are supposed to be used to combine two complete sentences into one. But I used "and" or "but" to begin many of the sentences in this book, including this!

FRAGMENTS

A sentence begins with a capital letter and ends with a mark of terminal punctuation (a period, question mark, or exclamation point), but not every string of words that begins with a capital and ends with a period is a sentence. For example, here is the excerpt from Eldridge Cleaver's *Soul on Ice* that you worked on in Chapter 8. Which word groups that begin with a capital letter are not complete sentences?

I lost my self-respect. My pride as a man dissolved and my whole moral structure seemed to collapse, completely shattered. That is why I started to write. To save myself.

A **fragment** is an incomplete idea that is punctuated to look like a complete sentence. Many professional writers use fragments for stylistic effects, as Cleaver does in the preceding paragraph in order to emphasize the essence of his point. However, fragments can be very annoying to read because they make it difficult for readers to see the connections among the writer's ideas.

Remember that a fragment is *not* simply a short sentence. If a sentence has a complete subject–verb unit, it is a sentence, no matter how short it is. The following three sentences are quite short, but each is a complete sentence:

"I came. I saw. I conquered."

Here is an even briefer sentence: "Go!" The verb is "go." The subject is not explicitly stated in the sentence, but it is understood to be "you."

Fragments may be long or short, and they often seem like complete ideas:

Studies show that biological heredity is very important for several traits. *Some of which I have already discussed in detail.*

Grammatically, however, fragments are not complete ideas, usually because they are missing a subject or a verb or both. If you read a fragment aloud, it usually sounds correct and almost always makes sense in its context. This is why it is so difficult to find fragments by reading sentences aloud. If you read your sentences aloud and cannot tell whether they are fragments, try examining each to make sure that it has at least one complete subject–verb unit. The **subject** is the person, thing, or idea that is doing the action or experiencing the condition expressed by the sentence:

In any society, unpleasant *work* must be done.
Some *people* must be persuaded or forced to do it.
Doing unpleasant work is dreadful.

The **verb** is the action that the subject is doing or the condition that it is experiencing:

In any society, unpleasant work *must be done.*
Some people *must be persuaded* to do it.
Doing unpleasant work *is* dreadful.

If you are not sure whether a sentence has a complete verb in it, perform this test on it: Find the word that you think is the verb of the sentence. Try putting one of the following pronouns—*I, we, he, you, it,* or *they*—in front of this word. Does the verb make a complete thought with the pronoun? Does it make sense?

In any society, unpleasant work *done*. ("Work done"="It done" and "It done" doesn't make sense.)

In any society, unpleasant work *is done*. ("Work is done"="It is done," which makes sense.)

or

In any society, unpleasant work *must be done*. ("Work must be done"="It must be done," which makes sense.)

Another special feature of English verbs is that they can function as other parts of speech as well as verbs. For example, what part of speech is the word "doing" functioning as in the sentences below?

1. Those people were *doing* unpleasant work.
2. *Doing* unpleasant work is dreadful.
3. The people *doing* unpleasant work were miserable.

In sentence 1, *doing* is functioning as half of the two-part verb. Notice that *were* is the first half of this two-part verb and it expresses the time of the action (in the past). *Doing* is the "main" or the "principal" verb, and it expresses the activity that was occurring. In sentence 2, *doing* is functioning as a noun—it is the subject or the thing that is being discussed in this sentence. (The verb in sentence 2 is *is*.) In sentence 3, "doing" introduces a modifying phrase that describes the subject of the sentence. It lets the reader know *which* people were miserable. (The verb in sentence 3 is *were*.)

Verbal Fragments

To be complete, a sentence needs a verb that expresses what the action is and when the action occurred. If a writer omits the helper verb in a two-part verb, he or she has created a **verbal**, a form that looks like a verb but does not function as a verb. Unlike most verbs, verbals do *not* change their form to indicate the number of subjects in the sentence or the time expressed by the sentence. When you use verbals as verbs, you create fragments instead of complete sentences:

Lower class people *excluded* from competing for good jobs. (fragment)

Lower class people *are excluded* from competing for good jobs. (complete sentence)

Lower class people, *excluded* from competing for good jobs, *are forced* to do society's unpleasant work. (complete sentence)

If you have a habit of using verbals instead of verbs, you should look for verbs that end in "ing" or in "ed" and make sure that you include a helper verb *or* add a complete verb.

WRITING ACTIVITY REVISING FRAGMENTS

Here is an advertisement for a sports network. On a separate piece of paper, rewrite the entire ad, turning every fragment into a complete sentence.

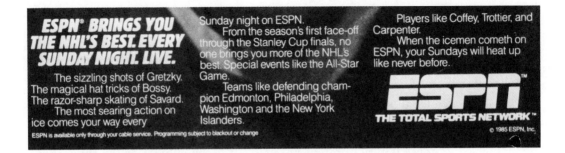

Which communicates the ad's message more effectively: the fragments or your complete sentences? Why?

Subordinator Fragments

Using a verbal instead of a verb is one way of creating a fragment. Another common way of making a fragment is writing a **subordinator fragment.** A subordinator fragment is a subject–verb unit that begins with a subordinator but that is not combined with another complete sentence:

The nature/nurture controversy goes on century after century. *Despite all the research on the effects of genetic inheritance.*

Reread the fragment that begins with "Despite" by itself. If you do this, you will see that it is not a complete idea. It should be connected to the sentence before it:

The nature/nurture controversy goes on century after century, despite all the research on the effects of genetic inheritance.

Often, subordinator fragments include a relative pronoun:

Studies of identical twins show that biological heredity is more important for particular traits. *Which I have already described.*

This kind of fragment should also be corrected by connecting it to the sentence before it:

Studies of identical twins show that biological heredity is more important for particular traits, which I have already described.

Methods of Correcting Fragments

There are several ways of correcting or eliminating fragments.

1. If the fragment is a subordinator fragment, (a) combine it with the sentence before it or with the sentence after it, *or* (b) omit the subordinator:

Studies of identical twins show that biological heredity is more important for particular traits. *Some of which I have already described.*

a. Studies of identical twins show that biological heredity is more important for particular traits, some of which I have already described.
b. Studies of identical twins show that biological heredity is more important for particular traits. I have already described some of these traits.

2. If the fragment has a verbal instead of a verb, (a) add a helper verb, (b) change the verbal into a verb, *or* (c) add a complete verb:

Studies of identical twins showing that biological heredity is important for particular traits.

a. Studies of identical twins are showing that biological heredity is important for particular traits.
b. Studies of identical twins show that biological heredity is important for particular traits.
c. Studies of identical twins, showing that biological heredity is important for particular traits, have proven that heredity is a critical factor.

3. If the fragment is missing a subject or a verb or both, add the missing part:

The effects of heredity on identical twins.

a. The effects of heredity on identical twins have been examined in recent studies.
b. I have read several studies showing the effects of heredity on identical twins.

EXERCISE   CORRECTING FRAGMENTS

Here are three uncorrected paragraphs from a student essay. Identify each fragment and correct it using one of the methods discussed above. You may have to add new words to some of the fragments to make them into complete sentences.

All societies have norms of behavior. They also have
deviant behavior. Behavior that violates the society's norms.
All normal people are occasionally deviant. Doing things, for
instance, that other members of their community might
disapprove of. But truly deviant behavior is behavior that is
forbidden by the community's laws. Because it threatens the
safety or the social order of the community. Thus, all
societies punish deviants who act criminally. Some
punishments ranging from ridicule to imprisonment to death.

However deviance can be a positive factor in a society.
Because it may slowly change the norms of the society.
Especially if the deviant behavior is not extreme. The
deviant behavior of a few people may be adopted. By more
people and then by larger groups. This behavior may then
become the beginnings of a new norm. As more and more people
participate in the deviant behavior. People in power slowly
begin to accept and even justify the behavior. And eventually
it becomes a norm. One striking example of this change from

deviance to norm. The earliest Christians were ridiculed, denounced, tortured and killed for their belief in Christ. Their behavior deviated greatly. From the norms of their surrounding Jewish and Roman communities. Slowly as more and more people joined them. Christianity became a respected behavior.

Another example of the way that deviance helps change the norms of society. Twenty years ago, independent women with minds of their own who refused to be bossed around by their husbands. They usually ended up divorced. And married women who worked because they wanted to were considered strange. And married men who stayed home to take care of the children. They were considered really crazy. Their deviant behavior couldn't be understood. Or tolerated by most of our society. Today independent strong women and women who work are everywhere. And more and more men becoming house-husbands. Yesterday's deviants are today's yuppies!

RUN-ONS

Just as a fragment is not simply a short sentence, a run-on is not merely a long sentence. This passage contains a famous sentence that is 313 words long and grammatically perfect:

Perhaps it is easy for those who have never felt the stinging darts of segregation to say, "Wait." But when you have seen vicious mobs lynch your mothers and fathers at will and drown your sisters and brothers at whim; when you have seen hate-filled policemen curse, kick and even kill your black brothers and sisters; when you see the vast majority of your twenty million Negro brothers smothering in an airtight cage of poverty in the midst of an affluent society; when you suddenly find your tongue twisted and your speech stammering as you seek to explain to your six-year-old daughter why she can't go to the public amusement park that has just been advertised on television, and see tears welling up in her eyes when she is told that Funtown is closed to colored children, and see ominous clouds of inferiority beginning to form in her little mental sky, and see her beginning to distort her personality by developing an unconscious bitterness toward white people; when you have to concoct an answer for a five-year-old son who is asking: "Daddy, why do white people treat colored people so mean?"; when you take a cross-country drive and find it necessary to sleep night after night in the uncomfortable corners of your automobile because no motel will accept you; when you are humiliated day in and day out by nagging signs reading "white" and "colored"; when your first name becomes "nigger," your middle name becomes "boy" (however old you are) and your last name becomes "John," and your wife and mother are never given the respected title "Mrs."; when you are harried by day and haunted by night by the fact that you are a Negro, living constantly at tiptoe stance, never quite knowing what to expect next, and are plagued with inner fears and outer resentments; when you are forever fighting a degenerating sense of "nobodiness"—then you will understand why we find it difficult to wait.

Martin Luther King, Jr.
"Letter from Birmingham Jail"

Dr. King's 313-word sentence that begins with "But" and ends with "wait" is not a run-on. The final eleven words—"then you will understand why we find it difficult to wait"—is a complete sentence, which is preceded by a series of subordinated ideas (each beginning with the subordinator "when") that are correctly combined with semicolons. A run-on, on the other hand, consists of two or more sentences that are incorrectly punctuated as one sentence. Here is an example of a run-on:

Discrimination is the treatment of people on the basis of their group classification rather than their individual characteristics, it is usually practiced by a group in power in order to preserve its privileges. (run-on)

The run-on above is a special kind of run-on called a **comma splice**: two sentences incorrectly joined with a comma. In Standard Written English, two complete sentences cannot be joined with a comma. The correct way to join two or more complete sentences is to use a coordinator, a subordinator, or a semicolon. A semicolon is usually used to join two complete sentences when the second sentence continues the idea expressed in the first sentence:

> Discrimination is the treatment of people on the basis of their group classification rather than their individual characteristics; it is usually practiced by a group in power in order to preserve its privileges.

This sentence could also have been separated into two complete sentences:

> Discrimination is the treatment of people on the basis of their group classification rather than their individual characteristics. It is usually practiced by a group in power in order to preserve its privileges.

Unlike fragments, run-ons are almost never used intentionally for special effects. Long run-ons, in particular, are too difficult to read. For instance, try to make sense of this run-on (which is an adaptation of a sentence in a student's essay):

> Although I was born in America and grew up here most people whom I meet for the first time ask me how long I have lived in America as if I were a new immigrant it is almost as if they believe that Asians aren't born in this country that we all came over on a boat this is only one of their stereotypes about Asian Americans many people also think that Asian Americans are a "model minority" we are quiet studious over-achievers shy and nonconfrontational we don't make waves I always shock people by asserting myself sometimes too aggressively but I don't apologize I just confront them with my own stereotype I'm a New Yorker.

This run-on could be punctuated as ten complete sentences:

1. Although I was born in America and grew up here, most people whom I meet for the first time ask me how long I have lived in America, as if I were a new immigrant.
2. It is almost as if they believe that Asians aren't born in this country, that we all came over on a boat.
3. This is only one of their stereotypes about Asian Americans.
4. Many people also think that Asian Americans are a "model minority."
5. We are quiet, studious over-achievers.
6. Shy and nonconfrontational, we don't make waves.
7. I always shock people by asserting myself, sometimes too aggressively.
8. But I don't apologize.
9. I just confront them with my own stereotype.
10. I'm a New Yorker.

Here is how the writer combined these ideas to make six complete sentences:

Although I was born in America and grew up here, most people whom I meet for the first time ask me how long I have lived in America, as if I were a new immigrant. It is almost as if they believe that Asians aren't born in this country-- that we all came over on a boat. This is only one of their stereotypes about Asian Americans. Many people also think that Asian Americans are a "model minority": we are quiet, studious over-achievers; shy and nonconfrontational, we don't make waves. I always shock people by asserting myself, sometimes too aggressively, but I don't apologize. I just confront them with my own stereotype: I'm a New Yorker.

Run-on sentences most commonly occur when the second complete idea begins with a pronoun or with a transition:

A stereotype is an image of a group of people that is shared by another group of people, *it* is applied indiscriminately to all members of the stereotyped group. A stereotype bears some resemblance to the characteristics of the stereotyped group, *however*, it is always exaggerated and distorted.

In the first run-on above, the pronoun *it* refers to the subject of the first idea (a stereotype), so some writers feel that they should join both ideas in one sentence. These ideas can be joined, but *not* with a comma:

A stereotype is an image of a group of people that is shared by another group of people; it is applied indiscriminately to all members of the stereotyped group.

Transitions can be used to link ideas, but *not* with a comma:

A stereotype bears some resemblance to the characteristics of the stereotyped group; however, it is always exaggerated and distorted. (Another way to link these two ideas correctly is to put a period after *group* and begin the second idea with *however*.)

Methods of Correcting Run-ons

There are several ways of correcting or eliminating run-ons.

1. Find the end of the first complete sentence (subject–verb unit) and put in a period, a question mark, or an exclamation point. This turns the run-on into two separate sentences.

Stereotypes can be positive or negative, usually they are used to emphasize the imperfections of the stereotyped group. (run-on)

Stereotypes can be positive or negative. Usually they are used to emphasize the imperfections of the stereotyped group. (two correct sentences)

2. Find the end of the first complete sentence and put in a semicolon:

Stereotypes can be positive or negative; usually they are used to emphasize the imperfections of the stereotyped group. (one correct sentence)

3. Combine the two sentences with a comma and an appropriate coordinator:

Stereotypes can be positive or negative, *but* usually they are used to emphasize the imperfections of the stereotyped group. (one correct sentence)

4. Combine the two sentences with the appropriate subordinator:

While stereotypes can be positive or negative, usually they are used to emphasize the imperfections of the stereotyped group. (one correct sentence)

Stereotypes, *which* can be positive or negative, are usually used to emphasize the imperfections of the stereotyped group. (one correct sentence)

EXERCISE **CORRECTING RUN-ONS**

Here are three uncorrected paragraphs from an essay. Identify each run-on, and correct it using the method that you think is most appropriate.

People who stereotype are committing injustices, they are depriving other people of their humanity. A stereotype is an image that one group of people share about another group of people, it can be negative, positive, or mixed. When people stereotype, they apply the image to all members of the stereotyped group, they don't see each member's individual characteristics and differences. Although stereotypes are always distorted or exaggerated, they usually bear some resemblance to the characteristics of the stereotyped group. (Otherwise, the stereotype wouldn't be recognized.)

Stereotyping is a very basic means of discrimination. If you stereotype someone as a "cold WASP," a "cheap Jew," or a "lazy Black," you aren't really seeing that person, all you

are doing is looking for instances of behavior that prove **your**
stereotype, also you are ignoring behavior that contradicts
the stereotype. Treating people on the basis of a stereotype
lets you discriminate against them, it makes you feel that
it's okay to reject them. In reality, of course, stereotyping
is a sign of ignorance, people who stereotype are unwilling or
incapable of finding out the facts about other people.

    Not only is stereotyping a form of ignorance, it also
reveals a lack of emotional maturity. One classic study done
by T. W. Adorno showed that insecure and immature people were
more likely to accept stereotypes than mature people, another
of Adorno's studies showed that people who do not stereotype
are more willing to accept others as individuals. They
interact with the real person not with the stereotype.

FAULTY PARALLELISM

Parallelism is a way of structuring a sentence so that it places similar ideas in similar grammatical forms. Faulty parallelism is distracting because it makes a reader stop to figure out the relationships between ideas that seem similar but that are not in parallel form:

Adorno's research showed that stereotyping is a sign of *insecurity, being immature,* and *people who ignore others.*

In the sentence above, the writer is listing a series of qualities that characterize people who stereotype. When a sentence includes words, phrases, or complete ideas in series, these must be in parallel grammatical form (all nouns, all verbs, all adjectives, and so forth):

- Nouns: Stereotyping is a sign of *insecurity, immaturity,* and *ignorance.*

- Adjectives: People who stereotype are often *insecure, immature,* and *ignorant.*
- Adverbs: People who stereotype may often act *insecurely, immaturely,* and *ignorantly.*
- Verbs: People who stereotype are often *feeling* insecure, *acting* immaturely, and *ignoring* others.
- Relative Clauses: People who stereotype are usually people *who have little confidence, who have not matured,* and *who have a tendency to ignore others.*

Note that a series of verbs or verbals must all be in the same form. If the writer had used different verb forms for this series, the sentence would not be parallel:

People who stereotype are often *feeling* insecure, *act* immaturely, and try *to ignore* others.

EXERCISE IDENTIFYING AND CORRECTING ERRORS IN PARALLELISM

The uncorrected paragraphs below have been adapted from a student essay. Underline each sentence that contains grammatical structures which are not parallel and write in a correction above each sentence you underlined.

Most people tend to have sterotyped views of men and women. People usually assume that men are more aggressive, more dominant, and they have more ambition than women. Women, on the other hand, are often stereotyped as being more passive and they show more emotions than men. These beliefs are stereotypes because they are inaccurate in many instances. Not all men are aggressive and ambitious, and not all women are characterized by passivity and show their emotions.

The only sex differences that research has uncovered are differences in upper-body strength, in mathematic skills, and spatially. In particular, males seem to do better than females in visual-spatial abilities and females are very

```
verbal.  In actuality, most sex differences are the results of

social training and not coming from biological inheritance.
```

DANGLING AND MISPLACED MODIFIERS

In Chapter 8, you practiced adding modifiers—descriptive words—to your sentences to make them more informative and more interesting. The placement of these modifiers is very important. If an adjective or an adverb is not next to the word it is describing, then the sentence may sound confusing or unintentionally silly. A **dangling** modifier is a word or a phrase that does not clearly modify any word in the sentence. Here is an example:

Being young and impressionable, cults can be very attractive to *teenagers.*

This sentence is confusing because it implies that cults can be young and impressionable. Improving this sentence requires rearranging its words:

Being young and impressionable, teenagers can find cults very attractive.
Cults can be very attractive to *teenagers who are young and impressionable.*

If a modifying word or phrase is not placed right next to the word it modifies, then it is a **misplaced** modifier. Look at how the misplaced modifier in the following sentence creates unintentional humor:

At an early age, my parents cautioned me about cults.

In this sentence, the initial modifier, "at an early age," sounds silly because it refers to "parents." Moving the modifier next to the word it describes corrects the problem:

My parents cautioned me *at an early age* about cults.

When I was at an early age, my parents cautioned me about cults.

EXERCISE   **IDENTIFYING AND CORRECTING ERRORS IN MODIFICATION**

The uncorrected paragraphs below are adapted from a student essay. Correct all of the misplaced and dangling modifiers.

What is a "cult" and how is it different from a religion? Defined as deviant groups, sociologists have noted that cults conflict with a society's established religions. Having existed throughout history, people have looked to cults for peace, salvation and mystical experiences. Shrouded in secrecy in today's world, cults are booming. Standing on street corners in every major American city, you can see cult members asking for contributions and trying to get new recruits.

Cults usually recruit members from colleges who are lonely and insecure and seeking easy solutions to the problems of becoming an adult. Using highly sophisticated techniques, the feelings, thoughts and behaviors of new recruits are manipulated. As soon as they enter the cult, cult leaders start their brainwashing. While being deprived of food, sleep and privacy, other cult members put intense peer pressure on the new recruits who are not allowed to discuss their former lives. Within a few weeks, the new recruits undergo a complete personality transformation. By swearing complete allegiance to the cult leader, the leader becomes their new parent. Completely in control, cult members are told what to eat and wear, when to have sex, and even how many children they can have.

CONFUSING SUBORDINATION

Sometimes writers try to pack so many ideas into a sentence that they lose track of where the sentence is going. Here is an example of a sentence which has very confusing subordination:

I think that a society in which a religion functions to control the government, like what is going on in Iran now causes serious problems.

Because this sentence seems to be going in several different directions at once, readers get confused about the writer's meaning. Here are three different ideas that I can disentangle from this sentence:

1. I think that when a religion functions to control a society's government, it causes serious problems.

   or

   I think that a society whose government is controlled by religion has serious problems.
2. What is going on in Iran now is an example of a society's government being controlled by religion.
3. What is going on now in Iran now causes serious problems.

I am genuinely unsure of the writer's meaning, but I can think of several ways of rewriting this sentence to make it clearer:

I think that when a religion controls a society's government, as in Iran now, it causes serious problems.

or

I think that a society whose government is controlled by religion, as Iran's is now, has serious problems.

In earlier chapters of this book, you practiced combining ideas by subordinating a part of a sentence to another sentence. Sometimes, when you subordinate several complex ideas, you may accidentally omit a word or phrase that would clarify the relationships among your ideas or you may add words that confuse readers. Most subordinators lead readers to expect specific sentence structures, and if these structures do not follow, readers get confused. For example, read this sentence, and think about how its subordination confuses its meaning:

By deposing the Shah of Iran enabled Muslim leaders to create a religious revolution.

When readers see a sentence that begins with "By" followed by an "ing" verb and a noun, they expect the next word in the sentence to tell who or what is doing the "ing" verb. In the sentence above, readers expect to find out who is "deposing the Shah of Iran" immediately after the word "Iran":

By deposing the Shah of Iran, Muslim leaders were able to create a religious revolution.

If the writer wanted to keep the word "enabled" in the sentence, he would have to change the "By":

Deposing the Shah of Iran enabled Muslim leaders to create a religious revolution.

When you edit your sentences for problems, reread each one aloud to make sure that it states your meaning clearly and that it doesn't mix up the subordinated sentence parts. If a sentence seems very mixed up, reword it or cross it out and rewrite it.

EXERCISE **IDENTIFYING AND CORRECTING CONFUSING SUBORDINATION**

The paragraph below is adapted from a student essay. Correct each sentence that contains subordination problems.

Although the Middle East is experiencing a major Islamic revival, but Islam has always been a strong independent religion in Iran. By serving the Iranians directly as leaders of the congregations allowed Islamic mullahs to meet the people's needs and to take public positions. During the 1970's, more and more Iranians turned to Islam in which was an outlet for their grievances against the Shah. In January 1979, Ruhollah Khomeini's supporters revolted against the Shah, and he fled to America. Although many Iranians, they supported Khomeini as a symbol of opposition to the Shah, but they didn't really approve of his fundamentalist programs. They were shocked when Khomeini forced the government and courts, which these things functioned democratically, to conform to Islamic laws. Because he was a fundamentalist, Khomeini wanted that the government to be ruled by religious

```
authorities who would rule according to God's (Islam's) laws.

Iran is now a total Islamic theocracy.
```

SENTENCE STRUCTURE CORRECTION SYMBOLS

You might not want to use these symbols to edit your own writing, but you may need to use them to edit a classmate's writing or to understand your teacher's comments.

Error	Problem
Frag	Fragment (a part of a sentence that is incorrectly punctuated like a complete sentence)
RO	Run-on (two or more complete sentences incorrectly punctuated as one sentence)
CS	Comma Splice (two or more complete sentences incorrectly joined with a comma)
//	Parallelism Error

EDITING WITH A WORD PROCESSOR

Here are some guidelines for editing the sentence structure of your word-processed revisions:

1. If your word processor has a BUST sub-program, use it to break each paragraph in your revision into separate sentences. Check each sentence to make sure it is a complete sentence, not a fragment or a run-on. Decide which sentences might sound better combined.
2. Use the SEARCH function key to find verbals (search for "ed" and "ing") and determine whether each verbal is correct or whether it needs a helper verb.
3. Print a copy of your revision and ask a friend to help you identify and correct any sentence structure errors.

WRITING ASSIGNMENT WRITING, REVISING, AND EDITING AN ESSAY ABOUT STEREOTYPES

Here is an essay by an English teacher about the stereotypes commonly used to describe English teachers. Read the essay and check off the stereotypes that you think are true.

O WAD SOME POWER THE GIFTIE GIE US . . .

After reading Stevenson's "The Sire de Maltroit's Door," my class decided that while the characters were romantically conceived, they were not complete stereotypes. Although we expected Denis to act as a hero should act and "do the right thing by Blanche," still he was more than just your everyday shining knight. And while Blanche was a beautiful maiden in distress (has anyone ever seen an ugly maiden in distress?), she had a nobility that somehow lifted her above the typical heroine tied to the railroad track. Even though the Sire was an evil uncle, or perhaps just an overly suspicious one, he was more interesting and more carefully developed than the fellow in the black cape who wants the rent.

We went on to discuss the idea of stereotypes and managed to get several good ones on the board. Then, in a second's lapse of sanity, I jokingly suggested that it might be fun to make a list of common stereotypes used to describe English teachers. What follows is a list that may amuse and instruct, with some comments I couldn't resist adding.

1. They push books. (I can think of worse things to push.)
2. They always give homework. (But some of them are so dizzy they forget to ask for it.)
3. They lecture a lot. (Time out for soul searching.)
4. They know everything. (About what?)
5. They all wear glasses because when they were little kids they wore out their eyes reading all the time. (Is this any worse than a generation with hearing aids at age 30 from all that rock music?)
6. They tend to be artsy. (Arty?)
7. Their desks are always covered with books and junk. They call this "being creative." (Never trust anyone with a clean desk.)
8. They carry rulers around to whack kids on the knuckles. (I thought math teachers did this.)
9. They are cultured. (See arty, not buttermilk.)
10. They drive junky cars. (We all know the reason for this. Don't we?)
11. They never make mistakes. (The retort to this one is so obvious that I'll leave it to you.)
12. They know how to spell everything. (Don't consult your dictionary; ask your friendly English teacher.)

13. They always have rubber bands around their wrists. (For holding all those homework papers.)
14. Females are usually unmarried and mean. (Some are married and mean.)
15. Males always wear those tweed jackets with reinforced leather patches on the elbows. (They get them from the thrift shop where college professors sold them. This is called "trickle-down economics.")
16. They grade papers all the time.
17. They *say* they grade papers all the time.
18. They carry books around all the time.
19. They have big vocabularies and use words like *nadir*. (That's what comes of carrying all those books around.)
20. They are smarter than other teachers. (Well, of course, we wouldn't go so far as to say that, but . . . .)

Carolyn Estes

After you finish reading this essay, do some prewriting for an essay about stereotyping. Think about the stereotypes associated with a particular group (such as elderly people, teenagers, men, women, blacks, homosexuals, Hispanics, Jews, Wasps, Orientals, Italians, Poles, "Moonies," Russians, conservatives, liberals, and so forth). Choose one group and think about the ways in which the stereotypes associated with this group hurt or impede individual members of the group.

If you cannot think of much to say about this topic, do some research: watch different television programs *or* examine different magazine advertisements for stereotypes. Pick one of the groups listed above, and take notes about the ways in which group members are portrayed on television or in advertisements. Are they major or minor characters? How are they treated and how do they treat others? How active or passive are they? How do they speak and behave? How educated are they and what are their jobs or professions? How are they dressed and groomed? After you take notes on these details, draw some conclusions about their implications: what stereotypes about the group do the television programs or magazine advertisements uphold or negate? The essay that you develop should be an analysis of the stereotypes about the group or an explanation of the impact of these stereotypes on individual members of the group. When you are finished writing your discovery draft of this essay, revise it using the techniques that you learned in Chapters 6, 7, 8, and 9. Next, proofread this essay by following the proofreading tips described earlier in this chapter. Then, edit the sentence structure of this essay according to the following directions:

1. Reread the essay and circle every fragment that you can find. Correct each one by using one of the methods for correcting fragments discussed in this chapter.
2. Reread the essay and underline every run-on that you can find. Correct each by using one of the methods for correcting run-ons discussed in this chapter.
3. Reread the essay, looking for problems in parallelism and in modification. Correct each error that you find.
4. Reread the essay one more time, looking for confused subordination. Revise or rewrite each sentence that seems confusing.

ISSUES FOR YOUR JOURNAL

1. How important is "correctness"? Do you spend too much or too little time correcting the errors and problems in your writing? Are your attitudes toward correctness in writing related to your attitudes about correctness in other aspects of your life?
2. How do you decide when to stop revising a piece and start editing it? How do you decide when to stop editing it?
3. Have you used a computer and a word processing program to write, revise, or edit your writing? If so, what were your reactions? If not, would you like to do this? Why or why not?
4. Do you ever see a commercial or read an advertisement and find yourself drawn to the product being advertised? Why? What kinds of images and words do advertisers use to attract and manipulate you?
5. Reread some of your earlier journal entries. How is your writing changing? How are you changing?

CHAPTER ELEVEN

EDITING GRAMMAR AND USAGE

Every person has a grammar which is just a little bit different from anybody else's— grammars are like snowflakes—and we all sort of get together and decide on what things we have enough in common to call a language.

SUZETTE HADEN ELGIN

You can be a little ungrammatical if you come from the right part of the country.

ROBERT FROST

THE IMPORTANCE OF EDITING GRAMMAR AND USAGE

As the linguist Suzette Elgin says, "Every person has a grammar." All people with normal hearing will have mastered the rules of their language's grammar by the time they are five years old. This unconscious grammar—which enables us to speak, and eventually, to write our language—is different from the lists of rules in the "Grammar and Usage" sections of handbooks and textbooks. So why am I devoting a chapter to grammar and usage? Because the grammar that some students use in writing may not follow the conventions that readers expect to see in academic or business writing, and if readers get distracted by nonstandard forms, they will not attend to meaning. For example, consider your reactions to the following sentences, only one of which has been edited for correct Standard Written English (SWE) grammar and usage:

1. The reader ain't got no idea what the writer mean in that essay.
2. The reader don't have any idea what the writer mean in that essay.
3. The reader doesn't have any idea what the writer means in that essay.

The meaning of these three sentences is basically identical. How do they differ? How do you think a teacher or an employer might respond to each of them?

Most readers expect to see SWE grammar and usage in writing, and many readers get annoyed when their expectations are disappointed. Writers who use unconventional forms of grammar in their academic writing make it more difficult for readers to understand their ideas. Thus, part of the process of communicating ideas effectively in writing involves expressing these ideas in grammatical forms that do not violate readers' expectations.

PAIRED EDITING TASK ANALYZING PROBLEMS IN GRAMMAR AND USAGE

Work with a classmate on this task. Below is an uncorrected placement test essay written by a college freshman. Read it carefully and then circle every nonstandard grammatical form that you find. Above each circle, write in the correct SWE form.

CHILDREN AND VIOLENCE

I believe that children learn violent behavior from their

parents. Children, especially a young child, is influence by

parental behavior. Children look up to their parents and tend
to imitate him.

Children also are influence by television (TV) and movies
but to a less degree. If a child from a non-violent home see
violence on TV, he don't automatically assume that the TV
characters are acting appropriate. However, the child who
been condition to seeing adults act violent may think there is
nothing wrong with the violent behavior he see on TV, and he
may try to imitate them.

Children learn way of coping with frustration and anger
from their parents, not from their TV heros. Therefore,
parent should be less worry about television and more about
they own behavior.

VERB FORMS

Every English verb has three forms that are called its "principal parts." These forms are the **present**, the **past**, and the **past participle**. All of the verb tenses in English are made from these three principal parts. When you look up a verb in the dictionary, you will find the present tense form listed first, the past tense form second, and the past participle third.

The Present and Future Tenses

The **present** tense in English indicates that the action or the condition expressed by a sentence is happening right now or is a general truth. For most verbs, the present is the form of the verb that can follow the word *to*. (This form is called the infinitive.) It is the form of the verb that is listed in the dictionary:

(to cause) Certain tests *cause* problems for some foreign-born students.

(to require) These tests *require* fluency in English.

In order to form the **future** tense of verbs, simply put "will" **or** "shall" in front of the present tense form:

These tests *will cause* problems for them in college because college tests also *will be written* in English.

USING THE PRESENT AND FUTURE TENSES

Write a paragraph describing your usual method of getting to school each day. If you live in a school dormitory, describe the way you get from your room to your first class. (Describe the hallways, corridors, staircases, and streets.) If you walk or drive to school, describe the route that you take. Do you use public transportation? If so, which buses and trains do you usually take? Where do you get on and off them? Use specific details and exact names. For this description, all of your main verbs should be in the present tense because the present is the form that is appropriate for actions that are repeated habitually (for example, "Every Monday at 8:15 a.m., I *walk* to the bus stop at the corner of First Street and Maple Avenue, and I *wait* for the number six bus").

When you are finished revising and editing your paragraph, circle every main verb. Above each one, write its future form. Then cross out all of the references to time in the paragraph, and above each one that you crossed out write "next week." By doing this, you will be changing your paragraph from a description of your general method of getting to school to a description of how you will get to school next week. Here is an example:

Next Monday
~~Every Monday~~ at 8:15 a.m., I ~~walk~~ *will walk* to the bus stop at the corner of First Street and Maple Avenue, and I wait for the number six bus.
will wait

The **past** tense indicates that the action or the condition expressed by a sentence happened in the past and is over. It is expressed by means of the past form, which usually ends in "ed." In fact, you can produce the past form of most verbs by merely adding *ed* or *d* to their present forms:

Multiple-choice tests *caused* problems for those students because the tests *required* fluency in English.

However, a number of verbs do *not* follow this rule. Instead, their past form is produced by changing the spelling of their present forms.

These verbs are called **irregular** verbs, and they cause many problems for students who have not yet memorized how to spell them:

Those students *found* multiple-choice tests difficult because they *were* not familiar with the procedures for answering these tests.

See page 294 for a list of verbs with irregular past tense forms.

In contrast to the past tense, which expresses actions or conditions that were completed in the past, tenses using the **past participle** express actions or conditions that began in the past and that are still occurring. The past participle is the form of the verb that follows a helping verb such as *have, has, had, am, is, are, was,* and *were.* Note that these helping verbs are all forms of "to be" and "to have." You can use these verbs as the main verb of a sentence or as a helping verb with the past participle form of another verb:

| Main Verb: | I *have* a house in Nassau County. |
| Helping Verb: | I *have* lived in my house since 1989. |

| Main Verb: | I *am* a proud homemaker. |
| Helping Verb: | I *am* planning to live here for many years. |

Like the past form, the past participle of most verbs is produced by adding *ed* to their present forms. In other words, the past and the past participle of most verbs look exactly the same:

Past: These tests *caused* problems recently because they *required* fluency in English.

Past participle: These tests *have caused* problems for the past fifty years, and some of these tests *have required* fluency in English.

However, many irregular verbs have different past and past participle forms:

Past: Many students *chose* incorrect answers on the test.

Past participle: Many students *have chosen* these incorrect answers before.

An important part of editing grammar and usage is learning to identify and correct unconventional verb forms. If you are ever unsure about the past or the past participle of an irregular verb, look up the present form of the verb in the dictionary. Almost every dictionary lists the present, the past, and the past participle forms of every irregular verb (in that order).

The English language enables you to use or to combine different verb forms to refer to different times. For example, if you want to refer to an action that is occurring as you are writing, you can use the present tense form ("I ask myself that question now") or you can use the *-ing* form ("I am asking myself that question now"). If you want to refer to an action that has been occurring over a period of time and is still occurring, you can combine the past participle form and the *-ing* form ("I have been asking myself that question for quite a long time now").

TWENTY-FIVE COMMONLY USED IRREGULAR VERBS

Here is a list of the principal parts of twenty-five irregular verbs—verbs whose past and past participle forms are created by changing their spelling rather than by adding *ed*.

PRESENT TENSE	PAST TENSE	PAST PARTICIPLE
am	was	been
begin	began	begun
break	broke	broken
bring	brought	brought
choose	chose	chosen
do	did	done
drink	drank	drunk
eat	ate	eaten
fly	flew	flown
freeze	froze	frozen
give	gave	given
go	went	gone
know	knew	known
ring	rang	rung
run	ran	run
see	saw	seen
sing	sang	sung
speak	spoke	spoken
steal	stole	stolen
swim	swam	swum
take	took	taken
tear	tore	torn
throw	threw	thrown
wear	wore	worn
write	wrote	written

Below is a student's report of an interview with a computer "hacker." Only the first paragraph has been edited for correct SWE verb forms. As you read the report, circle every nonstandard verb form, and write in the correct SWE form.

I interviewed Martin X four times. He is twenty years old and he lives in New York City. During the past two years, he has been a student at City College, majoring in computer programming.

Martin X is a "hacker"--a person who illegally taps into other people's computer systems and reads or steals their data. This delinquent career begun with Martin's desire to solve computer puzzles. He seen his older brother and sisters tap into computer bulletin boards across the country and he has wanted to prove that he could do it too. He always been mathematically talented, and he learn how to program a microcomputer by the time he was ten. Although his family forbid him to do anything illegal, he had did his first "hacking" at the age of twelve--he tap into employee data bank of the company where his mother worked and he discover confidential information about every employee in the firm. Slowly, he become addicted to the challenge of unlocking the security systems of the major computer networks in his neighborhood. He spended more and more of his time at his computer terminal, despite the adverse effects that hacking had on his schoolwork and his social life. He brang his friends over to see his accomplishments, but they all thought he was weird. His family worry about him too, although he had swore to them that he wasn't doing anything illegal.

Martin was unable to admit that hacking had became an obsession. It was only after he had broke the security code of his bank that his hacking was discovered. The bank didn't press charges against Martin, but they did threatened to do so if he resumed his illegal trespassing. His parents become so upset that they taken him to a psychiatrist. During therapy, Martin stop hacking, but then he begun doing it again after he stopped seeing the doctor. He claims that he has never stoled any valuable information from anyone and that he has not made any profits from his activities. He believes that hacking is a "harmless educational pursuit."

WRITING ACTIVITY USING THE PAST PARTICIPLE

Have you ever thought about what you might be doing now if you had not gone to college? Would you have stayed home? Would you have worked? What job would you have chosen? Why? Would you have been happy or unhappy? On a separate piece of paper, do some prewriting about these questions. Then, write an essay about what you would have done if you had not gone to college. Use as many past participles as you can. When you are finished writing, revise your essay to make it clearer, more specific, and more interesting. After you revise your essay, edit it for Standard Written English verb forms. Use a dictionary to check the spelling of every past participle.

-Ed Errors

In casual or rapid speech, most people do not pronounce the *ed* sound at the end of past tense verbs and past participles. Indeed, speakers usually skip this sound when the word that comes after the verb or the participle begins with a consonant: "Yesterday, I *ask* the teacher if I was *suppose* to revise my essay." Most listeners do not notice the missing *ed* ending and they understand that the speaker is talking about the past tense. However, the omission of *ed* endings in writing can confuse readers and is a serious Standard Written English error. So remember to proofread your past tense verbs and past participles and add *ed* or *d* endings wherever they are necessary.

EXERCISE **EDITING -ED ENDINGS**

Below is an unedited student paragraph. Circle every past tense verb form and every past participle. Add an *ed* or a *d* ending wherever it is missing. The first one has been done as an example.

When I master my computer's style checker program two years ago, the correctness of my writing really improve. Although I had learn to proofread for grammar errors in high school, I use to write many incorrect pronoun and verb forms. However, my grammar problems never bother me because I receive good grades in English. So when I got back my first college essay, I was shock that it had fail. The teacher note on it that my ideas were excellent but it had fail because of all the grammar errors.

At my conference with this teacher, I ask him what to do, and he suggest that I start word-processing my essays. He said that seeing sentences on a screen had help many of his students to identify grammar errors and that style checker programs had improve students' ability to find and correct their errors. He believe that I would benefit from using a computer program so I decide to try one.

I learn RightWriter and I have use its style checker on my essays ever since. It has help me edit my errors and improve my correctness. This has raise my grades and increase my confidence in my writing ability.

WRITING ACTIVITY **WRITING AND EDITING PAST TENSE AND PAST PARTICIPLE FORMS**

Write an essay about a serious problem that you experienced during the past five years. Explain the causes of the problem and how it affected you. Describe what you did (or tried to do) to solve the problem or to cope with it. Also explain what you learned from dealing with this problem.

Since you are writing about the past, most of your verbs will be in the past tense or past participle form. When you finish revising your essay, proofread the verbs for *ed* endings.

SUBJECT–VERB AGREEMENT

Another important editing skill is checking to see that all of one's verbs "agree" with their subjects. **Agreement** means that the form of the verb matches the **person** and the **number** of the subject of the sentence. **Person** is a grammatical term that refers to the speaker's or the writer's relationship to the subject of his or her sentence. If the writer is talking about herself, she must use a *first person* subject—*I* (if she is talking about herself alone) or *we* (if she is talking about herself as part of a group):

I rushed out to join the crowd, and *we* began marching.

If the writer is talking *to* someone or *to* something, he or she must use the *second person* subject—*you. You* can be used to address a single person or a group.

You are the person who must lead the march. The rest of *you* are all courageous and unyielding.

If the writer is talking *about* someone or *about* something, he must use a *third person* subject—*he, she,* or *it* (for a single person, thing, or idea) or *they* (for a group). If the subject of a sentence can be replaced by the words *he, she, it,* or *they,* then it is a third person subject. Each italicized subject in the following paragraph is a third person subject:

Nancy West leads this march on the White House. *The rest of the group* follows her. *The rally* is scheduled for 1:15 p.m. *Some marchers* may arrive early. *They* should wait for the rest of the group before raising their placards.

Remember that the term "person" has nothing to do with humans ("a house" can be a third person subject).

The subject of a sentence also has "number." A subject can be **singular**—one person or thing (*I, you, he, she, it,* or *one thing*) or **plural**—more than one (*we, you, they, several things*). Problems in subject–verb agreement usually arise in the present tense with *third person singular* subjects since these subjects require a verb with an "s" ending. Look at each of the italicized third person singular subjects in the paragraph that follows; each one needs a verb ending in "s":

Nancy West lead**s** this march on the White House. *The group* follow**s** her. *The rally* **is** scheduled for 1:15 p.m. If some marchers arrive early, they are to wait for the rest of the group before raising their placards.

Here is a chart of present tense verb forms:

Present Tense Verb Chart		
	Singular	*Plural*
First person	I walk	we walk
Second person	you walk	you walk
Third person	she/he walks	they walk
	it walks	

In the present tense of Standard Written English, a third person singular subject needs an "s" ending on a regular verb.

The verbs "to be" and "to have" may cause confusion about present tense agreement because they form the present tense differently than other verbs. Here is a chart of these two irregular verbs:

Present Tense Verb Chart		
	Singular	*Plural*
To be		
First-person	I am	we are
Second-person	you are	you are
Third-person	she/he is	they are
	it is	
To have		
First-person	I have	we have
Second-person	you have	you have
Third-person	she/he has	they have
	it has	

EXERCISE **USING PRESENT TENSE VERBS**

Here is a paragraph that was written in the present tense. Fill in each blank space with the present tense form of any verb that makes sense.

Computers _____ in a variety of sizes and prices. Some people _____ intimidated by computers. They _____ that a computer _____ a powerful machine with many mysterious buttons. Other people _____ it to be an overgrown calculator. In reality, a computer _____ a machine that _____ many types of arithmetic and logical operations. The computer _____ complex and powerful operations and it _____ them quickly, efficiently, and reliably. The heart of the computer _____ the Central Processing Unit or CPU. It _____ all of the "memory" needed to interpret instructions and to perform operations. Memory _____ the amount of information that the computer can store. Computers _____ two types of memory: "random access memory" or RAM and "read only memory" or ROM.

SPECIAL PROBLEMS IN SUBJECT–VERB AGREEMENT

There are several sentence structures that make it difficult to determine whether the subject is singular or plural.

When Words Separate a Subject from Its Verb

Words that come between a subject and its verb do *not* affect the number of the subject. You must determine which word is the sentence's subject and then use it to decide whether the verb needs an "s" ending.

The *color* of that computer *seems* drab.

The *colors* of that computer *seem* drab.

Be particularly careful editing subject–verb agreement when the words that separate a singular subject from its verb sound as though they are making the subject plural. These words include expressions such as "in addition to," "as well as," "including," and "together with." These expressions do *not* make the subject plural even though they sound as though they do.

A *microcomputer*, as well as a main-frame, *uses* silicon chips.

A *microcomputer and a main-frame use* silicon chips.

EXERCISE   **IDENTIFYING AND CORRECTING AGREEMENT ERRORS**

In the uncorrected paragraph that follows, underline the subject of each sentence and put two lines under the main verb of the sentence. Then, circle every verb that does not agree with its subject and write the correct form of the verb above each error that you have circled. The first sentence has been corrected as an example.

Recently, the number of computer programs for

preschoolers (have) increased dramatically. Most types of this
has

so-called "toddler software" uses music, color, and animation

to attract young children. The typical program prepared by

many publishers teach shapes, colors, and reading readiness.

The program, including the disk and the directions, are easy

to use. Furthermore, the features that make this software so

attractive to a parent is that it is easy to use and it is

very entertaining. A child between the ages of three and five

need to be instructed only once in how to use the program.

Then the child, together with his or her parents, simply work

through the "game" hitting number and letter keys. Programs

that require a child to make a decision or to solve a problem

seems to be the most popular. This type of program, as well

as programs that ask children to create imaginary things, also

foster reading readiness.

When a Subject Comes After Its Verb

In some sentences, you may reverse the order of the subject and its verb in order to achieve an interesting effect. When you do this, remember that the subject determines the form of the verb regardless of whether it precedes or follows the verb:

At the end of the list *is* the *toddler program.*

At the end of the list *are* the *toddler programs.*

In other sentences, you may want to begin with the words "There" or "Here." These sentence openers move the true subject to a position after its verb:

There *is* one significant *reason* why these programs are fun.

There *are* many *reasons* why these programs are fun.

When you edit your verbs, make sure that you check for these types of sentences to find the subject and to determine the correct form of its verb.

When Two or More Subjects Are Joined by "or" or "nor"

When two or more subjects in a sentence are joined by *or* or *nor,* the verb form is usually determined by the subject that is closest to the verb.

Neither the child nor her *parents like* the program.

Neither the parents nor their *child likes* the program.

EXERCISE   **IDENTIFYING AND CORRECTING AGREEMENT ERRORS**

In the paragraph that follows, fill in each blank space with the correct SWE form of any verb that makes sense in the sentence.

While there _are_ no up-to-date figures on the number of

English teachers using computers, it _seems_ that many teachers

are incorporating them in their lessons. Either a creative

writing program or drill and practice programs ~~for~~ _enable_ a teacher

to provide individualized instruction for each student. In

addition, there _are_ some software programs that _have_ a
teacher to tailor the lesson to each student's needs. A drill
program or a set of tutorial lessons _with_ questions for
students to answer and also _for_ each of their responses. A
good tutorial that provides many appropriate options _shows_
students plenty of opportunities to practice their skills at
their own pace.

When the Subject Is a Singular Pronoun

When used as subjects, the following pronouns are always considered singular and need verbs with "s" endings on them in the
present tense:

each	anyone
either	anything
neither	somebody
every	someone
everybody	something
everyone	nobody
everything	none
anybody	nothing

Everything contributes to the program's success.

Someone doing remedial work *is* likely to enjoy the computer's
endless patience and flexibility.

Either, neither, each, and *every* are always singular subjects unless
they are used with *or* or *nor*.

Neither tutorial *is* difficult.

Either this program or those *drills are* appropriate.

When Words Separate
a Singular Pronoun Subject from Its Verb

When a singular pronoun such as *either, neither, each,* and *every*
is separated from its verb by other words, it is easy to get confused

about the form of the verb. Remember that words that come between a subject and its verb do *not* affect the number of the subject or the form of the verb.

Neither program *is* difficult.

Each of these programs *has* a different focus.

The pronouns *some, none, any,* and *most* may be either singular or plural depending upon the meaning of the sentence.

Some of the software packages *are* empty.

Some of the software *is* broken.

EXERCISE **IDENTIFYING AND CORRECTING AGREEMENT ERRORS**

In the paragraph that follows, fill in each blank space with the correct SWE form of any verb that makes sense in the sentence.

Some of the most interesting educational software _are_

"creativity" programs. Each of these programs _have_ users

to stretch their imagination as they solve complex problems.

None of these programs _are_ exactly the same as any other.

One particularly challenging one _is_ "The Robot Factory."

This program _allows_ you to design a robot. Each of your robots

are to move through a maze that _is_ on the screen. You

make the robot move by selecting thrusters, grabbers, eyes,

wheels, and many other components for it. Every robot that

you create _is_ different, and each _has_ different

technological concepts.

When the Subject Is a Collective Noun or a Quantity

A collective noun is the name of a group that usually functions as a single unit. Some examples include *family, class, audience, committee,* and *group.* If you are referring to the group as a single unit, then the noun is a singular subject (and needs an "s" ending on its verb). If you are referring to the individual members of the group, then the noun is a plural subject.

This *group* of programs *is* known as "Creativity Software."

That *group* of programs *have* been separated onto different disks.

Like collective nouns, words that state a quantity or an amount usually function like singular subjects, but they can function like plural subjects when they refer to individual items. Words of quantity include amounts of time, money, height, length, width, space, and weight.

Two hours is the usual time it takes to complete a whole program.

Two-thirds of the programs *are* made by the same manufacturers.

When the Subject Looks Plural but Is Singular in Meaning

There are many subjects that look plural (in other words, that end in "s") but that are singular in meaning. These include names of some school subjects, names of some diseases, titles, and miscellaneous words like *politics* and *news*.

Mathematics is the focus of the *news* that *is* on television now.

Computing Professionals is an excellent journal.

EXERCISE   **IDENTIFYING AND CORRECTING AGREEMENT ERRORS**

In the paragraph that follows, fill in each blank space with the correct SWE form of the verb provided after the space. The first one has been done for you.

Computers *have* [to have] become indispensable in solving crime. The number of crime labs in urban cities _____ [to be] increasing each month. A recent report entitled "Computers and Law Enforcement Agencies" _____ [to offer] some reasons for the growing use of computers. First, the most recent group of crime-fighting computer programs ~~are~~ *is* [to be] able

to analyze a variety of unidentified substances. Moreover, a

number of these programs ~~have~~ *contain* [to contain] millions of

records about people who have been officially accused of

crimes. Finally, $500 *is* [to be] not too much money to pay

for programs that *has* [to access] information from thousands

of state and local law enforcement agencies. These programs,

which *are* [to be] growing in number, *save* [to save] time,

money, and energy.

VERB TENSE CONSISTENCY

After you edit your writing for verb forms and for subject–verb agreement, check to see that your verbs are consistent in tense. The verb tense that you select—past, present, or future—lets your reader know the time frame of the events that you are discussing. If you switch verb tenses without any logical reason, you will confuse your reader. For example, read the following excerpt from the uncorrected first draft of a student paragraph about writing:

Many teenagers today do not write very well. Most of the

blame for this problem can be attributed to a society that

permits children to be promoted year after year without

learning basic literacy skills. Teachers were not accountable

for their students' failures. And technology made it easy to

communicate without writing. However, writing skills will

always be necessary learning tools.

This paragraph makes me want to ask the writer, "Why did you switch from the present tense to the past and then to the future?" This

is the exact question that a classmate posed to the writer, and he revised his draft. Below is his revision. How does it differ from his first
draft above? Why is the last sentence in both versions written in the future tense?

```
    Many teenagers today do not write very well.  Most of the

blame for this problem can be attributed to a society that has

permitted children to be promoted year after year without

learning the basic literacy skills.  For years, teachers have

not been accountable for their students' failures.  And

technology has made it easy to communicate without writing.

However, basic writing skills will always be necessary and

valuable learning tools.
```

WRITING ACTIVITY   MAKING VERBS CONSISTENT

On a separate piece of paper, do some prewriting activities to help
you plan a brief essay that compares the high school that you attended
to the college (or other learning institution) that you are currently attending. The readers for this essay are seniors in your old high school
who want to know more about your current school. Choose *one* specific
feature to compare in this essay: the teachers (in both schools), the
cafeteria, the course registration process, the students, the library, the
classes, or some other feature of the two schools. When you discuss
your high school, use the past tense, and when you discuss your current school, use the present tense. Write your first draft of the essay on
a separate piece of paper. When you are finished writing, revise your
essay and edit it for SWE verb forms and verb consistency.

PRONOUN FORM, REFERENCE, AND AGREEMENT

A **noun** is a word that names a person, a place, a thing, a quality,
an action, or an idea. A **pronoun** is a word that can replace a specific
noun or that can be used instead of a noun. Usually a pronoun is used
to replace a previously stated noun (called its *antecedent*). Pronouns

help writers avoid repetition and they provide connections among sentences. For example, read the following student paragraph to see how pronouns help knit sentences together:

> The computer center in my high school was very small and
> uninviting. <u>It</u> didn't have many programs and the <u>ones</u> <u>it</u> did
> have were very old. <u>It</u> was directed by an ogre of a director
> <u>who</u> wanted to protect the disks from <u>us</u>. <u>He</u> didn't like the
> way <u>we</u> handled <u>them</u> and <u>he</u> was forever criticizing <u>us</u>.

When editing your writing, you may want to refer to the pronoun chart below. It shows the correct forms of three different types of SWE pronouns: *subject*, *object*, and *possessive*:

Chart of Pronoun Forms			
	Subject	*Object*	*Possessive*
First person			
Singular	I	me	mine, my
Plural	we	us	ours, our
Second Person			
Singular and Plural	you	you	yours, your
Third person			
Singular	he	him	his
	she	her	hers, her
	it	it	its
Plural	they	them	theirs, their

Every pronoun that you write should refer clearly to an antecedent noun stated earlier in the same sentence or in a preceding sentence. Unclear pronoun references confuse readers. If a pronoun doesn't have an obvious antecedent, or if the reader might be unsure about the pronoun's antecedent, replace the pronoun with the specific noun (even if this means that you have to repeat the noun a few times):

In my high school, *they* loaded the programs for *you* in advance. (Who loaded the programs for whom?)

In my high school, the *computer teachers* did the *students'* program loading in advance.

Just as verbs have to agree with their subjects, pronouns must agree with the nouns that they refer to or with the nouns that they replace. When you edit your pronouns, make sure that they agree with three characteristics of their antecedent nouns: **gender** (female, male, or neuter—*it*), **person** (first, second, or third), and **number** (singular or plural):

I liked my high school computer teacher the most out of all of my teachers. *She* knew every student by name, and *her* grading policies were fair. I owe *her* a great deal.

SPECIAL PROBLEMS IN PRONOUN–ANTECEDENT AGREEMENT

When the Antecedent Is an Indefinite Pronoun

Instead of referring to a noun, a pronoun may refer to another pronoun called an **indefinite pronoun**. Indefinite pronouns are usually used when speakers or writers do not know the name of the specific person or thing that they are discussing or when they want to discuss people in general. This group of pronouns includes the following:

anyone	nothing
anybody	everyone
anything	everybody
someone	everything
somebody	each
something	either
no one	neither
nobody	

These indefinite pronouns require a singular pronoun when referred to.

Everyone in my school likes *his or her* courses.

When *one* registers for computer courses, *he or she* has to consider who is teaching them.

When the Antecedent Is a Collective Noun

A collective noun—*family, group, audience, committee, team, class*—requires a singular pronoun when the noun refers to the group as a single unit. If a collective noun refers to the individual members of the group, it requires a plural pronoun.

> The *Computer Committee* usually makes *its* choices quickly, but the *members of the Software Committee* reach *their* separate decisions rather slowly.

When Two or More Antecedents Are Joined by "or" or "nor"

When two or more nouns are joined by *or* or *nor*, the pronoun should agree with the noun that is closest to it.

> Neither my professors nor my *tutor* allows students to be late to *his* programming sessions.

> Neither my tutor nor my *professors* allow students to be late for *their* programming sessions.

EXERCISE **DETERMINING PRONOUN FORM, REFERENCE, AND AGREEMENT**

Fill in each blank below with the correct pronoun.

Many teachers believe that most educational software is garbage. Much of this software has fancy colors and graphics but __it__ doesn't have sound enough educational content to justify __their__ high price. The developers of most software have tried to disguise __their__ programs' educational content with slick gimmicks __that__ attract attention but __they__ don't really teach anything. For example, each of the English programs that I have reviewed presents __its__ lessons in a video game format, but __it__ lacks a logical sequence of concepts and meaningful content. Each of these programs reflects the "game mentality" of the programmer who developed __them__: learning seems secondary to having fun. Teachers are the people __who__ ought to be directly involved in the

development of educational software. A teacher is the only
person who knows ~~the~~ *his or her* school's curriculum; thus, *he or she* is the
best person to determine the appropriateness of the content of
educational software for students.

PLURALS AND POSSESSIVES

It's easy to get confused about "s" endings. When you edit your
writing, look for the three types of words that need "s" endings: (1)
present-tense verbs that agree with singular subjects, (2) plural nouns,
and (3) possessives.

Plural Nouns

To form the plural of most nouns, simply add "s" to the end of the
noun.

teacher/teachers
day/days
Jackson/Jacksons

To form the plural of a noun that ends in "s," "x," "z," "ch," or
"sh," add "es."

boss/bosses
wish/wishes
Jones/Joneses

To form the plural of a noun that ends in "y" preceded by a consonant, change the "y" to "i" and add "es" (except for a proper name,
which keeps its "s" in the plural).

galaxy/galaxies
dictionary/dictionaries
Henry/Henrys

To form the plural of a number, a letter, or a symbol, add an apostrophe and an "s." If you write out the number, letter, or symbol, add
only the "s."

V/V's
8/8's
eight/eights

Possessives

To form the possessive of most nouns, simply add an apostrophe and an "s" to the end of the noun.

teacher/teacher's
no one/no one's
Bush/Bush's

To form the possessive of singular nouns that end in "s," again simply add an apostrophe and an "s" to the end of the noun.

bus/bus's
news/news's
Adams/Adams's

To form the possessive of plural nouns, add only the apostrophe.

boys/boys'
teachers/teachers'
Bushes/Bushes'

To form the possessive of a compound word, add an apostrophe and an "s" to the end of the last word.

father-in-law/father-in-law's
tennis player/tennis player's

Never add an apostrophe or an apostrophe and an "s" to possessive pronouns. The possessive pronoun that most writers make this error with is *its. It's* is the contraction of *it is,* not the possessive form of *it.*

EXERCISE   **USING PLURALS AND POSSESSIVES**

Below is an excerpt from a student's essay about computers and education. On a separate piece of paper, rewrite this excerpt, changing the word "computers" from plural to singular (that is, every time you see "computers," change it to "a computer" or to "the computer").

This change in the number of the subject of each sentence will require a change in the form of the corresponding verb. You will also have to make corresponding changes in the pronouns that refer to the subjects, and you may have to change the wording of some of the sentences.

Personal computers are an inevitable part of the future of education because of their many capabilities. Computers' abilities to organize information, to retrieve research, and to solve problems will probably make them indispensable to teachers and students alike.

What do computers have to offer for learners? First, they are fun to use, particularly for a generation whose best friends are television sets and video games. Second, thanks to their ability to present the same material over and over again endlessly, computers are infinitely patient tutors. Moreover, computers are "interactive"--they provide feedback appropriate to the users' responses. Thus, they can provide students with more individualized attention in one day than they can get from a month of classroom experience.

Furthermore, computers are able to store incredible amounts of data and information. For example, recent computers' hard disks are able to store entire encyclopedias, including diagrams, pictures, and photographs. And computers--actually computers' programs--have the ability to cross-reference all of this information and provide indexes of them.

In the not-too-distant future, students and teachers will tap computers' vast potential, and everyone will benefit.

EXERCISE   **IDENTIFYING AND CORRECTING ERRORS IN THE THREE DIFFERENT "S" ENDINGS**

In the essay below, circle all of the words that have incorrect SWE "s" endings (verbs, plural nouns, and possessives). Then write your correction above each error that you have circled.

Computers' cannot think. Or can they? Recently, Soft Path Systems' new creative software program, "Brainstormer," was introduced on the American market, and it enable computer to do much of the busy-work usually involved in creative thinking. Brainstormer don't actually comes up with original ideas, but it do create new combination of the basic ideas that a person type in. It's goal is to shuffle and display all of the possible variation of ones' original ideas.

In order to use the program, you types in a few basic themes and some variation on these themes. The program then mixs up the themes and variations, producing hundred of thousands of possible storys. These story's value is in helping you generate a multitude of options for developing your ideas. The program enable you to explore possibilitys and it helps you break out of ruts.

Brainstormer is also useful for teachers. It's ability to spew out endless variations can help a teacher to creates many different student's learning activitys. Furthermore, Brainstormer create individualized activitys to fit each students' needs so that different students' can work simultaneously on problem requiring different level of skills.

However, Brainstormer do has some drawback. It cannot develops original ideas, and it do not chooses the best or most logical combinations of ideas. In other word, it really

do not think! But for those writer who frequently experiences

difficulty in generating ideas, Brainstormer may be just the

answer. Its a tool that can helps them produce ideas and it

may improve their' creativity.

GRAMMAR AND USAGE CORRECTION SYMBOLS

Use these symbols to edit your own writing, to edit a classmate's writing, or to understand your teacher's comments.

Error	Problem
VERBS	
Vb	Incorrect verb form or verb ending
PP	Incorrect use of the past participle
Agr	Subject–verb agreement error
T	Incorrect verb tense
Vb Cons	Incorrect switch in verb tenses
PRONOUNS	
Pro	Incorrect pronoun form
Pro Agr	Pronoun–antecedent error
Pro Ref	Unclear pronoun reference or missing antecedent
PLURALS	
Pl	Incorrect plural ending on a noun
POSSESSIVES	
Poss	Incorrect possessive form or ending

EDITING WITH A WORD PROCESSOR

Here are some guidelines for editing the grammar and usage of your word-processed revisions.

1. The SEARCH function key can be used to help you identify a variety of grammar and usage errors. For example, you can search for troublesome verb forms (am, are, is, was, were, have, and has) and check to make sure that you have used the correct Standard Written English form of the verb and that it agrees with its subject.
2. You can also use the SEARCH function key to check for trouble-

> some pronouns (he, she, it, you, they, this, and whose) and check to make sure that you have used the correct form and that each pronoun clearly refers back to an antecedent.
> 3. If your word processor has a STYLE CHECKER or a STYLE ANALYZER program, use it to check for common usage errors in your revision.
> 4. Print a copy of your revision and ask a friend to help you identify and correct any grammar or usage errors.

WRITING ASSIGNMENT **WRITING, REVISING, AND EDITING AN ESSAY ABOUT COMPUTERS**

Below is an essay about computers by Lewis Thomas. After you read it, follow the directions below it and write an essay about computers.

TO ERR IS HUMAN

Everyone must have had at least one personal experience with a computer error by this time. Bank balances are suddenly reported to have jumped from 379 dollars into the millions, appeals for charitable contributions are mailed over and over to people with crazy-sounding names at your address, utility companies write that they're turning everything off—that sort of thing. If you manage to get in touch with someone and complain, you then get instantaneously typed, guilty letters from the same computer, saying, "Our computer was in error, and an adjustment is being made in your account."

These are supposed to be the sheerest, blindest accidents. Mistakes are not believed to be part of the normal behavior of a good machine. If things go wrong, it must be a personal, human error, the result of fingering, tampering, a button getting stuck. The computer, at its normal best, is infallible.

I wonder whether this can be true. After all, the whole point of computers is that they represent an extension of the human brain, vastly improved upon but nonetheless human, superhuman maybe. A good computer can think clearly and quickly enough to beat you at chess, and some of them have even been programmed to write obscure verse. They can do anything we can do, and more besides.

It is not yet known whether a computer has its own consciousness; it would be hard to find out about this. When you walk into one of those great halls now built for the huge machines, and stand listening, it is easy to imagine that the faint, distant noises are the sound of thinking, and the turning of the spools gives them the look of wild creatures rolling their eyes in the effort to concentrate, choking with information. But real thinking, and dreaming, are other matters.

On the other hand, the evidences for something like an *unconscious*, equivalent to ours, are all around in every mail. As extensions of the human brain, they have been constructed with the same property of error, spontaneous, uncontrolled, and rich in possibilities.

Mistakes are at the very base of human thought, embedded there, feeding the structure like root nodules. If we were not provided with the knack of being wrong, we could never get anything useful done. We think our way along by choosing between right and wrong alternatives, and the wrong choices have to be made as frequently as the right ones. We get along in life this way. We are built to make mistakes, coded for error.

We learn, as we say, by "trial and error." Why do we always say that? Why not "trial and rightness," or "trial and triumph"? The old phrase puts it that way because that is, in real life, the way it is done.

A good laboratory, like a good bank, or a corporation or a government, has to run like a computer. Almost everything is done flawlessly, by the book, and all the numbers add up to the predicted sums. The days go by. And then, if it is a lucky day, and a lucky laboratory, somebody makes a mistake: the wrong buffer, something in one of the blanks, a decimal misplaced in reading counts, the warm room off by a degree and a half, a mouse out of his box, or just a misreading of the day's protocol. Whatever, when the results come in, something is obviously screwed up, and then the action can begin.

The misreading is not the important error; it opens the way. The next step is the crucial one. If the investigator can bring himself to say, "But even so, look at that!" the new finding, whatever it is, is ready for snatching. What is needed, for progress to be made, is the move based on the error.

Whenever new kinds of thinking are about to be accomplished, or new varieties of music, there has to be an argument beforehand. With two sides debating in the same mind, haranguing, there is an amiable understanding that one is right and the other wrong. Sooner or later the thing is settled, but there can be no action at all if there are not the two sides, and the argument. The hope is in the faculty of wrongness, the tendency toward error. The capacity to leap across mountains of information to land lightly on the wrong side represents the highest of human endowments.

We are at our human finest, dancing with our minds, when there are more choices than two. This process is called exploration and is based on human fallibility. If we had only a single center in our brains, capable of responding only when a correct decision was to be made, instead of the jumble of different, credulous, easily conned clusters of neurons that provide for being flung off into blind alleys, up wrong trees, down dead ends, out into blue sky, along wrong turnings, around bends, we could only stay the way we are today, stuck fast.

The lower animals do not have this splendid freedom. They are limited, most of them, to absolute infallibility. Fish are flawless in everything they do. Individual cells in a tissue are mindless machines, perfect in their performance, as absolutely inhuman as bees.

We should have this mind as we become dependent on more complex computers for the arrangement of our affairs. Give the computers their heads, I say; let them go their way. Your average good computer can make calculations in an instant that would take a lifetime of slide rules for any of us. Think of what we could gain from the near infinity of precise, machine-made miscomputation that is now so easily within grasp. We could begin the solving of some of our hardest problems. What we need for moving ahead is a set of wrong alternatives much longer and more interesting than the short list of mistaken courses that any of us can think up right now. We need, in fact, an infinite list, and when it is printed out we need the computer to turn on itself and select, at random, the next way to go. If it is a big enough mistake, we could find ourselves on a new level, out in the clear, ready to move again.

Lewis Thomas

Do some prewriting for an essay about the importance of computers in your life. If you have never used a computer, think about whether you would like to learn how to use one. Why or why not? In what ways might computer programs help you? If you have used a computer, think about how the computer did or did not help you. Do you believe that computers are useful? Why or why not? Do you find them entertaining?

The focus of this essay is the current or potential value of computers in your life. Your readers are your classmates and your teacher. When you are finished writing your discovery draft, get feedback on it, and then revise and edit it using the techniques that you have practiced in this book.

ISSUES FOR YOUR JOURNAL

1. Has grammar been a problem for you? If so, why and how?
2. Are there any errors in your writing that you feel are impossible to correct, no matter how hard you try? What kinds of errors are these? Why do you think that they are so difficult for you to identify or to correct?
3. Did you enjoy reading and writing about computers? Why or why not?
4. What age is the drinking age in your state? What age do you think it should be? Why?
5. How do you feel about guns and about gun control? Who should be allowed to own guns? Who shouldn't be? Why?

CHAPTER TWELVE

EDITING SPELLING, CAPITALIZATION, AND PUNCTUATION

*A word is a design, once committed to
memory, we can recognize when we meet it
again. We do not learn to spell in obedience to
any "laws" of correctness. We learn to spell
merely because it is more convenient to
re-identify the picture we call the word if its
form, its outline, is standard and invariable
. . . two sum up the prakticle cas fer korekt
spelin and fer crekt punctueshn too deepens
on the advantejiz of won aksepted cod over
meny indavidule coads kurect speling savs the
tim of both reeder and riter.*

CLIFTON FADIMAN AND JAMES HOWARD

*Anyone who can improve a sentence of mine
by the omission or placing of a comma is
looked upon as my dearest friend.*

GEORGE MOORE

THE IMPORTANCE OF EDITING SPELLING, CAPITALIZATION, AND PUNCTUATION

The English language is difficult to spell because its spelling system is based primarily on meaning rather than on sound. Often, it is pointless to try to "sound out" the spelling of a word because a particular sound in it may be represented by several different combinations of letters. For instance, the "long a" sound can be spelled five different ways in English: "a" (paste), "ai" (bait), "ay" (may), "ei" (weigh), and "et" (bouquet). The playwright George Bernard Shaw once wrote that the word "fish" ought to be spelled "ghoti": "gh" can make an "f" sound (as in "rough"), "o" can make a "short i" sound (as in "women"), and "ti" can make an "sh" sound (as in "motion"). Complicating matters is the fact that there are very few useful spelling rules, and all of them have several exceptions.

Nevertheless, writers have to edit their spelling (and their capitalization and punctuation) because errors distract readers and can distort the meaning of a piece of writing so that it cannot even be understood. Furthermore, many readers have prejudices about people whose writing is filled with spelling, capitalization, and punctuation errors: the common stereotype is that such people are less intelligent and less educated than people who can write without these errors. Unfortunately, some teachers also believe this stereotype, and they fail essays that are intelligently written and coherently developed but are filled with spelling, capitalization, and punctuation errors. Don't let this happen to you. Proofread for your typical errors and correct them. In addition, don't let the fear of misspelling certain words keep you from using them. As you write and revise, choose words to convey your ideas and feelings and don't worry whether you have spelled them correctly. Just remember that you will have to look them up in a dictionary when you are finished revising.

PAIRED WRITING TASK **IDENTIFYING PROBLEMS IN SPELLING AND IN PUNCTUATION**

Work with a classmate on this task. Below is the essay by Sonja Rossini that was discussed in Chapter 8. This is how the essay looked *before* she edited it for errors in spelling and punctuation. Read the essay. Then, reread it and circle every error in spelling and punctuation that you can find. Work with your partner on correcting each error. When you are finished, compare your corrections to Rossini's edited version on page 207 of Chapter 8.

WOMEN WARRIORS

Margaret Mead, the famous anthrapologist, was once asked,
weather women should be permitted to be combat soldiers. She
answered, that they shouldn't because they are "Too Feirce".
I was intrigued by her answer; so I decided to do some reading
because I wanted to figure out what Mead meant.

I discovered many historical and modern myths about Women
Warriors. However in reality most primative and modern
societies, do not arm their women. Women can be drafted to
do non-combat service in offices. However they rarely take
part in any real combat or fight in wars. Still their not
fighting doesn't prove that they are "Too Feirce" to
fight.

Another notable anthrapologist Konrad Lorenz has pointed
out that, among most species of animals it is the males that
fight. He also stated that when female animals do fight
usually in defense of their babies they fight--to the death.
This may be a clue into Meads' comment; women may be feircer
deadlier fighters. In addition Lorenz noted, that threw
out history, in all kinds of cultures and civilazations men
and boys are the only ones who learn the rituels and the
rules of fighting. Maybe Mead means, that women don't know
these rituels and rules. If they were armed maybe they
would be so Feirce, that they would fight to the death of the
world.

Sonja Rossini

COMMON CAUSES OF SPELLING ERRORS

As Rossini's essay illustrates, writers usually have patterns of spelling errors that they repeat over and over in their writing. If a writer has *not* been diagnosed as learning disabled, then most of his or her typical spelling errors will result from one or more of the following causes:

1. *addition*—a letter is added to a word, usually because the writer pronounces the additional letter:
   inter*g*ration—integration
   ath*e*lete—athlete

2. *deletion*—a letter is dropped from a word, usually because the writer doesn't pronounce it:
   la*b*ratory—laboratory
   gove*r*ment—government

3. *transposition*—a letter is interchanged with the letter next to it, usually because the writer hasn't memorized a rule governing a tricky combination of letters:
   rec*ie*ve—receive
   effic*ei*nt—efficient

4. *substitution*—a letter is substituted for a letter that sounds similar, usually because the writer is unsure of the exact spelling of the sound:
   a*dd*itude—attitude
   civil*a*zation—civilization

5. *confusion about a spelling "demon"*—a word that is difficult to spell has been spelled incorrectly, usually because the writer didn't look up the correct spelling in a dictionary:
   di*s*sappear—disappear
   exist*a*nce—existence

6. *confusion with a homonym*—a word spelled like its homonym, usually because the writer doesn't know the spelling of the two homonyms (words that sound alike but that are spelled differently and have different meanings):
   principle—principal
   sight—cite—site

Here are some of Sonja Rossini's spelling errors. Can you figure out the most typical cause of her spelling problems?

anthr*a*pologist	anthropologist
prim*a*tive	primitive
civil*a*zations	civilizations
ritu*e*ls	rituals

These are "intelligent" spelling errors—each one represents the way that the writer pronounces the word. Rossini clearly has a pattern of problems with substitutions: all of these errors indicate confusion over the spelling of sounds that can be spelled several different ways. Since this type of error is so difficult to catch (because the writer isn't even aware that she has misspelled words), the only way to edit it is to ask someone else to help find the error. Most writing textbooks present lengthy lists of homonyms and spelling demons, but this seems pointless because each writer has his or her own set of troublesome words to look for and correct. Experienced writers don't refer to lists or homonyms or demons, and most of them don't memorize or use many of the rules of spelling. Instead, they proofread for their typical errors, they examine tricky words to see if these "look right," and they use a dictionary or a computer spell checker to check the spelling of troublesome words.

TECHNIQUES FOR IMPROVING SPELLING

Here are some suggestions for dealing with spelling problems and for improving spelling ability.

1. Don't worry about spelling while you are drafting or revising a piece of writing; wait until you are finished revising before you check your spelling. If you are writing an essay examination and you don't have time to edit, reread your paper carefully and look for any words whose spelling you are unsure of. If a dictionary is permitted on the test, look up each troublesome word; if not, try writing alternative spellings for each troublesome word and use the one that looks right.

2. Write down every word that you misspell in the Spelling Log in the appendix of this book. This is the best way to identify your own spelling problems. By listing every misspelled word (and its correct spelling), you will accomplish two important things:

(a) you will see the correct spelling of a word that usually confuses you and (b) you will see your typical patterns of errors (additions, deletions, transpositions, substitutions, "demon" confusions, or homonym confusions). If you have trouble determining your pattern of spelling errors, ask your teacher to help diagnose your problem. Once you have figured out the particular words or patterns that are causing problems for you, you will know exactly what to look for when you edit your spelling.

3. Use a standard college dictionary to look up the spelling and the punctuation of words when you are editing. If you don't know the first few letters of a word (which you must know in order to look it up), ask a classmate, a teacher, or a friend to help.

4. Create your own set of hints for remembering words that give you problems. For example, one student told me that she always uses the following sentence when she edits to help her remember how to spell the "there" homonyms: *They're* home in *their* house over *there*. And I still use the hints that my elementary school teacher taught me: The *principal* is my *pal* (not *ple*), and There's a *dance* in *attendance*.

5. Read material of increasing difficulty. Research on students' vocabulary development and on spelling skill indicates that both of these abilities are related to quantity and quality of reading. The more you read, the more words you will learn and the more easily you will be able to identify the correct spellings of words.

6. Do crossword puzzles and other word games that require you to match meaning and spelling. Do *not* do "word search" or "word hunt" puzzles since these don't include any information about the words' meanings and they only stress letter shapes.

EXERCISE   IDENTIFYING PATTERNS OF SPELLING ERRORS

Use the proofreading techniques discussed in Chapter 10 to find and circle every spelling error in the uncorrected paragraph that follows. Then write in the correct spelling of each misspelled word above the error, looking the word up in a dictionary if necessary. The first one has been done as an example.

```
If someone crashes into my car, destroying it and killing

me because I am not wearing my seat belt, so be it.  I made a
```

consequences

decision and I must take the (consquences.) I and millions of
other Americans are willing to do this, but our government
won't let us. Many states have past "seat belt laws" that
perscribe stiff fines for people who don't buckle up. I think
these laws are disasterous because they take away people's
indavidual rights. Each person has the right to decide how
much protection he or she needs. Its not fare for legaslators
to decide that every person in the state must wear a seat belt
at all times. I am an intellagent women and an excellent
driver, and I am capable of determining when I need to wear a
seat belt. Seat belt laws are more than an annoying
hinderance; they are an assault on our personal freedom.

SPELLING RULES

I have little faith in spelling rules. There are only three that I have found helpful in editing my own spelling:

First Rule: Doubling a Final Consonant

If you want to add a suffix to a word that ends in a single consonant, double this final consonant *if* three conditions are met:

a. The suffix begins with a vowel.
b. The original word consists of only one syllable or is accented on the final syllable.
c. In the original word a single vowel precedes a final single consonant.

Doubled	*Not Doubled*
control—controlled	peel—peeled
got—gotten	beat—beaten

The exception to this rule is any word that ends in an "x": tax—taxed.

Second Rule: Silent "e"

If you want to add a suffix to a word that ends in a silent (unpronounced) "e," drop the "e" *if* the suffix begins with a vowel, *but* keep the "e" if the suffix begins with a consonant.

hate—hating	hate—hateful
rare—rarity	rare—rarely

Some exceptions to this rule include the following words:

true—truly	mile—mileage
argue—argument	agree—agreeable

Other exceptions include any word that ends in an "e" that is preceded by a "g," "c," "o," or "y":

notice—noticeable
hoe—hoeing

An exception is the word "judge"—judgment.

Third Rule: Changing "y" to "i"

If you want to add a suffix to a word that ends in a "y," change this "y" to an "i" *if* the suffix begins with any letter except "i." (Keep the final "y" if the suffix begins with "i.")

marry—marriage	marry—marrying
satisfy—satisfied	satisfy—satisfying
pay—paid	pay—paying

Many teachers recommend that writers learn the "i/e" jingle ("i" before "e" except after "c" or when sounded like "a" as in "neighbor" and "weigh"). This jingle may be helpful, but it doesn't acknowledge all of the exceptions (including words like "either," "seize," "financier," and "height"). If "e/i" or "i/e" transpositions are a problem for you, resign yourself to looking up every word that contains these combinations.

EXERCISE **USING SPELLING RULES TO EDIT SPELLING**

Read the two uncorrected paragraphs below, and circle each misspelled word. Then try to use the spelling rules discussed on the preceding pages to correct each spelling error. When you are finished, use a dictionary to look up each word that you corrected in order to confirm that your spelling is correct.

Recently, more and more public institutions have stopped permiting people to smoke. Smokers are now restrictted to one small area in public rooms or they are forbiden to smoke at all. As a longtime smoker, I am more than annoied at these restrictions; I am outraged that my individual rights are being completly ignored. It has goten to the point where I am afraid to smoke in public for fear that some wierdo will attack me, demanding that I put out my cigarette immediatly. Since I hate getting into arguements with people I usually comply. But I am getting angryer and angryer at this denyal of my rights.

Although I smoke only occasionaly, I feel that smoking is my privilege. I know that smoking is bad for my health (and for my surviveal), but I have the right to do what I want to my body. I find it truely outragous that our government is granting non-smokers more legal rights than smokers have. This is irrational and inexcuseable. There has been a noticable decrease in the number of places where smokers are allowwed to smoke peacefully, and I think this is an illegal infringment of our rights.

PAIRED EXERCISE EDITING SPELLING

Practice your proofreading and editing skills by finding and correcting every spelling error in the following uncorrected essay. Work with a classmate on this essay and take turns looking up every word whose spelling you are unsure of.

Recently, there have been many laws passed aim at ensureing public safety: laws prohibitting drinking and driving, laws forbiding people to smoke in some areas, and laws requireing people to wear safety equipement in cars or motorcycles. Many Americans oppose these laws because they percieve them as infringments on their right to do whatever they want with their lives and their bodys. They feel that the goverment should not pass laws regulatting people's indavidual rights.

However, I beleive that the people who complian about the abridgement of their personal rights are basicly selfish and aren't considerring the consaquences of their actions. For instance, how many smokers consider how irratateing their habit is to non-smokers? Moreover, recent resaerch has shown that breatheing the smoke from someone else's cigerette can increase a nonsmoker's chances of getting cancer. Since when do smokers have the "right" to give other people cancer? And when the smokers themselfs get cancer or emphasyma, who has to pay their medical and hospital bills? All of us do, in the form of our medical insurence premiums and our taxes.

Moreover, I particuly rezent people who choose to drive without seat belts. In an accident, they will not be able to retane control of their cars and thus they are more likely to injure pedestrains and other drivers around them. Their

```
contemt for seat belts jepordizes other people's safety.

Therefore, when it is apparant than an indavidual's behavior

has (or can potentialy have) adverce affects on those around

him or her, then that behavior has to be controled.  This is

the principle reason why I support our societies' laws

protecting public safety.
```

CAPITALIZATION RULES

There are several rules governing the conventions of capitalization in Standard Written English. Since readers expect these conventions to be followed (and get distracted or annoyed if they aren't), writers have to memorize these rules or look them up when they are editing their writing.

1. Capitalize the first word of every sentence and of every sentence within a sentence.
   He said, "This is the book that I need."

2. Capitalize the names of specific people, places, groups, businesses, and events.
   Jack Logan was wounded in the Vietnam War while fighting in the Fifth Division in Cambodia.

3. Capitalize people's titles and their abbreviations.
   Karen L. Greenberg, Ph.D. or Dr. Karen L. Greenberg

4. Capitalize the names of specific courses, religions, languages, and organizations.
   This semester, I studied the Republican party in my Political Science 101 course, and I learned some Greek in my world religions course.
   (Note: If the writer of the sentence above had left out "101," then "political science" would *not* be capitalized.)

5. Capitalize titles of works (except words of three letters or fewer).
   "Women Warriors"
   Death of a Salesman

EXERCISE   **EDITING CAPITALIZATION**

Edit the following uncorrected paragraph by finding and correcting every error in capitalization.

although i am not the least bit suicidal, i believe that all humans deserve the right to die when and how they wish to. self-inflicted death is not murder. I strongly oppose new york state's law making suicide illegal and punishing people who help others commit suicide. Also, even though i am a devout protestant, i do not regard suicide as a violation of god's laws. For example, ten years ago, when dr. henry p. van dusen and his wife committed suicide, i felt that god would not damn them since they were simply exercising their free will. dr. van dusen was the president of the union theological seminary (the most famous protestant seminary in the world). the van dusens were famous here in america and in many european and african countries where they lectured extensively. however, no one knew how ill they had become and how much they depended on nurses for even basic functions like eating and bathing. their suicides, which were discussed in detail in the "people" sections of <u>time</u> and <u>newsweek</u> magazines, shocked and angered many people. however, many others, including myself, understood that the van dusens wanted to live and die with dignity and they did. everyone deserves these rights.

PUNCTUATION PROBLEMS

Many writers have one of the two basic problems with punctuation—underpunctuating and overpunctuating—and either problem can drive readers to distraction. Read each of the following "sentences" aloud to see an example of each problem:

1. Another notable anthropologist Konrad Lorenz has pointed out that among most species of animals it is the males who fight when females do fight usually in defense of their babies they fight to the death.
2. Another notable anthropologist, Konrad Lorenz, has pointed out, that among most species of animals, it is the males, who fight; when females do fight, usually in defense (of their babies), they fight—to the death.

Why did you have trouble understanding each of these "sentences"? One reason is that punctuation signals "chunks" of meaning. Here are the chunks of meaning in the preceding "sentence":

Another notable anthropologist / Konrad Lorenz / has pointed out that among most species of animals / it is the males who fight / when females do fight / usually in defense of their babies / they fight to the death

When we speak, we signal these chunks by pausing briefly after meaningful word groups and by stressing specific words. When we write, we use punctuation marks to represent these pauses and stresses. For this reason, it is difficult to grasp the meaning of the underpunctuated "sentence" above. For the same reason, an overpunctuated piece is even more difficult to read. In "sentence" 2, the unnecessary punctuation keeps forcing the reader to stop in the middle of a chunk of meaning, and this is extremely annoying. Some writers can read their writing aloud and hear where the various punctuation marks belong. For example, read aloud the correctly punctuated paragraph below, and consider whether you pause very briefly at the commas.

Another notable anthropologist, Konrad Lorenz, has pointed out that among most species of animals, it is the males who fight. When females do fight, usually in defense of their babies, they fight to the death.

Many writers have difficulty "hearing" punctuation, and they have to learn to punctuate by trying out all of the different punctuation marks and examining readers' responses to them. Punctuation serves six basic functions:

1. Punctuation ends sentences.
2. Punctuation connects sentences.
3. Punctuation separates items in a series within a sentence.
4. Punctuation separates words or phrases that modify a sentence.
5. Punctuation encloses or emphasizes interrupting material.
6. Punctuation separates quoted words or phrases from the rest of a sentence.

These six basic functions will be used to categorize the rules of punctuation that follow.

Ending Sentences

Once writers have decided whether their ideas should be expressed as statements, exclamations, or questions, they have to follow the conventions of Standard Written English punctuation. They must use a period to end each statement, an exclamation point to end a strongly worded statement, and a question mark to end a question. Here is an example of each "terminal" punctuation mark:

I think playing with punctuation can be fun.

I think playing with punctuation is terrific!

Is playing with punctuation really so interesting?

Connecting Sentences

The conventions of Standard Written English allow writers to use a semicolon, a colon, or a comma (with a coordinator) to connect sentences.

- A semicolon can be used to join two sentences when the idea in the second sentence is a continuation of the one in the first. It indicates a pause that is greater than a comma's but not as great as a period's.

    I just turned eighteen; now I am legally an adult.

- A colon can be used to connect two sentences when the second sentence contains an illustration of the first.

  I am now legally an adult: I can drive and I can be drafted to fight for my country.

- A comma and a coordinator can be used to link two sentences.

  I am legally an adult, but I am prohibited from drinking.

Separating Three or More Words or Phrases Used in a Series

In academic writing, a comma should be used to separate words or phrases or sentences in a series within a sentence.

New York, Connecticut, and Rhode Island have raised the drinking age from 18 to 21.

Separating Modifiers from the Rest of the Sentence

In Chapter 8, you practiced adding and moving descriptive words and phrases in sentences to make them more interesting and informative. Descriptive modifiers can be placed at the beginning, the middle, or the end of a sentence:

In New York and many other states, young people cannot drink until they are twenty-one years old.

Different handbooks give different rules about using commas to punctuate modifiers that are used to introduce or to end a sentence. In general, here are the conventional rules for punctuating material that introduces or interrupts a sentence:

- A comma should be used to separate an introductory word or phrase from the main sentence, but it is *not* necessary to separate a descriptive word or phrase at the end of a sentence.

  According to the law in New York, young people cannot drink until they are twenty-one years old.

  Young people cannot drink until they are twenty-one years old according to the law in New York.

- A comma can be used before *and* after descriptive words or phrases that interrupt the flow of a sentence, if these descriptive words or phrases are not necessary for identifying the subject of the sentence.

> Young people in New York, who may want to drink only rarely, cannot drink until they are twenty-one.

In this sentence, "who may want to drink only rarely," is not essential to the meaning. Do *not* use commas to surround interrupting modifiers that *are* essential to the meaning of the sentence.

> Young people in New York who want to drink illegally will always find a way to do so.

In this sentence, the phrase "who want to drink illegally" is necessary in order to let the reader know exactly which young people the writer is discussing.

EXERCISE   **EDITING COMMAS**

Proofread the following uncorrected paragraphs for comma errors. Insert commas where they have been omitted and cross out commas that are not necessary. Some of the commas are used correctly.

I have known how to use guns, since I was ten years old. My dad taught me how to shoot a gun, just as, his dad had taught him when he was ten. When I was younger, my family would go hunting, in the woods, every fall and spring. We would set traps, to catch rabbits raccoons and muskrats, and we would use rifles to shoot deer and birds. Shooting and trapping, was our way of life. These activities bound us all together, and provided us, with tons of food.

Recently, however, I have begun to question the "innocent" pleasure that I felt, in those days. I keep reading, about how hunting and trapping is making some animals extinct, and is destroying the breeding habitats of others. I think about animals that chewed their legs off, so as to free themselves from traps. I wonder about how animals who did not escape our traps felt, when we clubbed them to death. I

wonder how innocent, or how guilty I was. Lately when I read
all of the posters of the National Rifle Association, that
talk about the glories of hunting the rewards of trapping and
the joy of using guns I get a little nauseous. I think the
"gun tradition," has ended in my family. I will not teach my
son to shoot.

Enclosing or Emphasizing Interrupting Material

Parentheses and dashes are used to interrupt a sentence's structure to add information. Use dashes when you want to make the interrupting words stand out; use parentheses to deemphasize the interrupting material. Here is an example of each:

The Constitution protects the right of hunters to own sporting guns, but most of the guns used to commit murders (especially "Saturday night specials" and machine guns) are not recreational weapons.

The Constitution protects the right of hunters to own sporting guns, but most of the guns used to commit murders—especially "Saturday night specials" and machine guns—are not recreational weapons.

The first sentence focuses on "guns used to commit murders," and the parentheses are used to give two examples. The second sentence uses dashes to emphasize the two types of guns that are most often used to commit murders.

Separating Quoted Material
from the Rest of the Sentence

A pair of quotation marks should be used to set off the exact words that someone has spoken or written. Quotations of three or more words are usually preceded by a comma:

President Bush said, "I believe in raising the national drinking age to twenty-one."

When the quotation opens the sentence, the comma goes inside the closing quotation marks.

"I believe in raising the national drinking age to twenty-one," said President Bush.

The above quotations are "direct"; the exact words that someone has spoken are recorded. The following sentence contains an "indirect" quotation; a summary of what was spoken or written is presented. Quotation marks should *not* be used to set off an indirect quotation.

President Bush said he believed in raising the national drinking age to twenty-one.

A pair of quotation marks is also used to set off titles of stories, poems, magazine articles, and chapters of books:

I read an article called "Teenage Alcohol Abuse Today" in *Newsweek* Magazine.

Periods and commas are always placed inside the closing quotation marks:

The president said, "I will sign a drinking-age bill if Congress passes it."

Colons and semicolons are always placed outside the closing quotation marks:

The president said, "I will sign a drinking-age bill if the Congress passes it"; however, later he added that the bill "has to be bipartisan."

Question marks, exclamation points, and dashes are placed inside the closing quotation marks when they are part of the quoted material:

The president asked, "Will the bill be bipartisan?"

(The question mark is part of the direct question being quoted.)

They are placed outside the closing quotation marks when they are part of a larger sentence.

What does the president mean by "bipartisan"?

(The question mark ends the question in which the word "bipartisan" is enclosed.)

THE APOSTROPHE: USES AND RULES

The most frequent spelling error in student essays seems to be the incorrect use of the apostrophe. Incorrect apostrophes can distort your meaning, so proofread for them every time you edit a piece of writing. Here are some guidelines for using apostrophes:

1. Add an apostrophe and an "s" to form the possessive of nouns that do not end in "s."

    Dr. **Van Dusen's** suicide shocked the world, but his **family's** response was sympathetic.

2. Add an apostrophe to a singular noun that ends in "s."

    Reverend James **Lewis's** response was that "they died with dignity."

3. Add an apostrophe alone to form the possessive of plural nouns that already end in "s."

    The **Van Dusens'** suicide shocked the world, but their **friends'** reactions were sympathetic.

4. Do *not* add an apostrophe to a possessive pronoun.

    Although suicide is a way of dying with dignity, **its** effects are felt by family and friends.

5. Use an apostrophe to replace omitted letters in contractions.

    We **shouldn't** say that suicide is wrong because we **don't** have the right to judge other people's decisions.

Note: Remember that many teachers and employers think that contractions are inappropriate for formal writing. If you want to make your writing sound more academic or more formal, rewrite all of your contractions and any other abbreviations. For instance, read the sentence in the preceding example and then read the following sentence:

    We should not say that suicide is wrong because we do not have the right to judge other people's decisions.

The sentence with contractions sounds less formal than the one without contractions.

EXERCISE **EDITING APOSTROPHES**

Practice your skills at proofreading and editing unconventional uses of apostrophes by finding and correcting all of the problems in the following uncorrected paragraphs.

I just turned eighteen; now I am legally an adult. I can be drafted to fight for my country and die defending it's freedom. But I cannot buy a drink because most state's drinking age is now 21. The public and many congressmen and women believe a higher drinking age will save lives. They believe that most of the alcohol-related car crashes in this country are caused by drunken teenagers' aged 18-21. However they never cite evidence supporting their beliefs. And after extensive research on this topic, I have not seen one study that provides reliable scientific evidence for raising our countrys' drinking age from 18 to 21. Higher drinking ages do not reduce the number of accidents or deaths due to alcohol abuse.

In fact, the people responsible for most drunken driven accidents and fatalities are 21-24 year-old drivers'. Maybe our congresspeople would like to raise the drinking age to 25! Moreover, I think that Americas' history shows that prohibition is not an effective deterrent to alcohol abuse. If you make it illegal for people under 21 to drink in the open, they will drink anyway, and probably drink more and get into more trouble than if they could drink in places where their behavior could be supervised by adult's. I think congress should trust us and should lower the drinking age to 18.

EXERCISE   CHOOSING AND USING PUNCTUATION

Here are two uncorrected paragraphs without any punctuation.
Insert punctuation marks (periods, question marks, semicolons, co-

lons, commas, apostrophes, dashes, or quotation marks) wherever they are needed. Make sure that you capitalize the first letter of every new sentence that you create.

Why is the speeding limit in our nation cities 55 miles per hour has any study ever shown that this speed limit saves gasoline and if so how much gas does this speed limit actually save I have yet to see some solid evidence supporting a speed limit last week I heard our governor say that he wants to raise the highway speed limit to 60 miles per hour he said I believe that raising the speeding limit will lessen the number of fatalities on our states roads I disagree with him I doubt that a legal speed limit whether it is 55 or any other number of miles per hour really saves as many lives as our politicians tell us it does most accidents particularly fatal ones are caused by drunken or otherwise incapacitated drivers not by drivers who are speeding

As anyone who has ever driven in our major cities knows no one can speed the traffic is usually too heavy there are too many pedestrians and there are frequent traffic lights and stop signs thus the real issue is the speed limit on highways why shouldnt drivers go as fast as they want on Americas highways most highways in America are long open stretches of road you can drive for miles and miles on most highways and never even see a car except for the traffic cop who is hiding behind a billboard waiting to catch speeders all in all I think the 55 mile per hour speed limit is absurd.

EXERCISE **CHOOSING CORRECT PUNCTUATION**

The paragraph below is excerpted from an essay by the writer E. B. White. Each of White's punctuation marks has been replaced by a blank line. In each blank, write in the punctuation mark that seems most appropriate to signal the intended meaning (period, semicolon, colon, dash, parentheses, or comma). If you put in a period, capitalize the first letter of the word that follows.

There are roughly three New Yorks _____ there is _____ first _____ the New York of the man or woman who was born there _____ who takes the city for granted and accepts its size and its turbulence as natural and inevitable _____ second _____ there is the New York of the commuter _____ the city that is devoured by locusts each day and spat out each night _____ third _____ there is the New York of the person who was born somewhere else and came to New York in quest of something _____ of these three trembling cities the greatest is the last _____ the city of final destination _____ the city that is a goal _____ it is this third city that accounts for New York's high-strung disposition _____ its poetical deportment _____ its dedication to the arts and its incomparable achievements _____ commuters give the city its tidal restlessness _____ natives give it solidity and continuity _____ but the settlers give it passion.

When you finish this exercise, turn to page 343 to see the author's punctuation marks.

SPELLING AND PUNCTUATION CORRECTION SYMBOLS

Use these symbols to edit your own writing, to edit a classmate's writing, or to understand your teacher's comments.

Error	Problem
sp	spelling error
'	insert an apostrophe
:	insert a colon
,	insert a comma
—	insert a dash
=	insert a hyphen
.	insert a period
?	insert a question mark
"	insert a quotation mark
;	insert a semicolon

EDITING WITH A WORD PROCESSOR

Here are some guidelines for editing the spelling, capitalization, and punctuation of your word-processed revisions.

1. Always use your word processor's SPELLING CHECK program. This program has a built-in dictionary of correctly spelled words, and when the program finds a word in your text that does not match any words in its dictionary, it identifies the word as incorrectly spelled. The program will not automatically correct the word (because it may be a proper name, a technical word, or a word that is not in the program's dictionary). You must decide whether the identified word is correctly spelled, and if it is not, you must choose the correct spelling or type in a correction.
2. Most SPELLING CHECK programs will also identify words that are incorrectly capitalized.
3. Use the SEARCH function key to search for your "demon" words—words that you always misspell.
4. Use the SEARCH function key to search for apostrophes (and other troublesome punctuation marks) and make sure that you have used each one correctly.
5. Print a copy of your revision and ask a friend to help you identify and correct any errors in spelling, capitalization, and punctuation.

WRITING ASSIGNMENT   WRITING, REVISING, AND EDITING
AN ESSAY ABOUT INDIVIDUAL RIGHTS

Most of the readings and exercises in this unit concerned controversial "individual rights": smoking, drinking and driving, refusing to wear seat belts, committing suicide, and using guns. Choose one of these issues for an essay that will convince your classmates of the soundness of your opinions on the topic. Write a discovery draft and get feedback from your classmates. Then revise your draft using the techniques that you practiced in Chapters 6, 7, 8, and 9. Next, edit your revisions using the methods that you learned in Chapters 10 and 11, and in this chapter. When you are finished editing, exchange essays with a classmate. After you read your classmate's essay, circle every unconventional form and every problem and error that you find. Return the essays and discuss them. Then correct every problem or error that your classmate found in your essay.

Here is the punctuation that E. B. White used in his paragraph about New York. Compare these punctuation marks to the ones that you inserted on page 341.

> There are roughly three New Yorks. There is, first, the New York of the man or woman who was born there, who takes the city for granted and accepts its size and its turbulence as natural and inevitable. Second, there is the New York of the commuter—the city that is devoured by locusts each day and spat out each night. Third, there is the New York of the person who was born somewhere else and came to New York in quest of something. Of these three trembling cities the greatest is the last—the city of final destination, the city that is a goal. It is this third city that accounts for New York's high-strung disposition, its poetical deportment, its dedication to the arts and its incomparable achievements. Commuters give the city its tidal restlessness; natives give it solidity and continuity; but the settlers give it passion.

Note that White omitted the comma after "arts" in the second-to-the-last sentence. If this paragraph were a piece of academic writing, a comma would be required after "its dedication to the arts" in order to separate it from the final phrase in this series ("and its incomparable achievements"). (See page 334 for a discussion of this comma rule.)

ISSUES FOR YOUR JOURNAL

1. How do you feel about always having to look up troublesome words in a dictionary? Is doing this worth the effort? Why or why not?
2. What are your strengths and weaknesses as a student? How can you become a better student?

3. How effective are you at controlling time? How well do you plan and organize your time? Do you keep a daily list of things "to do"? Why or why not?

4. Are you continuing to write on a regular basis in your journal? Why or why not?

5. How have your writing processes and attitudes changed over the past semester?

PART FOUR

APPLYING YOUR WRITING SKILLS

CHAPTER THIRTEEN

APPLYING YOUR SKILLS TO COLLEGE WRITING ASSIGNMENTS

In writing the academic paper you are learning to select and organize the significant information of that discipline; by doing this, you make the information your own in a way that you never do when you memorize facts or formulas.

IRVIN HASHIMOTO
BARRY KROLL
JOHN SCHAFER

WRITING, REVISING, AND EDITING IN COLLEGE COURSEWORK

What does the epigraph by Hashimoto, Kroll, and Schafer mean? These three composition teachers are suggesting that students can use writing as a tool for learning the subject matter of their college courses. Many teachers agree with this suggestion and design writing assignments that help students find and solve problems in their disciplines. Typical college writing assignments require students to clarify, summarize, analyze, and evaluate the concepts and information that have been presented. Another type of writing frequently assigned in college is the research essay, which requires students to discover sources and to use the notes that they take from these sources to expand and illustrate their own ideas.

Although different disciplines require different strategies for organizing and presenting material, the techniques of effective writing are the same in every discipline. These techniques are the ones that you have been practicing in this book: prewriting; limiting a topic; writing a working thesis statement; considering focus, purpose, and audience; developing appropriate supporting details; and revising and editing.

CUES AND CLUES IN SPECIALIZED WRITING ASSIGNMENTS

Different disciplines organize and present material in different ways. How are students supposed to know these various approaches to presenting material? One way is to examine the cues and clues in the writing assignments of different courses. A **cue** is a word that suggests the strategy to be used in responding to the assignment. Cue words signal different methods of selecting, developing, and presenting details. Here are some cue words and the strategies that they suggest:

Possible Cues in a Summary:

Summarize: Select the main points and briefly describe them in a paragraph or two.

Describe: Give details about a person, object, or idea that will enable readers to experience it or understand your perception of it.

Outline: List the main ideas and the most important details within each idea.

Possible Cues in an Analysis:

Analyze: Describe each part of an object, an idea, or a problem separately and show how these parts relate to one another and to the whole.

Define: Explain what the object, person, or idea is and is not and give some examples of it.

Classify: Separate the parts of an object, an idea, or a problem into groups according to characteristics that group members share.

Compare: Describe each object, person, or idea and show how they are similar.

Contrast: Describe each object, person, or idea and show how they are different.

Trace: Begin with the first occurrence of the event and describe its progress up to the present.

Discuss: This catch-all term usually means define or analyze and illustrate.

Explain: Like "discuss," this also usually means define or analyze and illustrate.

Illustrate: Present several examples.

Possible Cues in an Evaluation or Argument:

Evaluate: Explain the worth or value of someone or something by examining its good and bad points.

Compare/Contrast: Describe objects, persons, or ideas to show which is better or more effective.

Argue: State your point of view and provide support or evidence for it.

GROUP WRITING TASK ANALYZING WRITING ASSIGNMENTS IN DIFFERENT DISCIPLINES

Get into a group of four and examine the assignments below. Underline the cue words in each assignment. In the space below each, write down what you think the assignment is asking writers to do. Be specific and don't merely repeat the words in the assignment. The first one has been done as an example.

1. (Sociology) <u>Select</u> any society that we have studied and <u>discuss</u> its social stratification.

Choose one society that the course included and describe its social classes. Explain how each social class is determined, and give examples of each class.

2. (Economics) Which of the various taxation policies that we have discussed is the fairest to all Americans? Justify your selection.

3. (Art History) In a concise, organized fashion, outline the contemporary art trends that we have discussed in the past five sessions. Then, choose two of these trends and compare them.

4. (Political Science) Select one of the congressional bills that we have discussed and explain its development from a draft bill into the current law.

SUMMARIES

Summary writing is the most frequently assigned type of writing in college courses *and* in most jobs. **A summary is a brief description of the main idea and key supporting points of something you have read, heard, or experienced.** Teachers often ask students to summarize lectures or reading material because summarizing is an excellent way of learning. Writing a summary requires a writer to identify the most important parts of an explanation or an argument and to present these parts in his or her own words. In order to write a summary of a discussion or a reading, you need to take notes on the main ideas and the most important details. Turn these notes into a summary by asking yourself what the main point of the reading or lecture was: "What was I supposed to learn from this?" State this main idea as the opening sentence of your summary. Then, in your own words, briefly state the key ideas and the important details. Present these ideas and details in the order in which they occurred in the material that you are summarizing.

Remember that a summary is not a paraphrase. When you write a summary, you should briefly describe the main points in the writer's explanation or argument. For a paraphrase, however, you should restate the writer's ideas, main points, and details in your own words. Thus a paraphrase might be as long as the original piece of writing, whereas a summary is almost always shorter. The length of a summary depends on your purpose. If you are summarizing a work that you will discuss in detail in an essay, you can write a one-sentence summary. You might also write a very brief summary of a work that you want to read for a research paper or for a test. Here is a student's brief summary of the essay about "labels" on pages 164–67 of Chapter 6:

> This essay describes how students who are labeled as learning disabled feel and act, and it discusses ways to help them ignore their labels and succeed.

If you are summarizing a work in order to refer to it in a research essay, you might want to write a summary that is a paragraph in length. Here is a student's paragraph-length summary of the essay on labels:

> This essay describes the problems caused by the labels that teachers and psychologists attach to students. Specifically, the author discusses the way in which students who are labeled as "learning disabled" feel and act. He notes that often these students come to believe that this label means they cannot do well in school, and they start to use the label as an excuse for not doing as well as they could or should do. The author also discusses ways of helping students ignore their labels and succeed.

Turn to Chapter 6 and reread the entire essay which is summarized above. Do you think the summary leaves out any important ideas? If so, what are they?

WRITING ACTIVITY **WRITING A SUMMARY**

Reread the essay by Sylvia Ann Hewlett on pages 95–97 of Chapter 4. On a separate piece of paper, write a one-sentence summary of the essay. Then write a one-paragraph summary of the essay. Describe the writer's points in the order in which she discusses them.

GROUP EXERCISE **COMPARING SUMMARIES**

Get into a group of three or four students. Read each other's summaries of the Hewlett essay and compare them. Make one list for the points that were present in all of your summaries and make a separate list for the points that were in some summaries but not in others. Decide whose summary is best and be prepared to say why.

WRITING ACTIVITY **COMPARING A SUMMARY AND A PARAPHRASE**

Choose one of the essays in this book and summarize it in one or two paragraphs. Then write a paraphrase of the essay. Be prepared to explain the differences between your summary and your paraphrase.

ANALYSES

Another type of writing frequently assigned in college and business is the analysis. **When you analyze something, you break it down to learn about its parts and to show how they are related to one another and to the whole.** Although you may not be aware of it, you are analyzing all the time that you are awake: noticing things and people and considering how they have or haven't changed, examining problems and figuring them out, seeing something enjoyable and thinking about why you liked it. Analysis is a basic human thought process.

Here are examples of assignments that call for analysis:

1. Write a critical analysis of William Faulkner's *The Sound and the Fury*.

    This assignment asks you to describe each part of the book (the plot, characters, setting, symbolism, and so forth) and to explain how these parts worked together to achieve the effect that the book had on you.

2. Explain the concept of artificial intelligence.
   This assignment asks you to define what artificial intelligence means and to give examples of it.

3. Analyze television advertisements in terms of their audience appeal.
   This assignment asks you to classify different subgroups of television ads, to describe the characteristics that these subgroups share, and to give examples of them.

4. Discuss the causes of the defeat of the Equal Rights Amendment.
   This assignment asks you to describe the major and minor reasons why this amendment was defeated.

A STUDENT RESPONSE

Here is a student's analysis of Sylvia Ann Hewlett's essay at the end of Chapter 4. Note that Hewlett's essay is itself an analysis.

In her essay "Running Hard Just to Keep Up," the economist Sylvia Ann Hewlett explains the impact of the current economy on working families. Not only do most American families have difficulty making money for their basic necessities, but they also have no time for each other. According to Hewlett, both of these problems impact negatively on the family structure and the children.

Hewlett cites several causes of today's problems. First, as the wages of male workers have declined, their wives have been forced to work, but the combined earning of most couples is still not enough to buy a house or health insurance or to pay for college educations. Recent increases in the tax rates have worsened this problem. In addition, increasing numbers of children come home to an empty house after school and when their parents do get home, there is not much "quality" time left in the day for family togetherness.

Hewlett makes several suggestions to remedy these problems, but I strongly doubt that our government will adopt any of them. Indeed, Hewlett's essay convinced me that things are going

to get a lot worse for American families before they begin to get
better.

Thomas Stapleford

WRITING ACTIVITY   WRITING AN ANALYSIS

In the essay on pages 226–229 of Chapter 8, Betty McCollister
analyzes the causes and effects of the "Neandertal Stereotype."
Choose a stereotype that makes you uncomfortable and analyze its
causes and effects. Do some brainstorming about the reasons why this
stereotype developed and about the consequences of this stereotype for
the people to whom it is applied.

WRITING ACTIVITY   ANALYZING DIFFERENT VIEWS OF A PROBLEM

For this activity, you will write two analyses of a problem that is
of great concern to students and administrators at your school. Select
a problem and then follow the directions below.

ANALYSIS #1

Analyze the problem from the students' point of view. Interview
friends and classmates about the factors that are causing this problem
or making it worse. Based on your interviews, define the problem and
analyze its causes *from the students' perspective*. Use the notes that you
took during your interviews to prewrite, write, revise, and edit your
analysis.

ANALYSIS #2

Analyze your school's problem from the administrators' point of
view. Interview several administrators about the problem and use the
information from your interviews to define the problem and analyze
its causes *from the administrators' perspective*.

EVALUATIONS

Teachers of every academic subject frequently ask students to
write evaluations, because the process of evaluating requires students
to explore topics in depth: one cannot judge something—an idea, a
viewpoint, a theory—until one truly understands it. **Typically, an eval-**

uation assignment asks writers to defend or attack a point of view or to compare it with competing viewpoints. Also, when an assignment asks writers to "respond to" or "react to" a viewpoint, it is asking them to evaluate it—to judge it according to criteria that are appropriate for the subject. When you do freewriting and brainstorming for an evaluation assignment, think about whether you agree or disagree totally with the view or if you agree or disagree only partially. If you agree with the view, you can defend it by using one or more of the following strategies:

- Explain your reasons for agreeing with it.
- Do research and offer supporting evidence for the view from experts in the field.
- Describe any criticisms of the view (that have been discussed in class or that you have read about) and show why each is not valid or conclusive.

If you disagree with the view, you can attack it by using one or more of the following strategies:

- Describe all of the problems in the view and explain why the view is not accurate or not logical.
- Do research and explain the criticisms of the view offered by experts in the field.
- Explain why the view has not been supported logically or with enough evidence.

If you have mixed responses to the view, you will have to provide reasons why you agree in part and disagree in part.

You can use the same prewriting techniques—freewriting, brainstorming, and clustering—that you would use for any essay to develop your initial responses to the issue or viewpoint. Then, write a working thesis statement that presents your subject and your evaluation or judgment of it. Next, write out the criteria or the standards by which you will evaluate your subject. In any evaluation, it is important for the writer to let the reader know, at the beginning of the essay, what criteria he or she is using. This lets the reader know what to expect. For example, what is your reaction to the following brief evaluation of a word-processing program?

"Volkswriter Deluxe is terrific. It's the best program that I've used and I recommend it highly."

This writer has given her judgment but hasn't provided any criteria—she hasn't told us *why*, or according to what standards, Volkswriter Deluxe is so good. Now look at her revision:

> "Volkswriter Deluxe is the best program on the market. It is easy to learn and use and it performs a wide range of tasks. And best of all, it's less expensive than its competitors."

This revision presents the three criteria that are most important to this writer: ease of learning and use, comprehensiveness, and price. Each discipline has its own set of criteria. For example, when you analyze a fictional work of literature, you might evaluate it according to criteria such as "believability of characters" or "effectiveness of language." If you were asked to evaluate an economic theory, you might use criteria such as "comprehensiveness" and "validity."

In order to write an effective evaluation, you need to choose criteria that are appropriate for your readers and that are most likely to convince them. Although your audience is usually your teacher, don't assume that he or she knows everything about the topic and that it is acceptable to leave out information. In fact, the first information that you should present is a precise, accurate statement of the view that you are evaluating. Then, give your opinion about it (in your introduction), so that your reader will know what to expect from your essay. Make a list of your criteria, and under each criterion list all of the reasons for your judgment. Then write a discovery draft of your essay. Your goals in this discovery draft are to judge your subject and to justify your evaluation according to appropriate criteria. If your reasons and evidence conflict with your working thesis statement, develop a new one. If you need to consult public sources, consult them, take notes, and incorporate these notes into your discovery draft.

A PROFESSIONAL RESPONSE

Here is a draft of an evaluation of a word-processing program. I wrote the evaluation for a magazine for writers. The program is the one that I used for this book.

```
AN EVALUATION OF VOLKSWRITER DELUXE

If you write for a living or for pleasure, you probably

do your writing on a computer with a word-processing program.

If not, you should get one immediately, and the one you should
```

get is Volkswriter Deluxe, version 2.1, from Lifetree
Software. The acid test for any word-processing program is
its power--how well and how quickly it performs a wide variety
of tasks. Volkswriter Deluxe is one powerful little program,
and--like its automotive namesake--it's also easy to learn,
fun to use, relatively cheap.

Volkswriter Deluxe is not a luxury program--it doesn't
create footnotes or endnotes, it doesn't have a spelling
checker in it, and it doesn't compute mathematics. However,
it does just about anything else you might want to do to a
piece of text--creating, modifying, formatting, and printing
quickly and easily. The program is packed with features for
creating, moving, adding, and deleting text. It uses the IBM
PC's function keys to invoke all editing commands, so you
don't have to worry about key combinations. If you forget any
function key's command, you can call up an on-screen outline
that tells you (in four short lines) what every key (and every
combination of keys) does.

I am not particularly adept with computers, and I almost
gave up word processing totally when I first tried to learn
Wordstar and Microsoft Word. Then I found Volkswriter Deluxe,
and life got easier. Its set-up is almost completely
automated, and its on-disk tutorials are excellent. It is
truly easy to use, and best of all, it offers power and fun
for a relatively cheap price (about $250). I recommend it
highly.

Karen L. Greenberg

1. What criteria did I use to judge this product?

2. What evidence did I provide to support my judgment? How convincing is this evidence?

Here are some points to remember when you write and revise an evaluation:

- Choose criteria that are logical and appropriate for your topic *and* for your audience.
- Communicate these criteria clearly and convince readers that these criteria are important.
- Communicate your point of view on the topic.
- Provide evidence (observations, experiences, facts, testimony, and statistics) to support each of the reasons for your viewpoint.
- Make sure that your evidence is relevant to your criteria and to your audience.

WRITING ACTIVITY **WRITING AN EVALUATION**

Choose one or more of the topics below to evaluate in an essay. Make sure that your point of view and criteria are clear to readers.

a. the quality of a novel that you read recently
b. the quality of your school's newspaper
c. the fairness of your school's grading policy
d. the city in which you are currently living
e. the quality of your high school versus the quality of your college
f. the advantages of living in a dormitory versus living in an apartment
g. the quality of different types of computers or computer programs
h. the effectiveness of different types of teaching methods

RESEARCH ESSAYS

Many college teachers assign research essays in order to help students learn to use sources intelligently. In Chapter 6, you learned how to consult public sources—people, books, periodicals, and reference works—to gather additional details for an essay and to revise a working thesis statement. Writing a research essay requires a writer to consult a wide variety of sources of information and to sort out, analyze, and organize this information logically and coherently. The process of producing an effective research essay is basically a process of becoming an independent learner: one learns where and how to get the best information about a question or a problem, and one learns how to evaluate and present this information. This process has eight steps:

1. selecting a topic and narrowing it down to a manageable question or problem
2. compiling a "working bibliography"
3. exploring these sources and taking notes
4. developing a working thesis statement and an outline or branched cluster
5. writing a discovery draft of the essay
6. revising the draft
7. editing the revision
8. preparing a list of sources

Selecting and Narrowing Down a Topic

Choose a topic that really interests you. You will have to read about it for several weeks, so you might as well start with a topic that is important to you. If you are assigned a subject to write about, use the techniques that you practiced in Chapters 2 and 3 to narrow down the topic:

- Do some freewriting about it and find a focus or two.
- Do some brainstorming to develop the focus and to clarify your purpose and audience.
- Do some clustering to elaborate details about your focus, purpose, and audience.
- Jot down notes about the topic's parts, characteristics, processes, or stages.
- Jot down notes about the topic's causes, effects, or implications for various groups of people.
- Do a brief discovery draft of your ideas about the focus.

A STUDENT RESPONSE

Here is an example of a student's effort to narrow down a topic that was assigned to him for a research paper in his communications course: "The Impact of the Media on Our Society." This topic is too broad for an eight- to ten-page essay.

Impact of Media

Effects on adults and children

Television

Audience – Communications teacher who knows the impact of media and television

Research Sources – Books and articles on how television programming (affects Americans)

(provides entertainment and news)

(teaches us certain values as kids & reinforces these values as we grow-up)

Focus – Effects of television programming on American children and teenagers (These effects are probably negative.)

Compiling a Working Bibliography

When you have an idea of the problem or question that you want to examine, go to the library and prepare a list of the possible sources of information about this focus. Begin with the **catalogue**, the alphabetical index of all of the materials in the library. In some libraries, the catalogue consists of cards in drawers; in others, these cards have been converted into pieces of data on computer terminals. The catalogue lists each of the library's books on three separate cards—by title, by author, and by subject. Here is an example of each card for the book *You and Media*:

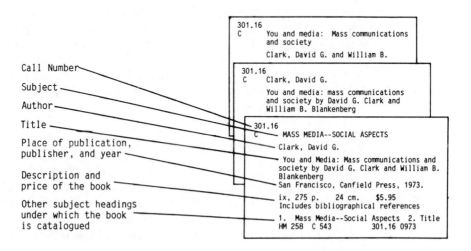

Begin your working bibliography by looking up all of the books on the subject of your topic. The subject card for each book indicates whether it has a bibliography. On a separate 3" by 5" index card, write down the author (last name first), title (underlined), date of publication, place of publication, publisher, and call number of each book that seems relevant to your topic. The catalogue will indicate the books on your topic that have bibliographies. Write down the call numbers of books with bibliographies, and find and examine each of them. Make out a separate index card for each of the books that you select from these bibliographies.

Next, check the appropriate indexes of periodicals—the journals, magazines, and newspapers—stored in the library. Since periodicals are current, they are valuable sources of information. In order to find periodicals that include information about your topic, consult several periodical indexes. The two most useful are the *Readers' Guide to Periodical Literature*, which is a monthly index of the articles in about 200 magazines and which lists articles under both subject and author, and the *New York Times Index*, which is a monthly index of major news events and feature articles and which lists articles by their subjects. Essays in academic, business, and professional journals can be found by consulting periodical subject indexes in specific fields, such as the

Humanities Index, the *General Science Index*, the *Business Periodicals Index*, and the *Social Science Index*.

When you consult these indexes, use a separate 3″ by 5″ index card for each article or essay that seems relevant to your topic and include the author (last name first), title of the article (in quotation marks), title of the periodical (underlined), volume number, complete date, and page numbers. The reference section of most libraries has additional resources that may be very valuable for compiling a preliminary working bibliography. These include guides to government publications, yearbooks, indexes of pamphlets, brochures, clippings, indexes of book reviews, and indexes of biographies. Many libraries also have indexes of audiovisual materials (such as film, videotapes, slides, records, and audiotapes).

Exploring Sources and Taking Notes

As you read the various sources of information in your working bibliography, keep your specific topic and your purpose for writing about this topic in mind. Select information that is relevant to this topic and record your notes on your index cards. Most often, your notes should be a summary, *in your own words*, of the information contained

Barnouw, Erik. *The Sponsor* NY: Oxford University Press, 1978. (301.161 B)

p. 105 – "the action in episodic drama can be quickly understood, and invites emotional identification" . . . "Such programming undoubtedly forms patterns of ideas and attitudes about the world" . . . "On television it is drama, not news programming, that takes the lead in setting patterns."

Barnouw, Erik. *The Sponsor*, NY Oxford
University Press, 1978. (301 .1618)

P. 105 – Barnow says that people
understand and identify with
episodic drama ("action/adventure"
shows) and this affects their
ideas and attitudes about life
more than the information
presented in news programs.

in the source. If you record an author's specific points—even in your own words—you are paraphrasing, not summarizing. Reread pages 350–351 of this chapter about the differences between a summary and a paraphrase.

When you take notes, remember to write down the page number of material that you paraphrase, because you will need to indicate it in your paper. If you think that the author's exact words are very important for clarifying a point, copy them exactly, put a quotation mark at the beginning and end of the quote, and note the page number from which it came. Here are two bibliographical note cards: the first shows the material from the source in a quotation, and the second shows a paraphrase of the quoted material.

WRITING ACTIVITY USING THE LIBRARY CATALOGUE

Use your library's catalogue to find out the following information about the book *News From Nowhere*:

Book's complete title_____

Author's complete name_____

Date of publication_____

Place of publication_____

Publisher_____

Subject headings_____

Call number_____

Developing a Working Thesis Statement and an Outline or Branched Cluster

As you read the various sources of information in your working bibliography, you may change your focus based on the material that you are reading and the ideas that occur to you when you think about the significance of what you have read. For example, here is a student's initial focus for her essay:

Most people watch several hours of TV every day and tend to accept the values portrayed in the shows.

And here is the working thesis statement that she developed after consulting several sources about her focus and after thinking about what she had read in these sources:

Television sponsors have become the ones who define society's values and who transmit these values through their commercials and their control of TV programming.

A working thesis statement helps you keep track of what your research essay will explain, describe, or prove. Remember that you can revise this thesis statement as often as you want while you are doing your research *and* while you are drafting and revising your essay. After you have done extensive reading about your focus, examine your note cards to get a sense of the kinds of information you have collected and to get an idea of what issues still need further research. As you read through your note cards, think about some ways in which you might apply the information that you have collected.

- Do you want to review prior research on the topic, pointing out areas of agreement or conflict among researchers?
- Do you want to compare the work of competing researchers and explain whose view(s) seems more logical and why?

- Do you want to use a theory (or a set of interrelated theories) to explain a specific phenomenon?
- Do you want to confirm or refute the assertions, methods, or findings of other researchers on the topic?
- Do you want to show how research in one field of study relates to research in another field?

As you clarify your purpose in doing research, you may have to modify your thesis statement. You may also want to write a branched cluster or an informal outline of the information that you have collected. One way to do this is to separate your note cards into groups pertaining to the same subtopics. Here is an example of part of an outline based on a group of note cards:

Section II. Sources of power of TV sponsors
(How does the sponsor transmit its idea of what is good, important, or valuable to viewers?)
  A. Commercials
    1. Spokespersons
      a. Entertainment or sports stars
      b. Authority figures
    2. Idealized world
      a. People always wealthy, clean, and happy
      b. People have plenty of time to relax, clean, and use the sponsor's products
  B. Programs
    1. Entertainment programs
      a. Idealized people, families, and lives
      b. Neat, clear solutions to every problem
    2. News programs
      a. Only "entertaining" news is shown
      b. Editorials and interpretations of news events depend on sponsors' values

The writer can use this outline to arrange her note cards so that she can start writing a draft of this section of the essay.

Writing a Discovery Draft of the Essay

A research essay calls for many of the strategies that you have been practicing: describing, defining, summarizing, explaining, comparing, contrasting, analyzing, and evaluating. As you reexamine each group of notes and try to make the information meaningful to a reader, you will have to choose the strategy that is most appropriate for your purpose and for the information. Think about ways of presenting the information that you have collected and consider the background details that should be presented before a specific piece of information is discussed in your draft. Consider why the information that you have collected is important. Also, think carefully about your point of view and about how the information makes sense in terms of your point of view.

Avoiding Plagiarism. Use your own words as much as possible. When you refer to your sources to support your points, paraphrase them or quote them and cite the source by author and page number(s). Remember, a paraphrase is a point-by-point summary of another writer's ideas—in your own words—and you should paraphrase more often than quote. In fact, you should only quote the exact words of another writer if these words are particularly striking or memorable. Otherwise, when you want to present the ideas or evidence from the sources you have consulted, paraphrase these ideas accurately, simply, and clearly. *And cite the source's author and page number(s).* If you do not cite the source of paraphrases and quotes, you are **plagiarizing**—borrowing someone else's ideas and words and trying to pass them off as your own. Put quotation marks around all of the source material that you quote directly (and cite the source) or paraphrase the material and cite the source. Here is an example of a piece of writing; a student's discussion of it, using accurate paraphrases and quotes; and another student's plagiarized paraphrase of the original piece:

EXCERPT FROM A SOURCE

The dependence on camera events, pseudo-events, gives enormous power to those in a position to create such events. No network dares ignore a White House rose garden "scenario" or a military "photo opportunity." Thus, in regard to current happenings, the arrangers tend to set the agenda for national discussions, directing our attention *to* some events, some problems—and, far more significantly, *away from* others.

STUDENT REFERENCE TO THIS SOURCE

Another subtle way in which the government controls the news is through the events that it plans. As Erik Barnouw has pointed out, "No network dares ignore a White House rose garden 'scenario' or a military 'photo opportunity' (127). National and local government agencies have the power to focus our society's attention on some events and to make us ignore other events (Barnouw 128).

STUDENT PLAGIARISM OF THIS SOURCE

The government has enormous power over network news. For example, no network can ignore an event at the White House or at the State Department or at a military base. Thus, government agencies can almost set the agenda for national discussions by focusing our attention on some events and, more importantly, away from others.

WRITING ACTIVITY PARAPHRASING

Here is a passage from a chapter by Paul Weaver on "Newspaper News and Television News" in the book *Television as a Social Force*. On a separate piece of paper, write a brief paraphrase of Weaver's points and include the appropriate citation.

Faced with a choice between two potentially newsworthy events, the American TV news organizations will prefer, other things being equal, the one for which there is better film. What film they have for an event tentatively identified as newsworthy ordinarily guides, and in some cases may completely determine, the way the event is defined and the theme chosen for a story—a practice which could easily cause the story to misrepresent the situation as it really was. And in rare instances, television news organizations have been known to "create" film, to stage spectacles for purposes of being filmed, in order to have something newsworthy to report (92).

Citing Sources Within a Research Essay

Different academic disciplines have different styles for citing the sources of paraphrases and quotations within a research essay. If your teacher does not tell you which style manual to use to cite your sources, use the 1988 edition of the *MLA Handbook for Writers of Research Papers*, published by the Modern Language Association. This style manual is the one used most often for essays in the humanities.

There are several ways of "documenting" or giving credit to the authors whose works or ideas you are summarizing, paraphrasing, and quoting. Below is an excerpt from a source, followed by different strategies for citing this excerpt.

Excerpt from page 358 of a book entitled *Public Opinion* by Walter Lippmann:

News and truth are not the same thing. The function of the news is to signalize an event; the function of truth is to bring to light the hidden facts, to set them in relation to each other, and to make a picture of reality on which men can act.

How to cite a paraphrase of or quotation from this excerpt:

1. If you do not mention the author's name in your paraphrase or quotation, then you must write the author's last name and the page number(s) of the source within parentheses at the end of the sentence. Note that the name and the page number are *not* separated by any punctuation mark.

   Example 1: News is a form of knowledge that is only tenuously related to the truth (Lippmann 358).

   Example 2: One news analyst argues that the news and the truth are not the same things: "The function of the news is to signalize an event; the function of truth is to bring to light the hidden facts, to set them in relation to each other, and to make a picture of reality on which men can act" (Lippmann 358).

2. If you do mention the author's name in your sentence, then write only the page number(s) of the source in parentheses at the end.

   Example 1: Walter Lippmann has pointed out that news cannot be likened to the truth: the truth reveals hidden facts, whereas the news only marks an event as important (358).

   Example 2: Lippmann distinguishes between the news and the truth. He points out that "the function of the news is to signalize an event; the function of truth is to bring to light the hidden facts, to set them in relation to each other, and to make a picture of reality on which men can act" (358).

Revising the Essay

A research paper should show the writer's mind at work: it reveals the significance of the information to the writer. An ineffective research paper merely strings together a series of paraphrases and quotations from experts on the topic. An effective one synthesizes the theories and views of experts in a field and uses this information to present a new understanding of the topic. As you revise your essay, make sure that you have incorporated paraphrases and quotations smoothly into your writing. Each one should be introduced by a brief comment and should serve a specific function (such as illustrating your point, backing up your assertion, or giving an example of the author's language).

Also, check to make sure that you have given credit to the author whenever you have used his or her ideas to support yours. Remember, if you have merely changed a few words of another writer's sentence or paragraph, you are plagiarizing, not paraphrasing. All of your paraphrases must state the original writer's meaning *in your own words*. Also, make sure that you give credit to the writer and that you have documented your paraphrases and quotations correctly according to the style manual that you are using. Then, revise your essay using all of the strategies that you have learned and practiced in this book.

Editing the Essay

A research essay has to be edited for errors and for unconventional forms, just as does any other essay you write for a teacher or an employer. Use the techniques that you have learned in this book to edit your sentence structure, diction, grammar and usage, spelling, and punctuation.

Preparing a List of Sources

At the end of your research essay, you must provide a bibliography that includes all of the sources mentioned in the essay, arranged alphabetically according to the authors' last names. According to the style of the *MLA Handbook for Writers of Research Papers*, this list is called "Works Cited," and it is the only place in your research essay where you should include all of the information about the sources you are citing. Thus, your list must be complete and accurate. Here is an example of part of a list of Works Cited.

```
                          Works Cited

Barnouw, Erik.  The Sponsor.  New York: Oxford University Press,

       1978.  [a book with one author]

Clark, David, and William Blankenburg.  You and Media: Mass

       Communications and Society.  San Francisco: Canfield Press,

       1973.  [a book with two authors]

Fisher, Walter.  "A Motive View of Communication."  Quarterly
```

Journal of Speech 56 (1970): 132-139. [an article in a scholarly journal]

Flynn, Alexander. Personal interview. 25 May 1991. [an interview]

Gewen, Barry. Rev. of _The News at Any Cost_, by Tom Goldstein. _The New Leader_ 27 Jan. 1986: 14. [a book review in a periodical]

Goodman, Walter. "Critic's Notebook." _New York Times_ 16 April 1991, sec. C: 16. [an article in a daily newspaper]

Griffith, Thomas. "From Monitor to Public Echo." _Time_ 13 Nov. 1984: 89. [an article in a weekly or biweekly periodical]

Weaver, Paul. "Newspaper News and Television News." _Television as a Social Force._ Ed. Richard Adler. New York: Prager Publishers, 1975. 81-96. [an essay in an edited book]

WRITING ASSIGNMENT WRITING, REVISING, AND EDITING A RESEARCH ESSAY

The topic for your research essay is legislation aimed at making English the country's official language. As of 1992, eighteen states have passed resolutions or constitutional amendments making English the state's only official language. Currently, a group called U.S. English, headed by the linguist and former senator S. I. Hayakawa, is seeking the passage of an English-only amendment to the U.S. constitution.

People who support this amendment believe that it would unite the country by encouraging everyone to learn and use English. Further, they think it would save taxpayers money if government legislation and voting ballots were printed only in English. Opponents believe that if the amendment passed, it would lead to the prohibition of other languages for governmental functions and for public advertisements and, thus, discriminate against everyone who did not learn English. The National Council of Teachers of English recently passed a resolution condemning the group U.S. English. An excerpt from this resolution is printed below.

. . . that NCTE urge legislators, other public officials, and citizens to oppose actively any actions intended to mandate or declare English as an official language or to "preserve," "purify," or "enhance" the language. Any such action will not only stunt the vitality of language, but it will also ensure its erosion and in effect create hostility toward English, making it more difficult to learn.

In order to write this essay, you will have to learn more about the U.S. English movement and about English-only legislation. Go to your library and look up these topics in the catalogue, in the *Readers' Guide to Periodical Literature*, and in the *Humanities Index*. Consult at least three books and five periodicals. After you have read extensively about this legislation, develop your own viewpoint about it. Then use the following guidelines to help you write, revise, and edit your essay.

Guidelines
1. Do some freewriting, brainstorming, and clustering about your reactions to English-only proposals.
2. Specify your focus:
    What does U.S. English want and why do they want it?
    How much do you already know about this issue?
    What else do you need to find out about it, and what kinds of sources should you consult?
3. Determine your audience:
    Who is your audience for this essay?
    What does your audience already know about this topic, and how do they feel about it?
    What kind of evidence will you need to present in order to convince this audience of your view?
4. Refine your purpose for writing this essay:
    What do you want your readers to understand?
    What do you want your readers to think, to feel, or to do when they are finished reading your essay?
5. Write a sentence that can serve as your working thesis statement. (Feel free to change this thesis statement as you do research and write a discovery draft.)
6. Carefully reread your freewriting, your brainstorming, and your clustering. Consider the ways in which your details relate to your focus, audience, purpose, and working thesis statement.
7. Take notes from the books and periodicals you consult, and keep a working bibliography.
8. Write a discovery draft of your essay.

9. Get as many responses to your discovery draft as you can (from classmates, teachers, tutors, friends, and family).
10. Revise your discovery draft by using the techniques that you practiced in Chapters 6, 7, 8, and 9.
11. Edit your essay using the techniques that you practiced in Chapters 10, 11, and 12.
12. Consult your library's copy of the *MLA Handbook for Writers of Research Papers*, third edition, edited by Joseph Ginaldi and Walter Achtert (New York: Modern Language Association, 1988). Follow its directions for the format of your essay and for documenting sources within the essay and at the end of the essay.

ISSUES FOR YOUR JOURNAL

1. What kinds of writing do professionals in your major (or in your current job) have to do? How do you feel about your ability to do these writing tasks?
2. Collect interesting quotations from lectures or from readings in your courses. Write them down in your journal, and write your responses to each one.
3. What books, journals, or magazines have you read in the past month? What do these reveal about your reading habits and your life?
4. How do you see yourself changing—as a student, an employee, a son or daughter, a parent, or a friend?
5. What do you most want to change about your life? How will you go about making this change?

CHAPTER FOURTEEN

APPLYING YOUR SKILLS TO ESSAY EXAMINATIONS AND WRITING TESTS

WRITING, REVISING, AND EDITING ESSAY EXAMS AND WRITING TESTS

This chapter will help you master the skills that you need to perform well on the two types of essay tests in college: essay examinations in subject-matter courses and writing competency tests. Teachers use essay exams to evaluate students' learning and to assess their ability to apply their knowledge to new problems and situations in a discipline. Writing competency tests have a very different purpose: they are used to determine whether students have the academic writing skills necessary to perform well in college and in the careers for which college is preparing them.

The writing skills that you have been practicing in this book are the same skills that you need to do well on both types of tests. In many ways, writing an essay exam is similar to writing an academic essay for a composition course. Like other academic writing, essay tests require students to do some thinking and prewriting about the topic, to develop a clear thesis, to provide specific details arranged in logical paragraphs, and to revise and edit the essay so that it is clear and coherent and follows Standard Written English conventions. Writing in a timed testing situation means that you will have to speed up the time that you devote to each stage of the writing process—prewriting, drafting, revising, and editing.

GROUP WRITING TASK   **ANALYZING ESSAY TEST TOPICS**

Get into a group of three students and examine the essay test topics below. Choose one person to write down what the group thinks each topic is asking students to write about and what strategies might be appropriate for developing an answer.

1. (Philosophy Exam) You have thirty minutes to analyze and evaluate the following statement by the French philosopher Helvetius: "Our ideas are the necessary consequence of the historical time and society in which we live."
2. (Sociology Exam) This is a two-part essay exam. First, define the "scientific method." Second, design an experiment that uses the scientific method to assess the effects of this course on students' understanding of sociological research. You have 75 minutes to complete both parts.
3. (Competency Test) You will have fifty minutes to plan and write the following essay: Older people bring to their work a lifetime of knowledge and experience. They should not be forced to retire,

even if keeping them on the job cuts down on the opportunities for young people to find work. Do you agree or disagree? Explain and illustrate your answer from your own experience, your observations of others, or your reading.

4. (Competency Test) You will have fifty minutes to write a four- to six-paragraph essay on the following topic: Discuss the influence of television on you and your family.

ESSAY EXAMINATIONS

Essay examinations are gaining in popularity among American teachers because they reveal the extent to which students can think critically and write analytically about a subject. There is no way that anyone can write an effective response on an essay exam if he or she has not studied and thought about the material being tested. Cramming the night before a test cannot substitute for doing the readings, taking notes on them, and discussing the readings and the class lectures or labs in study groups.

When you receive an essay examination, read it through carefully in its entirety. This will give you a sense of the number of questions you will have to answer, the amount of writing you will have to do, and the amount of time you should devote to each answer. Next, examine each question for its cues and clues. (Interpreting these cues is discussed in detail on pages 348–349 of Chapter 13.) If you misinterpret the question or ignore its directions, you will not be able to answer it correctly. Here are some sample essay questions with comments about the strategies that each seems to require:

1. "Discuss the concept of 'negative feedback' and its role in maintaining homeostasis (the steady state)."

   This question, from a biology final exam, begins with the vague cue *discuss*, which means summarize (or analyze) and illustrate. The question indicates that students should define "negative feedback" and give examples of it. Then, they should define "homeostasis" and give examples of the ways in which negative feedback helps maintain it.

2. "Most poets use musical devices (such as stress and tonal patterns) to achieve meaning and mood. Analyze the contribution of musical devices to the meaning and the mood of one poem by three of the following poets: Emily Dickinson, Walt Whitman, Robert Lowell, John Crowe Ransom, and Wallace Stevens."

This question, from an English literature midterm, requires students to present their personal interpretations. The question seems complicated, but the clues are clear: choose *three poets* and choose *one poem* written by each poet. Then for *each* of these three poems, describe how its stress, metrical pattern, rhythm, and rhyme schemes set up the mood and help communicate the meaning of the poem.

3. "Attack or defend this thesis: all fascist movements are really anti-movements—they define themselves by the things against which they stand."

This question, from a political science final, asks for an evaluation. It has no right or wrong answer; students' answers either make sense and are supported by appropriate evidence or they are unreasonable or unsupported. Students would have to explain what the thesis means and then give their opinion about its accuracy or validity, providing specific evidence for their judgment and their reasons.

Every essay examination question contains at least one cue about the strategy that students should use to respond to it, as well as clues about the information that should be included in the answer. Never write a response until you are sure that you know what the question is asking you! Analyze an essay exam question carefully before you begin answering it, try to relax, and remember that you have a large repertoire of strategies to use to develop your response. You can use all of the strategies that you have studied in this book which include the following:

- **Narrate** a story or an experience that reflects your ideas or feelings about the topic.
- **Describe** a person, place, thing, or process as it relates to the topic.
- **Define** the topic by explaining its distinguishing characteristics and by illustrating it with examples of what you mean by it.
- **Classify** people, things, processes, events, or concepts into groups according to a characteristic that is shared by all members of the group.
- **Compare** or **contrast** two or more people, things, processes, events, or concepts by noting points of similarity and differences between them.
- **Analyze** the parts or categories of a complex object, idea, or event, *or* explain the causes or the effects of an event or a behavior.
- **Evaluate** the worth or the value of an object or an idea according to criteria or values that you specify.

- **Argue** your point of view by using some or all of the strategies above.

Your goals in writing an essay exam are always the same: (1) to state your answer as clearly and as directly as possible and (2) to signal the relationships among your ideas so that your answer is easy to read. The time limits of essay exams force writers to compress the processes of writing: prewriting may consist of merely jotting down notes or making a scratch outline. Often, there is not enough time to revise and rewrite, so writers have to draft and revise simultaneously. In addition, on an essay exam, you can state your thesis statement immediately without worrying about getting and holding the reader's attention. Also your conclusion can be briefer, simply summing up your main points. Make sure that you leave time to reread your answers and to write your corrections neatly.

STUDENT RESPONSES

Here are some actual student essays written in response to essay examination questions. Be prepared to discuss why you think each one did or did not answer the questions effectively.

1. Discuss the various ways in which color is measured. Then describe the relationship between color and light variation.

Student's prewriting:

munsell's hue system — hue chrome
→ values
— more light → Describe each
(moonlight / daylight) → more color
light makes different effects

Student's answer:

The most widely used system for measuring colors is the

Munsell system named for its inventor Albert Munsell. The

system consists of a tree that shows the hue, chroma and value

of different colors. Hue is the basic quality of a color
(red, yellow, green, blue and purple). Value is each color's
degree of whiteness or blackness. Chroma is the color's
strength or degree of contrast. Color can also be measured in
math terms: the product of value times chroma is a color's
power.

Colors vary according to how much light hits them. The
more light that hits the color, the more the color is visible
to our eyes. If you look at a color picture in the moonlight,
you can't see the color in the picture. If you look at the
same picture in the day, the colors are sharp. Light produces
different effects on color and on its measurement.

2. Discuss the role of the Soviet Union in the Vietnam War.

Student's prewriting:

Student's answer:

For many years, the American government underestimated
the role that the Soviet Union played in the Vietnam War.

From 1965-1967, the Soviet Union sent hundreds of military advisors to Vietnam. These people trained the Vietnamese to fly combat missions and fire missiles. For the past 25 years, America assumed that this was the total extent of the Soviet Union's role in the war. But recent articles in the Soviet magazine Ekho make it clear that the Soviet Union sent weapons and millions of rubles to Hanoi to fund the war. So while the Soviets were saying that they were only advising the Vietnamese, in reality they were funding them, providing them with weapons, and teaching them how to kill Americans.

3. List the different types of galaxies and their characteristics. Then explain why the different shapes of galaxies do *NOT* represent stages in the life cycle of a galaxy.

Student's prewriting:

I. Elliptical (egg-shaped, old)
II. Spiral (circular, all ages)
III. Irregular (no shape, old & young)
Young and old stars in all 3 types.

Student's answer:

1. Elliptical galaxies are egg-shaped and they range from a full sphere to a flat narrow one. They contain mostly old stars.

2. Spiral galaxies have a circular center with spiral arms radiating out from them. They have young, middle aged, and old stars in them.

3. Irregular galaxies have no regular shape. They contain
   some young and old stars.

Some scientists believe that galaxies start out as
elliptical, then change to spiral and then end as irregular.
But this doesn't seem true because there are young and old
stars in all three types of galaxies. If irregular galaxies
were the last stage of a galaxy's life cycle, then it would
have only old stars in it.

WRITING ACTIVITY WRITING AN ESSAY EXAMINATION

Here is an essay examination from an introductory education
course. Follow the directions.

You have one hour to plan, write, and edit an essay analyzing the
cartoon on the opposite page. In your essay, you should (1) explain
what the cartoon implies about children and television, (2) evaluate the accuracy of the cartoon's implications, and (3) explain
your viewpoint on the impact of television on children.

WRITING COMPETENCY TESTS

Thousands of colleges across America are assessing students'
writing abilities and determining whether they have the necessary
skills to do upper-level college coursework or to graduate. Because the
consequences of this kind of test are more serious than they are for a
classroom exam, many students get so anxious about doing well that
they freeze and forget their natural writing processes. Try not to let
this happen to you. When you take a writing test, try to relax and tell
yourself that you know the strategies necessary to write well. Remind
yourself that you have a variety of prewriting strategies available to
use to begin developing your response to the test topic and a variety of
techniques for revising and editing your answer. All of the skills that
you have practiced in this book and in your writing courses have prepared you to do well on any test of your writing abilities.

There are several specific test-taking tips that may help you write more fluently and more effectively on writing tests. I have developed these tips from reading thousands of writing competency tests during the past 15 years and from interviewing the student authors of passing and failing tests. Here are Greenberg's Seven Tips for Doing Well on Writing Tests:

1. **Read the test topic or question over *twice*.** Then, on scrap paper, make a brief list of each task that the topic asks you to do. Here is an example of a tricky test topic that actually has three tasks that the student must complete to receive a passing grade.

   > Many people fantasize about being someone else, someone famous or a character in a book. If you were able to become someone else (living, dead, or fictional), whom would you choose to be? What are the reasons for your choice and what would your life be like if you could be this person?

   By reading this question over carefully, you can see that you have to do several things: (1) describe the person whom you have chosen, (2) explain your reasons for wanting to be that person, and (3) describe what your life would be like if you were to become that person.

2. **Do some prewriting.** Freewrite, brainstorm, cluster, or branch in order to get a sense of what you know about the topic and how to develop your response.
3. **Make your introduction brief.** Also, be sure that your introduction includes your thesis statement or point of view about the topic.
4. **Be specific and concrete.** Don't write vague generalizations or clichés. Use your personal experiences and the knowledge you have gained from reading to support and illustrate your assertions.
5. **Write one draft.** You will not have enough time to revise and edit your draft *and* to write it over again. Moreover, students often make mistakes when they copy over a draft in a hurry. Instead, skip lines and leave room to insert your revisions and corrections. Make your revisions and corrections legible, but don't worry if they look a little messy, because teachers often give credit to students for revising and editing their essay tests.
6. **Wear a watch and check the time.** Plan how much time you will need to write, revise, proofread, and edit your response.
7. **Leave time to proofread and edit.** A test essay with brilliant insights will not pass if the sentence structure is garbled or if it is filled with diction, grammar, and punctuation errors. Be particu-

larly careful to proofread and correct the errors that you know you usually make in writing.

WRITING ACTIVITY WRITING A COMPETENCY TEST RESPONSE

Here is a sample topic from the writing skills test of the Texas Academic Skills Program (the TASP). Follow the directions.

You are asked to prepare a writing sample of about 300–600 words on an assigned topic. The assignment can be found below. Read the assignment carefully before you begin to write, and think about how you will organize what you plan to say. Be sure to write about the assigned topic and use multiple paragraphs. Please write legibly. You may not use any reference materials during the test. Remember to review what you have written and make any changes you think will improve your writing sample. You have approximately one hour.

ASSIGNMENT

Some people say modern machines have made our lives better, while others argue that machines are ruling our lives so much that it is hard to maintain our individuality. Write an essay, to be read by a history teacher, arguing for one position or the other. Support your argument by referring to your own experience, observation, or reading. Your purpose is to persuade the reader that your view of the influence of machines is correct.

ESSAY EVALUATION

Essay examinations are usually scored by the classroom teacher using his or her subjective judgment about what constitutes a passing answer and about how much credit to assign each part of the answer. Writing competency tests, on the other hand, are usually scored by teams of teachers who rate each essay according to an evaluation scale that describes the characteristics of an essay at each score point. Here is a sample of the evaluation scale that we use at The City University of New York to score the writing competency tests of more than 25,000 students every year. In order for an essay to pass, at least two readers must give it a score of at least 4.

CUNY EVALUATION SCALE FOR THE CUNY WRITING SKILLS ASSESSMENT TEST

6

The essay provides a well-organized response to the topic and maintains a central focus. The ideas are expressed in appropriate language. A sense of pattern of development is present from beginning to end. The writer supports assertions with explanation or illustration, and the vocabulary is well suited to the context. Sentences reflect a command of syntax within the ordinary range of standard written English. Grammar, punctuation, and spelling are almost always correct.

5

The essay provides an organized response to the topic. The ideas are expressed in clear language most of the time. The writer develops ideas and generally signals relationships within and between paragraphs. The writer uses vocabulary that is appropriate for the essay topic and avoids oversimplifications or distortions. Sentences generally are correct grammatically, although some errors may be present when sentence structure is particularly complex. With few exceptions, grammar, punctuation, and spelling are correct.

4

The essay shows a basic understanding of the demands of essay organization, although there might be occasional digressions. The development of ideas is sometimes incomplete or rudimentary, but a basic logical structure can be discerned. Vocabulary generally is appropriate for the essay topic but at times is oversimplified. Sentences reflect a sufficient command of standard written English to ensure reasonable clarity of expression. Common forms of agreement and grammatical inflection are usually, although not always, correct. The writer generally demonstrates through punctuation an understanding of the boundaries of the sentence. The writer spells common words, except perhaps so-called "demons," with a reasonable degree of accuracy.

3

The essay provides a response to the topic but generally has no overall pattern of organization. Ideas are often repeated or undeveloped, although occasionally a paragraph within the essay does have some structure. The writer uses informal language occasionally and records conversational speech when appropriate written prose is needed. Vocabulary often is limited. The writer generally does not signal relationships within and between paragraphs. Syntax is often rudimentary and lacking in variety. The essay has recurrent grammatical problems, or because of an extremely narrow range of syntactical choices, only occasional grammatical problems appear. The writer does not demonstrate a firm understanding of the boundaries of the sentence. The writer occasionally misspells common words of the language.

2

The essay begins with a response to the topic but does not develop that response. Ideas are repeated frequently, or are presented randomly, or both. The writer uses informal language frequently and does little more than record conversational speech. Words are often misused, and vocabulary is limited. Syntax is often tangled and is not sufficiently stable to ensure reasonable clarity of expression. Errors in grammar, punctuation, and spelling occur often.

1

The essay suffers from general incoherence and has no discernible pattern of organization. It displays a high frequency of error in the regular features of standard written English. Lapses in punctuation, spelling, and grammar often frustrate the reader. Or, the essay is so brief that any reasonably accurate judgment of the writer's competence is impossible.

It is a good idea before taking a competency test to talk to your instructor or a counselor to learn how the test will be evaluated.

INDIVIDUALIZED PROGRESS LOGS

1. Writing Progress Log

2. Spelling Log

3. Conference Log

The three charts that follow will help you keep track of your writing progress and problems *if you use them.*

1. WRITING PROGRESS LOG

Every time your teacher returns a piece of your writing—in your writing course *and* in every other course—make notes about the piece in this log. By doing this, you will be able to see your progress and also focus on the areas that need further improvement. If you need more writing log pages, make copies of this page.

Date _____   Course _____

Title of Paper _____

Strengths:

Problems and Errors:

2. SPELLING LOG

List in this log every word that you misspell or that you are not sure how to spell. In your spare time, make up a sentence for each of the words in the log (on a separate piece of paper). If you need more Spelling Log pages, make copies of this page.

PROBLEM WORD (spelled correctly)	**MY MISSPELLING**	**TYPE or CAUSE** (of this spelling error)

3. CONFERENCE LOG

Every time you have a conference with your writing teacher, summarize that conference in the space below. Use the notes that you write in this log to help you remember your teacher's comments and suggestions and to help you keep track of your progress. If you need more Conference Log pages, make copies of this page.

Date of Conference _____

Material Discussed _____

Teacher's Comments, Suggestions, and Assignments:

Dear Student,

     Writing this book was a labor of love and anxiety for me. Now I need your help to revise it. When you are finished using this book, please write me a letter about its strengths and its weaknesses. What did you like about it? What did you dislike? How can I improve it? Please mail your letter to me at the address below. If you include your name and address, I will write back to you. Thank you.

                                    Gratefully,

                                    Karen Greenberg
                                    c/o College Division
                                    St. Martin's Press
                                    175 Fifth Avenue
                                    New York, NY 10010

Acknowledgments (continued from p. iv)

"Base Stealer" by Robert Francis. Reprinted from *The Orb Weaver*, copyright © 1948 by Robert Francis, published by Wesleyan University Press. By permission of University Press of New England.

"Survey: Work in the 1980s and 1990s" by Julia Kagan. Reprinted with permission from *Working Woman* magazine. Copyright © 1983 by Hal Publications.

Drawing by Donald Reilly; © 1981 The New Yorker Magazine, Inc.

"Running Hard Just to Keep Up" by Sylvia Ann Hewlett. Copyright 1990 by The Time Inc. Magazine Company. Reprinted by permission.

"Fable for Tomorrow" from *Silent Spring* by Rachel Carson. Copyright © 1962 by Rachel L. Carson. Reprinted by permission of Houghton Mifflin Company. All rights reserved.

Excerpt from *Life Manipulation* by David Lygre. Copyright © 1979 by David G. Lygre. Reprinted with permission from Walker and Company.

"Magnitudes" by Howard Nemerov. Reprinted by permission of the author's estate.

"Labels Like 'Learning Disabled' . . ." by John Kelly. Reprinted from *The Chronicle of Higher Education*.

"Careers That Promise Big Payoffs" by William Banks. Reprinted from *Money* magazine by special permission; copyright © 1985 by The Time Inc. Magazine Company.

Excerpt from *A Writer Teaches Writing*, first edition, by Donald Murray. Copyright © 1968 by Houghton Mifflin Company. Used with permission.

"Being a Man" by Paul Theroux. From *Sunrise with Seamonsters* by Paul Theroux. Copyright © 1985 by Cape Cod Scriveners Company. Reprinted by permission of Houghton Mifflin Company. All rights reserved.

Handycam ad, reprinted by special permission of Sony and McCann-Erickson.

Excerpt from *Television and Human Behavior* by Comstock, Chaffee, Katzman, McCombs, and Roberts. Reprinted by permission of the Rand Corporation.

"Correcting the Neandertal Stereotype" by Betty McCollister. Copyright © 1990. First appeared in the May/June 1990 issue of *The Humanist* and reprinted with permission.

"A New Era" by Theo Sommer. From *Die Zeit*, Hamburg. Reprinted with permission from World Press Review, Oct. 1985.

Excerpt from "Letter from Birmingham Jail" in *Why We Can't Wait* by Martin Luther King, Jr. Copyright © 1963, 1964 by Martin Luther King, Jr. Reprinted by permission of HarperCollins Publishers Inc.

"A Question of Language" by Gloria Naylor. Copyright © 1981 by Gloria Naylor. Reprinted by permission of Sterling Lord Literistic, Inc.

"To Err Is Human" by Lewis Thomas. Copyright © by Lewis Thomas. From *The Medusa and the Snail* by Lewis Thomas. Used by permission of Viking Penguin, a division of Penguin Books USA Inc.

Drawing by Steve Edwards. Reprinted from *Phi Delta Kappan*.

"CUNY Evaluation Scale for Writing Assessment" reprinted from *The CUNY Writing Skills Assessment Test: Student Essays Evaluated and Annotated by the CUNY Task Force on Writing*, The City University of New York, Office of Academic Affairs, 1983. Copyright © 1983 by The City University of New York. Reprinted with permission.

Excerpt from *The Joy Luck Club* by Amy Tan. Reprinted by permission of the Putnam Publishing Group. Copyright © 1985 by Amy Tan.

INDEX